THE REVOLT AGAINST GOD

The Revolt Against God

The Conflict Between Culture and Christianity

by

RUFUS WASHINGTON WEAVER, D.D., LL.D.

Former President, Mercer University; author of "The Christian Faith at the Nation's Capital," "The Vatican Envoy," "The Religious Development of the Child," etc.

NEW YORK

Fleming H. Revell Company

LONDON AND EDINBURGH

"I am convinced that the welfare of mankind does not now depend on the State and the world of politics; the real battle is being fought in the world of thought, where a deadly attack is made with great tenacity of purpose and over a wide field upon the greatest treasure of mankind, the belief in God and the Gospel of Christ."—WILLIAM E. GLADSTONE.

"Some day people will learn that material things do not bring happiness and are of little use in making men and women creative and powerful. Then the scientists of the world will turn their laboratories over to the study of God and prayer and spiritual forces. When this day comes, the world will see more advancement in one generation than it has in the past four."—CHARLES STEINMETZ.

Preface

THE CHAPTERS which follow present an attempted interpretation of the molding of Christianity by contemporary cultures—an historical process which to-day is culminating in an assault upon the idea of God, backed by the resources of powerful military nations. These governments have taken the position that faith in deity is a menace to both social and political progress.

The academic source of this modern Revolt against God can be traced to a type of humanistic culture which, in all of its assumptions, refuses to adopt any hypothesis that presupposes the existence of God. The extension of this negating attitude to the areas of life, where moral and religious behavior is the subject of scientific study, is creating a new form of godlessness which, as it becomes dominant in organized society deadens and even destroys the moral restraints that an awareness of a righteous God produces, and stifles the motives to higher living which are always aroused by a sense of the presence of a loving God.

The book is an introduction to another work, a new type of apologetic for the Christian faith—an inductive or scientific approach to the problem of religion—grounded upon the harmony and the consistency of the evangelical experience with the observable processes of our phenomenal world, as these are described by competent scientists.

The powers which to-day are striving to destroy the belief in the idea of God, an effort which has assumed the character of a Blitzkrieg against God—a lightning-like war upon the Judge of the Nations—have developed within the past quarter of a century a God-defying nationalism, which is the basic cause of World War II. No one can study the impact of successive linguistic cultures upon Christian thought and practice without discerning through the centuries the growth of the Revolt against God. An historical continuity is clearly in evidence. Beyond question, the climax of the age-long conflict between human culture and divine provi-

7

dence is being reached. If the perusal of this book awakens a deeper interest in the study of this conflict the writer will be fully rewarded.

Among those to whom thanks are due are Hon. Walter M. W. Splawn, former Dean of the Graduate School of The American University, to Professor F. W. Collier, head of the Department of Philosophy in the same institution, who gave the writer the opportunity of presenting a major portion of the interpretation given in this book to post-graduate classes, composed of serious-minded men and women, to Dr. W. O. Carver, of the Southern Baptist Theological Seminary, to Dr. W. O. Lewis, General Secretary of the Baptist World Alliance, to Dr. Ernst Correll, The American University, and to Ellis Meredith, the well-known newspaper woman, who read the manuscript and offered highly valued suggestions.

R. W. W.

Washington, D. C.

Contents

		PAGE
INTRODUCTION	. . . .	11
I. THE RELIGIOUS SCENE PREVIOUS TO THE WORLD WAR FOR HUMAN FREEDOM	. . . .	19
II. THE BLITZKRIEG AGAINST GOD	. . . .	30
III. THE MIND OF CHRIST	. . . .	40
IV. THE APOSTOLIC MIND	. . . .	50
V. THE JUDAIZING MIND	. . . .	59
VI. THE GENTILE MIND	. . . .	70
VII. THE HELLENISTIC MIND	. . . .	81
VIII. THE THEOLOGICAL MIND	. . . .	91
IX. THE ROMAN MIND	. . . .	102
X. THE SACERDOTAL MIND	. . . .	112
XI. THE ECCLESIASTICAL MIND	. . . .	122
XII. THE MYSTICAL MIND	. . . .	133
XIII. THE PROTESTANT MIND	. . . .	144
XIV. THE NATIONALISTIC MIND	. . . .	156
XV. THE EMANCIPATING MIND	. . . .	169
XVI. THE DENOMINATIONAL MIND	. . . .	181
XVII. THE SCIENTIFIC MIND	. . . .	193
XVIII. MODERN SCIENCE AND THE CHRISTIAN GOD	. . . .	203
XIX. THE TEMPTATION AND THE FALL OF MODERN NATIONS	. . . .	216
XX. THE MIND OF CONTEMPORARY CHRISTIANITY AND THE FUTURE OF THE WORLD	. . . . . .	225
REFERENCES	. . . .	237
INDEX	. . . .	241

9

Introduction

THE MOST portentous phenomenon in modern history is not the global war in which all peoples and nations are involved; it is not the threat of world-wide enslavement to whose prevention the free governments of earth are lavishly spending their wealth, their man-power and their material resources; it is not the possible destruction of European and Western civilizations with its unprecedented impoverishment of human culture. The most portentous phenomenon in modern history is the Blitzkrieg against God.

On January 1, 1943, forty-three per cent of all the people on earth were under the rule of governments that were then actively engaged in the effort to destroy, especially in the minds of youth, the idea of God as the deity who rightfully possessed the claim to an allegiance superior to that given to the State. The authority of the State, so these rulers asserted, was without a rival, and therefore there was no place for either the Jewish, the Moslem, or the Christian God. The militant blasphemers that control the governments of Japan, Turkey, Russia, Germany and other states, in their eagerness to establish each a New Order, exhibit a type of political atheism which has no parallel in human history.

The assault upon the idea of God has its immediate motivation in a nationalism that claims for itself an absolute sovereignity, beside which religion is permitted to function only on the condition that it subserves distinctly governmental ends. Any nation that seeks to use religion for its own selfish purposes develops inevitably a repugnance to the idea of the God. The striking fact that needs recognition and emphasis is that for the first time in human history governments, openly, avowedly and violently are undertaking to eradicate the idea of God from the thinking of those over whom they rule. They are doing this, so they claim, because the idea of God, whether it be Moslem, Jewish or Christian, is a hindrance to public welfare and a menace to national progress.

11

Kemal Ataturk, the founder of the new Turkey, led in the over-throw of Mohammedanism and set up a government which in no respect recognizes the existence of God. Japan declares her Emperor to be divine, the bodily representative of heaven and earth, ruling a divine people who are destined to conquer the whole world. Germany illustrates the modern outreach for a deity whose supreme manifestation is found within the blood of a chosen people—the Nordic race. Russia, through its communistic leaders, has sought the destruction of all religious institutions and agencies, and the government itself has given approval and financial support to a vigorous atheistical propaganda. Italy has had a concordat with the Pope of Rome, but Mussolini, who began his public life as an avowed atheist, in the heyday of his power, declared Fascism to be above the Roman Catholic Church.

Nations in other days have sought through persecution and conquest to impose a form of religion upon their own and other peoples. In this our day the resources of governments are being brought to bear to destroy the very basis of religion—the belief in the supernatural. This is the Blitzkrieg against God. A study, based upon the principle of continuity in history will throw light upon this startling and terrifying situation, and should show that the Revolt against God has developed in an intelligible and logical way through the reaction of cultural forces that have helped and have hindered the progress of religious faith.

During the past nineteen centuries, the Christian movement has penetrated, one by one, new and radically different cultures. It has not only acted upon these cultures beneficially but has been acted upon by them, sometimes with lasting injury to the pristine Christian faith. Each culture has its own language, thought-patterns and prevailing popular philosophy that create the distinguishing characteristics of the culture itself. The thesis is maintained that the simple Christian faith, as it passes out of the environment of one culture into that of another, is in the process molded into somewhat different form and expression and that, in so far as these changes are a departure from the teachings of Jesus, the Christian religion loses something of its essential character and its inherent power. These changes today bulk large in the many and strikingly different ecclesiastical organizations that promote the Christian religion, and these differences are traceable in large measure to the impact [somewhere] of a culture, sometimes more than one, upon the Christian movement as it has made its way through the generations that make up the Christian era.

A Christian is one who by his own personal choice is engaged in the culture of the consciousness of Christ. The goal of his endeavors is to reproduce the mind of Christ, so that his outlook upon life may be in harmony with that of Jesus. This is a difficult undertaking. The language he uses, with its words whose meaning he apprehends, fixes the control and limits the range of any expressed interpretation of his own personal experience. General ideas come to him in the form of the thought patterns of his contemporary world. His mental background is largely a reproduction of the views on all matters, religion included, as these are held and declared to be true by those who dominate the thinking of his social environment. He lives and moves and has his being in the stream of current thought. The Christian, however zealous he may be in his efforts to reproduce the consciousness of Christ and to express in action his devotion to the ideas that Jesus taught, is limited, if not bound, by the cultural limitations of his times.

Christian history is the portrayal of the process through which the mind of Christ is more or less reproduced in single individuals, in various groups and in the total body of professing Christians, covering the past nineteen centuries. Ideally, the history of the Christian religion is the record of the impact made by the mind of Christ upon humanity since he emerged as a wandering teacher in Palestine. The actual account of this impact, modified by many human influences, is given, subject to the limitations of human knowledge, in the discipline called Church History.

A survey of Church History shows that in the Christian movement there have been five major conflicts, and today we are in the midst of the sixth, the most fearful of them all. The first of these conflicts resulted in the crucifixion of Jesus. The Pharisees were the educated leaders of the Jewish people. They were united in the carrying forward of a seemingly worthy purpose, the success of which involved the continuance of the Jews as a social unit. So long as each succeeding generation maintained the traditional customs, kept the regulations as taught by the rabbis, honored the

Mosaic Law and observed the festivals and the ceremonies that the Law required, the Jewish national consciousness continued to be effective in its control of the Jewish religious life.

Jesus came into direct conflict with the leaders of this program. He discredited their authority, he scorned their interpretations, he exposed their hypocrisy and he flouted their most cherished beliefs. Therefore, the Jewish leaders conspired to destroy him. Later, when the Gospel of Christ penetrated the Gentile world, many Jewish Christians, under the influence of Pharisaic culture, sought to crib, cabin and confine the Christian movement within the framework of the Mosaic Law. The conflict with these Judaizers is writ large in the Acts of the Apostles and in the Epistles.

When Christianity entered the Græco-Roman world, paganism was established everywhere. Beautiful temples rose in every town and city; sacrifices by priests, festivals, processions and other elaborated forms of worship were associated with every temple. Idolatry and polytheism were an important part in the social life of all peoples. Though few in number, the Christians set themselves against all forms of idolatry and they did not desist from their effort until every heathen temple was legally closed and pagan worship had been prohibited.

The persecution of the early Christians by the Roman emperors often has been misinterpreted. The Roman Empire was an established order, covering nearly the whole of the then known world. Civilization and the Empire were practically synonymous. Every religion was granted toleration, and the Roman government was indifferent to the number of religions that might be accepted by the individual or the group. The Christian religion was never persecuted solely as a religion. Universal reverence for authority, centering in the Roman emperor, was one of the basic principles in the Roman regime. This reverence the Christians were unwilling to show. They acknowledged as Lord of all an obscure Jew, concerning whom they said that he had been crucified and afterward had been raised from the dead. Thus the Christians arrayed themselves against the established order and openly opposed, by their recognition of the supreme authority of Jesus, a government which made possible commerce among widely separated peoples and guaranteed the safety of her citizens as they journeyed throughout the Empire. The blessings of peace, justice and civilization itself grew out of the administration of Roman law. The Christian movement refused to give unqualified support to this established order. A definite issue was raised by the demand of the Roman government that the Christians burn incense before the statue of the Roman Emperor, and where they refused, their persecution followed. When the conflict ended, the Roman Empire had ceased to exist.

For a thousand years the Roman Catholic Church established order, maintained discipline, crushed so-called heresies, erected asylums for the suffering and the oppressed, and supported schools in order that the ecclesiastically approved Christian doctrines might be perpetuated through the priesthood from generation to generation. The overthrow of this established order in large portions of Europe, we call the Reformation. "The Bible and the Bible only" became the battle cry of the Protestants. Men turned to their inner life to discover the truth and the strength of the Christian faith. Habakkuk and Paul gave to Luther the message, "The just shall live by faith." Men again sought to reproduce the spiritual experiences described in the Bible. Through their protestations, the absolute power of the Roman Catholic Church over northern Europe and Great Britain was forever broken.

The establishment of the State Churches, based upon the union of Church and State was the work of the rulers of the various territorial sovereignties whose emergence and development followed the Reformation. Their power was great and their rule was severe. However, there were Christians who could not accept the creeds and the practices of the State Church, and these opposed the religious intolerance exhibited by the ecclesiastical and civil powers. A love of freedom was growing. Persecution could not stay this mighty spiritual movement. Democratic governments were formed. The United States of America led in the incorporation of religious liberty as an essential part of its fundamental law. In lands where the State Church was the spiritual arm of government, freedom of worship was embodied into law and the rights of religious minorities were recognized. The trend in civilized lands was for the time toward the enjoyment of increasing religious liberty.

As we review this brief survey of the conflicts in history, we see that Christianity found liberation from Jewish tradition through the attack of Jesus upon Pharisaism; from the polytheistic priesthoods, through the assault of Apostolic and post-Apostolic leaders upon idolatry; from the Roman imperial rule, through the resistance of the Early Church to the worship of the Roman Emperor; from the ecclesiastical tyranny of the Papacy, through the revolt called the Reformation, and, last, from the legalized intolerance of the State, through the successful establishment of the principle of religious liberty and the separation of the Church from the State.

Today Christianity faces a problem beside which Pharisaism, Gentile Paganism, the Roman Empire, the Roman Catholic Hierarchy and the State Establishments fade away into comparative insignificance. This problem has had its origin in a materialistic science, so strongly entrenched in the culture of the modern world that governments, choosing the dicta of the scientists rather than the truths of divine revelation, are directing their powers to the obliteration of the idea of God in the minds of those over whom they exercise authority. The civilized world is witnessing the growing dominance of organized forces that seek the destruction of those social institutions and agencies that have safe-guarded and encouraged the spread of religious faith; among these institutions, in many respects the most powerful, is government.

World War II, whatever it may have been when it first began, is not merely a conflict for the preservation of democracy as a form of government, but a conflict for the preservation of man's most precious right, the right to love and to serve God according to the dictates of his own conscience. Totalitarianism which always claims, if its sovereignty be limited, and which always exercises, if its sovereignty be unchallenged, the power to enforce absolute submission, seeks the complete obliteration of the religious liberty that preconditions the free consideration of the claims that religion makes. "The essence of religion," say Chief Justice Charles E. Hughes, writing the dissenting opinion in the famous Macintosh case, "is a belief in a relation to God, involving duties superior to those arising out of any human relation. One cannot speak of religious liberty with a proper appreciation of its essential and historic significance without assuming the existence of a belief in a supreme allegiance to the will of God."

The suddenness with which the modern dictators brought under their sway so large a part of the world's population sent a shiver through the free peoples of earth, and the boldness with which they named the conditions under which they would desist from their works of destruction compelled thoughtful men everywhere to visualize the gulf into which they sought to plunge the whole of Western civilization.

The backgrounds of this modern Blitzkrieg against God need to be carefully studied; then, and not until then, can a proper and adequate consideration be given to the Christian program for the realization of a just and durable peace.

I

The Religious Scene Previous to the World War for Human Freedom

*"The Present Time—youngest born of Eternity, Child and heir of all Past Times with their good and evil, and parent of all the Future—is ever a 'New Era' to the thinking man. * * * * * To know it and what it bids us do, is ever the sum of knowledge for all of us."—*THOMAS CARLYLE.

THE CONSIDERATION of religion is coincident with the rise of reflective thought; the science of religion is the youngest of the major sciences. The oldest books in human history are religious books. Temples and altars are seen in every ancient civilization. No human group has been found so low in the scale of human development as to be lacking altogether in religious ideas and practices. The universality of religion is an established fact. Certain Australian tribes were reported as possessing no definite religious feeling, but a closer study has proved beyond question that ceremonies of a distinctly religious character exist among them. Mankind is "incurably religious." Everywhere men have sought the supernatural. Religion therefore is as inherent in the human mind as intelligence or morality, and in its reach is higher than either of them.

Since religions vary greatly as to forms, beliefs, and objects of worship, it follows that they cannot be of equal grade and value. Some are debasing and harmful; others possess only limited truth; while the adherents of no religion, not even Christianity, are in perfect accord as to faith and practice. "What religion, then, is worthy of acceptation by all mankind?" is the question to be answered. The inquiring student hesitates to accept the testimony of any religious adherent who, affirming the finality of his own religion, does not welcome the consideration of the claims and arguments of other religions. The supporters of Christianity should be every ready and glad to accept investigation and comparison.

New social and economic conditions are making possible the secondary education of an increasing proportion of American youth. Hundreds of thousands of young men and women are passing through our institutons of higher learning. They are meeting the problems raised by science and philosophy, and these involve religion. They are being trained in the sciences by experts; and even within institutions under the control of some religious body they receive more thorough instruction in the sciences than in the subject of religion.

American college graduates are much better prepared in the physical and the social sciences than in the field of religion. Where courses that bear upon religion are given particularly in philosophy and psychology, the frequent effect is to weaken, if not to break down altogether, the faith the student had when he entered college.

Modern communication has compressed the world to the dimensions of a neighborhood. As a result, we have an acquaintance with the non-Christian world which enables us to interpret and to value fairly the so-called heathen religions. The beliefs and the practices of the ancients are now so well known that the history of their religions is a recognized field of study. There are books on comparative religion written for popular use. "The evolution of religion" is a phrase widely used to describe a genetic explanation of the variety of religions in the world, and efforts have been made to show how, in a purely natural way, Christianity has evolved from earlier religious movements.

The writing of history is dominated today by the scientific method. This involves the acceptance of the law of continuity, or cause and effect, in the interpretation of the past. The historical method has gained the ascendency in many theological seminaries and is strongly intrenched in the work of scholarly interpreters of the Bible. The development of doctrine, or theology, is explained as a series of reactions made by religious thought to a concrete social or intellectual situation which, in some period of the past, created a problem for the ablest thinkers of that day. The particular doctrine, when it was formulated and officially approved, was then set forth as the true and final solution of the existing theological problem. The historical method, it may be noted in passing, lends little support to an inerrant divine revelation.

The tendency of nearly all modern writers is to interpret the history of religion as a natural human process, through which the individual or the group seeks satisfying adjustments with the superhuman powers or Power believed to exist. The most important decision which the student of religion makes in beginning his investigations is one the truth of which cannot be proved or disproved by an appeal to accessible data, namely, the reality of the supernatural. Following the present trend in this field, the student may assume that every religion of mankind "is a product of human evolution and has been conditioned by social environment"; that there is in the religious experience itself no evidence of the presence of the supernatural, and that the belief in a spiritual world cannot be based upon any sound, reliable footing. The study, then following the scientific method, is limited to human behavior in the field of religion. The provincial character of this assumption is readily seen; for the most important issue that religion raises— namely, the validity of the objects or Object of worship—is excluded from consideration before the investigation is actually started.

Every religion undertakes to satisfy some human needs. The development of man fixes the bounds of his desires and the limits of his needs. His mental progress contributes to the enlargement of his religious aspirations, and as a result the religion he accepts must contain new elements in order to satisfy his growing intellectual, moral and spiritual needs. Religious customs, rites, creeds, and institutions thus arise in response to these demands.

The work of the student who follows the scientific method is limited to the description of the practices, the beliefs, the feelings and the attitudes as exhibited by the adherents of any religion; to a comparison of these with similar data furnished by the investigation of other religions and to the framing of generalizations based upon these observations of the religious behavior of mankind. This is the clearly circumscribed field of the science of religion.

The recognized authorities in this realm of scientific study insist that it is impossible for them to assume the existence of God, the verity of the claims of the Christian religion, or the integrity of the Bible, because these assumptions lie outside the field of scientific investigation, which is limited by them to the consideration of observable physical and psychic facts. Therefore, all personal presuppositions and religious beliefs must be carefully eliminated by the scientific investigator, in order that the religious data he considers may be made the sole factor in determining the conclusions that may be reached. In order to maintain the scientific character of the study of religion, the investigator declines to take into his calculations the truthfulness of the basis on which all religions rest, namely, the reality of the supernatural. The scientist in the field of religion therefore prefers not to take sides upon the only issue which gives to religion any genuine interest or permanent value.

The students of science, philosophy, and religion take experience as the subject of study and create their several systems of thought. Each of these disciplines has its own techniques and objectives. All three groups of students are investigating experience, but each with a different purpose. Before going further, we recognize that a definition of experience is needed.

Experience is known to us only in the finite centers of the individual consciousness. Experience is all that is felt, perceived, understood, remembered, and willed.

The student of science is engaged in the measurement of experience and the basis of his study is mathematics.

The student of philosophy is seeking to discover the meanings of experience and the basis of his study is the laws of reason.

The student of religion posits an interpretation of experience that assumes an other-than-human relationship, the goal of which is the transformation of the mysterious, the transcendent, the divine into helpful ministries, and the basis of his study is the mystical in the religious experience. In simple phrase, religion is reverence in action, inspired by the belief that a helpful relation with the supernatural is humanly achievable.

In studying experience, the scientist asks the question, "How?"

The philosopher asks the question, "Why?" The religionist asks the question, "Whence cometh my help?"

The work of the scientist ends with description. Since there is uniformity in the changes which the scientist observes, the description becomes prediction for all future situations of like character. The work of the philosopher ends with the systematized explanation of the universe as a whole. He presents a world-view, in which are outlined the meaning of history and the realm of values. The religionist seeks the enhancement of life, and, on the highest level, his *summum bonum* is a satisfying relationship "with the Power that produced him, the Authority that is over him, and the Unseen Being with whom he is capable of communion." [1]

The scientist, discovering natural laws, directs man in the harnessing of natural forces, thus increasing the might of mankind. He seeks knowledge and power. The philosopher, discovering fundamental principles, enables men to recognize, at least to some degree, the unity and the harmony of all things, visible and invisible. He seeks wisdom. The religionist, discovering in his environment forces that threaten his peace and within himself aspirations that he cannot satisfy, offers an interpretation and proclaims a revelation that affords a hope of immediate benefit and assured blessedness. He seeks a lasting security and an everlasting salvation.

Each of these systems of thought—science, philosophy, and religion—presents a different interpretation of the universe, based upon a study of human experience. The scientist reaches a mechanistic interpretation of the universe; the philosopher, a metaphysical interpretation; the religionist, a mediatorial interpretation which posits the visible world as partly revealing and partly concealing the process, the meaning, the purpose, and the goal toward which the whole creation moves. The mediatorial interpretation in Christianity attains in Jesus Christ its fullest expression, as the divine Mediator between God and man. All three of these systems cultivate the same ground, but each sows different seed, and each reaps its own different harvest.

The scientist looks for an ever-changing universe in which law is uniform and ever present. If this gives a complete picture of the cosmos, the image of a machine more nearly describes the universe than any other figure.

The philosopher looks for a universe in which the existing dissonances within human experience may be harmonized, or at least rationally explained. If this is a complete picture of the cosmos, the proper and adequate interpretation of the universe is metaphysical.

The religionist, with mingled feelings of awe and submission, seeks adjustment with the unseen superhuman world which he has been taught to believe exists; he longs for a revelation in which he may trust, for a divine reinforcement which will endue him with more than human strength, and, on the higher moral levels, he hopes for a deliverance from sin and the possession of eternal life. If this be a complete picture of the cosmos, the true, the complete, and the final interpretation of the universe is mediatorial.

Religion is frequently described as a life, a creed, a worship. Religion is indeed all three. It is a way of living in the presence of the imperfectly known; it is expressed intellectually in a body of beliefs, and socially it manifests itself in forms of worship, in addition to creating its own institutional organizations for its perpetuation and its special agencies for world-wide propagation.

All religious phenomena have their rise in the religious experience of the individual, and the continuance of a religion is ever dependent upon the reproduction of this religious experience in the individuals of the generations that follow. As the form of thought in articulation is determined by the language of the group of which the individual is a member, so the visible and outward manifestations of the religious experience are determined by the religious modes of expression, characteristic of the religion to which the group adheres. The more highly a religion is organized, the greater is the social pressure which it brings to bear upon the individual life. There is a tendency in nearly all religions to compel assent and submission by some kind of external compulsion, and this has often taken the form of physical force.

Religious liberty is the recognition, the establishment, and the safeguarding of the rights of the individual, to the end that in all matters pertaining to religion he may act freely in giving expression to his religious attitudes and convictions; that he shall be neither enjoined nor molested as he associates himself with others holding to like beliefs and that those so associated shall enjoy as their natural right the propagation of their religious opinions and convictions, unhindered by any civil authority.

There has never been a time in American history when the individual enjoyed so much of freedom in the expression of his personal attitudes toward any and all organized religions as today. Those who assume common attitudes form groups. Racial and social inheritances, cultural attainment as well as personal temperament are factors to be recognized in any classification. Rightly interpreted, these groups picture in broad outline the modern religious mind. Christianity, embracing in our own country more than two hundred and fifty divisions, called denominations, is from the point of view of the wealth, the culture, and the power of the nations whose citizens have accepted it, the foremost of all religions.

These divisions of Christianity grow out of differing forms of government, varying interpretations of the sacraments or ordinances, competing claims as to ecclesiastical authority, and the divergent doctrines upon which these differences are based. The significance of this statement will appear later. All Christians are agreed as to the truthfulness of the teachings and the rightfulness of the claims of Jesus Christ, the benefits which will come to everyone who centers his trust in him as Lord and Saviour, and the desirability of extending Christianity throughout the world. They differ widely in the methods used to secure the ends upon which they agree.

Absolute uniformity of belief and action is unattainable under the existing conditions, for the Christian's religious experience is always the experience of an individual, with personal attitudes distinctly his own. The stronger the individuality, the greater is the strain in conforming to ecclesiastical demands. Such men and women, strong in their likes and dislikes, submit with increasing reluctance to denominational restrictions. The religious experience, however, demands a social expression, without which it is weakened in vigor and emotional power. If the individual represses his religious experience, it is at the cost of serious impairment. Religious freedom, with all its benefits, creates new and

disturbing problems, both for the individual Christian and for
organized Christianity, and these problems become more evident
when a division of mankind is made upon the basis of common
personal attitudes, whose unhampered expression is conditioned
upon the enjoyment of religious liberty.

The disciples of Jesus, according to the New Testament, had a
religious experience, made a confession of it and were given a
task which grew out of the experience and the confession. The
classic illustration of a functioning discipleship was given in connection with the declaration of Jesus regarding the founding of
his church. He asked his disciples what was the opinion of the
people generally as to himself. When they had answered, he
again asked, "But whom say ye that I am?" Simon Peter promptly
answered: "Thou are the Christ, the Son of the living God."
This was Peter's creed or confession of faith. Jesus gave priority
to the religious experience in saying, "Flesh and blood hath not
revealed it unto thee, but my Father who is in heaven." Then to
this disciple was given, based upon his experience and his confession, a commission, a task, to be shared with all others having
a like experience and making a like confession.

New Testament Christianity began as an experience, a confession, and a task. The experience grew out of the voluntary acceptance of Jesus Christ as Messiah and Lord. The phrase, "the
Lord Jesus Christ," was the earliest Christian confession of faith.
The task, given to Peter and to all the followers of Jesus Christ,
was the carrying of his Gospel to all nations—world-wide and age-
long evangelization. The continuance of primitive Christianity
thus depended upon the reproduction of the New Testament
experience, the New Testament confession, and the directing of
co-operative effort toward the accomplishment of the New Testament task.

The major problems of early New Testament Christianity arose
out of the attitudes and the presuppositions of the disciples, whose
minds had been molded by Jewish thought, largely of the Pharisaic type. Those who sought to unite the old Judaism and the
new religion which centered in the Messiahship and the Saviour
hood of Jesus, formed a party called the Judaizers. These endeavored to make the acceptance of the new faith conditional

upon the Gentile believer's, at least, partial submission to the restrictions imposed upon the Jews by the Mosaic law. The presence of the controversy is evident in the Acts of the Apostles and in the Epistles, especially the Epistle to the Galatians.

When Christianity came into contact with the Gentile world, it found the Greek mind in the ascendancy. Placing the greatest emphasis upon wisdom, it was natural for the Greek-speaking Christians, responsive to their intellectual environment, to give the foremost place to the confession or creed, the philosophical aspect of Christianity, and to concern themselves with orthodoxy, or right thinking.

The union of the Christian church and the Roman Empire led to the development of the Church under the direction of the Roman mind, skilled in organization; and under the influence of the Church of Rome, the task of the speedy and forcible propagation of the Christian religion throughout the known world was made the primary objective of organized Christianity. Identifying membership in and submission to the authority of the Church with the acceptance of Christianity, the Roman Church closed the doors of redemption to all who were outside its fold, by making Christian baptism the condition of salvation.

The movement called the Reformation was basically the recognition of the primacy of the Christian experience: "The just shall live by faith." It proclaimed the right of the individual to lay hold on salvation by a personal trust in Jesus Christ. The Bible was declared to be "the sole rule for faith and practice." Differences of belief, growing out of divergent interpretations as to the teachings of the Bible, divided the Protestants into the modern denominations.

This brief survey, general in character, suggests a division of modern organized Christianity in which the religious experience of the individual is made the basis of differentiation.

1. The Mystical Mind, including all Christians and all Christian bodies who make the personal acceptance of Jesus Christ primary.

2. The Theological Mind, including all Christians and all Christian bodies who make orthodox belief primary.

3. The Ecclesiastical or Sacerdotal Mind, including all Christians and all Christian bodies who give the Church and its clergy

the primary place. The principal member of this group is the Roman Catholic Church.

The non-Christian religions may be classified as tribal, nationalistic, ethical, and redemptive, the division being made on the conviction that in each there may be found a distinguishing loyalty in the religious experience of the individual. They are grouped under the following headings:

1. The Tribal Mind, embracing practically all the adherents of the animistic religions.
2. The Nationalistic Mind, best illustrated in the syncretistic religions of ancient civilizations.
3. The Ethical Mind, the religions that make the observance of ceremonial and moral laws the primary matter.
4. The Redemptive Mind, of which primitive Buddhism, in its desire to escape from the evils of life, is the most important.

The two groups, the Christian and the non-Christian, make up "this believing world"; but they do not include all mankind. There are those who, like Gallio, have no interest in religious discussion; others affirm that all religions are grounded in superstition and exert a baneful influence upon human life; and still others, keenly interested in the subject, assume the attitude of the suspended judgment or take openly an agnostic position.

The typical modern man, in intimate touch with the present tendencies of thought and in sympathy with the scientific method as the one reliable means for the acquiring of tested knowledge, is fascinated by evidence of the power that religion as a social force has always exerted. It presents a vast variety of phenomena; it exhibits everywhere tremendous and incessant activity, and it possesses a mighty and universal hold upon humanity. Religion also challenges his way of thinking and living. He feels bound to uncover its sources, to measure its energies, and to explain its activities.

If there are many interpretations of Christianity, as indicated by the number and variety of the denominations, there are also many interpretations of the meaning of life by those who are frankly and openly opposed to religion. Every writer, speaker and thinker has his own special point of view regarding this vital matter; and the power that religion awakens is present in the very emotion that marks his opposition, and in the difficulty he experiences in writing or speaking with restraint. Thus the modern skeptic, though he rejects all religion, is inescapably religious.

The mental attitudes of those who ally themselves with no religious body may be grouped under the headings: 1. The Scientific Mind; 2. The Hedonistic Mind; 3. The Confused Mind; and 4. The Hostile Mind.

1. The Scientific Mind is the characteristic attitude of an increasing number of cultivated men and women who have accepted the principle of causality as a sufficient explanation of religious phenomena. These affirm that the scientific method is the fairest and best in the pursuit of religious truth, since science "does not dogmatize; it observes. It deals only with phenomena—single phenomena or facts; group phenomena or laws." This attitude of mind is exhibited by many living philosophers as well as by nearly all scientists working in the field of religious phenomena.

2. The Hedonistic Mind embraces a large proportion of the non-religious population in Christian lands who, without serious reflection, accept the philosophy of happiness as crudely expressed in the phrase, "having a good time." These make pleasure an end, and resent the moral restraints which the Christian religion imposes.

3. The Confused Mind is the typical attitude of a multitude of college and university students and of serious and thoughtful men and women everywhere who are informed upon the issues which the modern study of religion has raised and find themselves bewildered as they try to relate their inherited faith with modern thought.

4. The Hostile Mind represents in this country a small but very active group who reject every religion, who denounce it as an inherited superstition, and who are vigorously opposed to all religious organizations. The Russian Communists and their sympathizers throughout the world form the most militant of all groups, hostile to every form of organized religion.

This concludes a survey of the religious scene during the Indian summer that separated World War I from World War II, the World War for Human Freedom.

II

The Blitzkrieg Against God

*"Two worlds are in conflict, two philosophies of life. * * * * One of these two worlds must break asunder."*—ADOLPH HITLER.

NEW WORDS are constantly breaking into popular use; the latest of such is "ideology," with its accompanying phrase, "the war of ideologies." Ideology once had a quiet, obscure place in the dictionary and belonged to the ponderous vocabulary of the philosophers, especially those who founded their systems upon biological evolution. If it had not been for the pundits of the press, the near-omniscient columnists, whose oracular effusions are syndicated and published in many American journals, this word would probably have remained true to its early meaning and usage, a philosophical pearl, such as "the deep, unfathomed caves of ocean bear," for the original definition of the word is "the science that treats of the evolution of ideas."

Usage is the final determiner of definition. Popular use is changing the word to mean "any system of thought which through propaganda, education or coercion is used to change and to dominate some area of human society." Ideologies, as thus defined, tend to create friction and collision within the social order, and whenever their supporters attempt by the use of force to impose these systems in the reorganization of society, either within the framework of a state or beyond its territorial boundaries, warfare is the natural outcome.

Since the intention of those who champion a new ideology is to change radically the structure of some well established social order, through the introduction of a carefully thought-out plan, the first stage is the stressing of the benefits that will inevitably follow the adoption of the plan. Thus modern ideologies have had their origin in civilized countries, where the masses are longing for social betterment.

The inauguration of a new ideology, in terms that appeal to social unrest and marked by active propaganda, is followed by the training of groups enthusiastically committed to its advancement. The last stage is the gaining of the control of the government and the use of force in the imposing of the new system upon those who are governed. Persuasion, education and coercion are the steps that lead to its successful establishment.

Civilization is the co-operative effort of men to create, to use, and to enjoy whatever is needed, useful and humanly satisfying. The five chief factors in every civilization are Mother Earth, language, co-operative activity, ordered life involving government and a sanctioning purpose, or religion. The basic problem of every civilization has been, and is, the proper correlation and the harmonious integration of all these factors. From this point, it is seen that the study of civilization must include the following:

1. The history of the development and the employment of the material resources available for use by man.

2. The study of the language through which literature, art, philosophy and religious thought assume nobler forms.

3. The account of the extension of co-operation, through an increasing division of labor, resulting in the multiplication of useful things, the exchange of goods, the creation of wealth and the higher spiritual values.

4. The description of the growth of social organization, culminating in a form of government fashioned so as to be a collective social instrument for the protection of the rights and the promotion of the security and the general welfare of the governed.

5. A survey of religion, as the ultimate source of that through which all that is reverently cherished and highly prized is given a supernatural sanction.

The essential character of these five basic factors are clearly seen. The bodies of men need sustenance. This earth on which we dwell is carrier of all the sustaining elements of physical life. Language is the carrier of ideas and thereby furnishes the sustaining elements in the thought life of man. The division of labor, the distribution of goods and the production of wealth are the carriers that support and perpetuate the economic order, without which the civilization could not survive. Government is the carrier of social security, which, through the making and the enforcement of just laws, suppresses disorders and preserves a stable society. Religion is the cement of civilization, and at its best is the carrier of human hopes for divine aid and guidance, for a world ruled in righteousness and for a lasting and durable peace on earth.

As the ancient civilizations, those sublime creations of the human spirit, pass in review, we see each bearing an appropriate title —the Egyptian, the Sumerian, the Cretan, the Babylonian, the Assyrian, the Persian, the Phœnician, the Greek, and the Roman; each adapting itself to its particular physical environment; each creating its own language, modes of written expression, literature, art and world-view; each cultivating the soil, inventing tools and machines, thereby increasing its wealth and extending its domain; each developing approved customs, standards of conduct, modes of government, and, quickened by the inescapable sense of dependence, each observing the ceremonies and supporting the institutions of the religion which binds into a spiritual unity the people, creating thereby a social solidarity, grounded in common worship.

Thoughtful men recognize these five essential elements in the genesis and growth of every civilization, and have chosen one or another of them as the basis of philosophical systems. Physical science, limiting its survey to Mother Earth, describes natural processes and postulates the law of continuity. Philosophers, grounding their conclusions upon the results of scientific study in the realm of the physical, evolve the various systems of Materialism. Others, recognizing a fundamental difference between matter and mind, have asserted that the mind has a reality that the changing phenomenal world does not possess, and beginning with Plato, develop systems of thought, under the general title of Idealism. Others still, more concerned for the preservation of the values of life, the objects of desire for which man is ever striving as having for him the highest and most enduring significance, create philosophies that range from the Practical Reason of Immanuel Kant to the various modern forms of Pragmatism.

Religious thinkers have formulated two systems of thought, with a third that is a principle rather than a finished system. The clergy of the Roman Catholic Church hold that this Church is by divine right above all human institutions, including the State, and that its approved doctrines embody a philosophy that is free from all error. Certain churches, national in their scope, assert that the Church is co-equal with the State and each is to support the other. The Free Churches are agreed in denying the totalitarian claims of the Roman Catholic church and in opposing the union of Church and State, but they have evolved no clearly outlined philosophy for the social order, save that they seek to leaven the whole of mankind with the spirit and the purpose of Jesus Christ. They place a little child in the midst, and declare that the civilization that undertakes to make central the physical, intellectual, moral and spiritual welfare of this child can provide the social order most needed by mankind, and that none other can.

Every civilization rests upon a system of values that embodies the principles of action that control the lives of the people, who, through co-operation and support, enjoy and perpetuate the particular culture that the civilization seeks to express.

Our American civilization, according to many students of political theory, is grounded upon the principle of the perfectibility of human nature. Out of this principle have evolved five corollaries which are believed to control social action. These are Freedom— the inalienable right of man to life, liberty and the pursuit of happiness; Democracy—political sovereignty is inherent in the will of the people; Popular Education—the dissemination of knowledge among all the people, irrespective of their station in life, is the most effective means of safeguarding and preserving democratic institutions; Modern Science—man has discovered in the scientific method the way through which all the forces of nature may be utilized in the promotion of human welfare; Unlimited Progress—the extension of man's freedom, the creation of material wealth and the enrichment of culture irresistibly contribute to human betterment. As these conceptions have become central in the thought and action of the people of the United States, the American way of life has been evolved.

The incorporation of the separation of Church and State, through the First Amendment of the Federal Constitution, has freed the people of the United States from coercion in the realm of religion, granting to every one "full liberty in religious concernments." All faiths stand upon an equality before the law of the land. Religious liberty guarantees the right to hold to any religious belief or to reject the claims of any and every religion. Within this land of the free, the religious and the irreligious are fully protected in the proclamation of their personal convictions. Our fathers never used the word ideology, yet it is proper to describe the principles that they wrought into the structure of our social order as the American Ideology.

Freedom of religion has given an opportunity for the development of three types of atheism: 1. Academic Atheism, based usually upon scientific materialism; 2. Practical Atheism, whose adherents act as if there were no God; 3. Militant Atheism, whose advocates hold that the belief in a personal God is a menace to the welfare of mankind.

Bertrand Russell illustrates the first: "God and immortality, the central dogmas of the Christian religion, find no support in science."

Practical Atheism is a way of living in which God is ignored. It has been estimated that at least fifty per cent of the people of the Western world today are practical atheists.

Militant Atheism asserts that the idea of God is a hindrance to public welfare and a menace to national progress. Its exponents are in general agreement with the declaration of the well-known historiographer, Dr. Harry Elmer Barnes, who says: "It is the thesis of the writer that the orthodox religious complex is, in its multifarious ramifications, the most active and pervasive menace to civilization that confronts mankind today, compared to which war and poverty are unimportant details." [2]

The growing skepticism regarding the existence and the sovereignty of God has not had a significant part in the political life of the English-speaking peoples. This is not true of Japan, Turkey, Russia, Germany and to some degree Mexico, where the assault upon the belief in God has assumed the character of open hostility.

Japan illustrates the outreaching of modern nationalism for a deity whose concern centers upon a single chosen race. Her Emperor, the bodily representative of heaven and earth, is divine; the land over which he rules is divine and the Japanese alone, of all peoples, are divine. Shrewd, subtle, ambitious and treacherous, the rulers of Nippon long had planned their Blitzkrieg against the idea of God. They appropriated every scientific discovery and invention made in other lands that could in any way be used in the equipping of their armed forces for world conquest. They taught their youth that if they died for their Emperor, they would become in another life gods in the Japanese Lotus Heaven. Their astonishing victories over trained British and American soldiers, in 1942, proved the power of this incentive; for the Japanese fought with a fanaticism born of this union of religion and patriotism. Among the nations now warring against God the Japanese are the least capable of acknowledging the sovereignty and the grace of the Christian God, whose fatherhood would embrace all races, kindreds and tribes.

Kemal Ataturk, the founder and later the dictator of the new Republic of Turkey, inaugurated the Blitzkrieg against God in the land where for centuries the Sultan, as the Caliph, had exercised spiritual authority over the entire Moslem world. He did not desist from his assault upon Allah, the God of Islam, until he had banished the reigning Caliph, Abdul Majid; forbidden the reading of the Koran, the Moslem Bible, made the wearing of the fez, a headpiece necessary to Moslem worship, a penal offense; stripped the veil from the faces of Turkish women and expunged all Arabic words from the language, supplanting the Arabic with the Roman alphabet. He set up, in place of the antiquated religious and civil courts, a modern legal system. He made his country into a modern state, and in so doing he created a nation without God. Desiring to become a world power and adopting science as a trustworthy guide, the Turkish people permitted the deportation of the Arab Allah. Turkish nationalism suppressed the fanatical and once militant Mohammedanism so completely that Kemal Ataturk, before his death, exultingly declared, "Islam, this theology of an immoral Arab, is a dead thing." [3]

The Blitzkrieg against God in Russia is the logical consequence of the acceptance of the teachings of Karl Marx, the pioneer of modern Communism. He declared in 1844 that "the beginning of criticism is the criticism of religion." Bakunin, another Communist leader, asserted that "if God exists, then man must be a slave. But man can and must be free. Therefore God does not exist."

The Bolshevists have repeatedly declared that "before capitalism can be destroyed, God must be toppled from his throne."

The Russian Revolution disestablished the Russian Orthodox Church, confiscated its landed estates comprising 19,000,000 acres, and its bank funds amounting to nearly $1,500,000,000. According to the findings of General Denikin's Commission, twenty-eight bishops and 1,215 priests were shot during the years of 1918-19. Atheism was taught in all state schools, and under governmental sponsorship the Union of Atheists, carried on its atheistic campaign throughout the wide expanses of the Soviet Union, using every available means for its propaganda. The Pope of Rome said in his encyclical of 1937: "For the first time in history we are witnessing a struggle, cold-blooded in purpose and mapped out to the least detail, between man and all that is called God." [4] The suppression of religious instruction and the persecution of religious leaders was conducted, under legal machinery, on a scale perhaps never known before in history. They attacked the idea of God on the ground that He was the enemy of the masses, the main support of capitalism and of economic enslavement; that the Bolsheviks, in making this attack, were fighting against fanaticism, superstition and ignorance and for economic freedom and the establishment of scientific truth.

There were three periods of religious suppression, 1922-23, 1929-30, and 1937-38. The official theory was that the religious leaders were counter-revolutionaries. The Russian Orthodox Church was the chief sufferer. The Baptists, the Evangelical Christians, and other groups, having in 1933, 3,000 registered communities and several million communicants, became the object of attack in 1929, when all religious propaganda was made illegal. Under severe persecution, their members rapidly declined and their ministers were imprisoned, exiled or put to death. The Union of Atheists, with 80,000 organizations, reported in 1932, 7,000,000 members, not including 1,500,000 Godless children.

Faith in God survives in Russia. From 1937 onward, there have been signs of a revival of religion. The Soviet press has recognized the growing strength of Christian faith in the U.S.S.R. The power of the Union of Atheists is waning. Baptists and Evangelicals have been permitted to appeal to their brethren throughout the world to pray for the victory of the United Nations. Russian diplomats are stressing the fact that their Constitution grants freedom of worship. The Communist atheists, who inaugurated the Blitzkrieg against God, have not won a complete victory.

Hitler had little to say about religion in his *Mein Kampf*, though he did assail sending missionaries to inferior races. Apparently he hoped to destroy the Jews without calling down upon himself the condemnation of German Lutherans and Catholics on this racial persecution. He expected these two religious bodies to submit to the government's policy because they were being financially supported from the public treasury.

The National Socialist Party declared in its program: "We demand the liberty of all convictions in the State, so far as this does not endanger or militate against the customs or moral feelings of the German race." Attributing to the moral feelings of the German race the final determination in all religious matters opened the way for a religion grounded upon the presence of God within German blood and race, and that reversion to a tribal religion is today in process of formulation.

The National Reich Church of Germany has been organized, limited in membership to those of Nordic descent; no deed is to be approved by this Church which does not serve to safeguard the nation; along with the Jews, the Old Testament must be banished from Germanic religion and culture; the prime object of the Church is the religious renewal of the people out of their specific German inheritance, and the goal of this German Faith Movement, in the words of President Roosevelt, is to "abolish all existing religions, Catholic, Protestant, Mohammedan, Hindu, Buddhist and Jewish alike."

The plan for the National Reich Church, drawn up by Alfred Rosenberg, Hitler's most trusted adviser in the field of German culture, has received the support of the powerful Nazi Youth organizations. Goebbels, Himmler, and other Nazi leaders gave full endorsement to the Thirty Point Plan of the new Church. Point Five asserts that the National Reich Church is determined "to exterminate irrevocably and by every means the strange and foreign Christian faiths imported into Germany in the ill-omened year 800." All church buildings are to be confiscated and on their altars there will be neither the Bible nor the crucifix but *Mein Kampf* and a shining sword—*Mein Kampf*, it is solemnly declared being, "to the German nation, and therefore to God, the most sacred book." The swastika is to replace the Christian cross on all cathedrals, churches and chapels within the Reich. Hitler is heralded by some Nazi leaders as the German Messiah, and children are taught to pray for him and to him.

Alfred Rosenberg, whose book *The Myth of the Twentieth Century*, published only in German, has had a sale of more than a million copies, on page 146, 94th edition, declares that the concept of national honor is "the beginning and end of our thoughts and actions. It does not tolerate any rival source of influence, whether it be Christian love, Masonic humanitarianism or Roman philosophy."

A pall hangs over religion throughout the world. No nation is free from the confusion, the dislocation, the strife that arises out of the conflict between organized religion and organized society. The United Nations have not, and indeed cannot, unite in endorsing the Four Freedoms, of which Freedom of Religion is one. Within Great Britain, Canada, and the United States, every effort is concentrated upon the prosecution of the war, but competent observers report no marked deepening of interest in religion. Some students of history are saying that this is the darkest hour the Christian religion has faced.

Academic Atheism pervades wide circles of the English-speaking intelligentsia; Practical Atheism controls the lives of multitudes in all lands, who act as if God did not exist; Militant Atheism, which in its most effective expression is the denial by governments of the right of God to the supreme allegiance of mankind, is suppressing organized religion, unless it actively serves some ideological system that the ruling power would enforce. These three forms of atheism create, combine and produce a crisis for Christianity that involves its very existence.

The situation is thus described by George Terrell in a recent issue of the *Hibbert Journal*; "Science by rejecting the supernatural has made orthodox religion unintelligible so long as it is taken to be true in the absolute sense which it claims; orthodox religion in consequence hangs in a mist of unreality, preserved like a museum piece, rapidly acquiring the tender charm of fairyland."

We are standing on the brink of the abyss. We look downward and we are frightened. If we seek to understand, if we seek to know how to bridge that abyss, it may be wise for us to look backward and study the linguistic cultures that have extended, but, at the same time, have weakened the Christian faith. We turn for the present from the Blitzkrieg against God to the study of the molding of Christianity through the historic impact that successive cultures have made upon the first-century faith and the Christian way of life.

III

The Mind of Christ

"Let this mind be in you which was also in Christ Jesus."—PAUL.

MIND, as used in this work, is the point of view of large groups of individuals, often myriads in number, who have been able to influence and in a measure control the course of Christian history. The only exception is in the study of the Mind of Christ. The thesis is maintained that, in so far as the simple Christian faith departs from the point of view of Jesus, the Christian religion loses thereby something of its distinguishing character and inherent spiritual power.

The purpose of the studies which follow is the interpretation of the changes in the Christian religion, as recorded in Church History, that evidence the influence of a contemporary environment upon the existing forms of organized Christianity—a survey of the human factors that have transformed the simple, vitalizing faith portrayed in the New Testament into the competing and often conflicting expressions that the Christian religion assumes today.

The approach to the study of the Mind of Christ is attended by many difficulties. He was limited in his teachings by the language he used, by the religious thought-patterns of his day and by the ascendancy of the Pharisaic group-mind. The Messianic idea of his day was wrapped up in an apocalyptic program which involved an earthly kingdom and the conquest of the world by the Jews, while the current conception of religious service to God centered in the meticulous observance of ceremonial and moral laws. Closing his earthly ministry, he was forced to say to those who understood him best, "I have yet many things to say unto you, but ye cannot bear them now."

The problem is further accentuated by the fact that the materials which throw light upon the mind of Christ are so scanty, limited to the four Gospels and a few reported sayings in the Epistles and elsewhere. Furthermore, all the teachings of Jesus are addressed to an Oriental people, far removed from the modern Occidental mind, so that often it is no easy task to pour his real meaning into the molds of contemporary thought.

Scholars divide hopelessly in their interpretations. Speaking in general terms, the final viewpoint adopted rests upon the attitude and the personal presuppositions of the individual scholar. If he approaches the materials to be studied, convinced that Jesus is merely a man, the product of his age, he applies to the record the scientific principles which control the historical method and seeks to explain everything as a natural process, dismissing as untrustworthy any item that cannot be seen as illustrating the law of historical continuity. His estimate of Jesus will vary from that of a deluded enthusiast, dreaming of himself as Israel's Messiah, to that of him as the last of the great Hebrew prophets, setting forth profounder moral objectives than any of the earlier seers of Israel. If the scholar represents one of the great Christian bodies of today, whose creeds define the person and the work of Jesus Christ, the whole of the material available for study will be interpreted in harmony with the accepted historic creeds.

Yet there is enough in the Gospels of teaching and incident that reveal clearly the mind of Christ, that make possible the formulation of the point of view that Jesus sustains with reference to all the significant problems of human life; and this is the goal of the present study. The quest is to discover the principles that determine the conduct of Jesus.

The first recorded words of Jesus, given by Luke, "Wist ye not that I must be about my Father's business?" are a pregnant and significant utterance: 1. "I," the affirmation of self-consciousness, involving personal relations to other selves; 2. "Must," the affirmation of duty-consciousness, involving a moral order whose sovereignty he recognizes; 3. "Father," the affirmation of God-consciousness, involving his participation on the side of God in the activities of the world.

The first glimpse we have of the growing youth Jesus reveals a mind in which the service to God is the primary duty. This sentence also gives the natural divisions for the study of the Mind of

Christ: 1. How and What He Thought of Himself and Others;
2. How and What He Thought of Moral Obligations; 3. How
and What He Thought of Religion and of God.

1. The truly great teacher creates, within the minds of his students, an increasing evaluation of all mankind. By this test Jesus is
pre-eminent. He is the world's greatest believer in the worthfulness of man. In asking, "What shall it profit a man, if he gain the
whole world and lose his own soul?" he places the noblest conceivable valuation upon the human personality and suggests that the
eternal welfare of man is the ultimate goal in the cosmic process.
The universe is interpreted by him as a means to an end. He im-
plores men to live upon the upper level of human experience,
namely, the religious consciousness, by bringing into operation the
principles that inhere in the perfect and holy character of God,
so that their lives may be controlled by these principles and they
may thus realize in themselves the fulfillment of the supreme purpose of creation. The universe is made for man, to the end that
man may voluntarily find his fullest self-realization in God.

The possibility of ordering the individual life in harmony with
the will of God is the ground on which Jesus rests his appreciation
of the human personality. All men are potentially the sons of God.
In himself Jesus makes the experiment of exhibiting under human
conditions a life nourished and dominated by the purpose to do
the will of the Father, on the basis of which he calls to mankind,
"Follow me." Jesus reveals the capacity of man to extend hospitality to God, and his whole message is summed up in the words:
"If a man love me, he will keep my word; and my Father will love
him, and we will come unto him and make our abode with him."

Since God holds man in such high esteem, all men should make
reverence for personality the governing principle in all human relationships. "Thou shalt love thy neighbor as thyself" is not fulfilled
unless it is accompanied by the unceasing effort to "become neighbor" to everyone. This is the teaching of the parable of the Good
Samaritan. Reverence for personality, finding its expression in
seeking the good and only the good of others, underlies all the
teachings of Jesus. Love is the natural expression, wherever such
an appreciation of personality exists. Love is the desire to bless
another, and, when it has complete ascendancy, it evokes all the

resources of the individual personality in the fulfillment of the endeavor. The brotherhood of man does not rest upon ties of blood, but upon the fact that every man possesses a personality worthy of reverence by all his fellows, and brotherhood becomes a living fact, not merely a theory, when and only when this reverence finds its expression in practical, loving ministries.

Jesus ignores social gradations and approaches the various groups of his day seeking only their good. He mingles alike with the rich and the poor, the most respected members of the community and the despised publicans and sinners. Crowds touch his sympathies and sometimes move him to tears. The Jewish people are sadly oppressed. Their taxes, civil and religious combined, are estimated by competent scholars to have absorbed one-third of their annual income. Poverty and suffering are found everywhere. The discontent of the times is linked to the hope of an earthly Messianic King. A few years later the country will flame into revolt. Yet Jesus offers no immediate panacea. In his thought, these evils are superficial and secondary. The source of all the ills in human life is the naughty heart of man. He has come to seek and to save the lost, and his mission is accomplished when the individual, denying self by repudiating all selfish and unholy desires, becomes his disciple. Jesus refuses to settle an issue between two brothers involving the distribution of property. He makes a clear-cut distinction between the duties which the individual owes to Cæsar and those which he owes to God. He is not a social reformer; he is a soul-regenerator.

Jesus seeks to improve society by bringing its individual members into right relation with God and thereby with one another. The ideal society he proclaims is the Kingdom of God, the rule of God voluntarily accepted by all who, one by one, enter into the Kingdom. Human relations, of whatever kind or character, are the field of action in which is expressed within human limitations the rule of God. The Gospel Jesus preaches is individualistic in its appeal but socialistic in its practice. Jesus gives to the individual the highest value and commits to him a social program in which he may prove the verity of this evaluation.

2. The desire to do good to others must have ascendancy over the inner life if conduct is to measure up to the requirements of

Jesus. The test of all moral acts is whether they are inspired by an altruistic motivation. Enemies must be loved and the injury another does must be met by an invincible generosity. Each individual is under obligation to be the center of a radiating beneficence. Everyone who asks forgiveness must have his request granted and the wrong forgotten. The generous-hearted, who express their good-will in loving ministries to all who are in need, shall enter into an eternal blessedness. In the mind of Jesus, love is not a kindly, philanthropic emotion; it is the dedication of all of one's powers to the practical and generous expression of good-will, without the expectation of any objective earthly benefit to be gained thereby. It is on this high level that Jesus meets those of his day, and his behavior toward them perfectly illustrates the principles he teaches. He is put to death because of the irreconcilable conflict between his way of living and that of his contemporaries.

Jesus denies that self-interest, however intelligently guided, has the right to control conduct. He refuses to use his miracle-working powers for his personal advantage. He will not employ spectacular methods to gain popular applause, and he indignantly repudiates the suggestion of a compromise with evil as the means of attaining success. Selfish motives he rejects altogether.

The secret of the moral grandeur of Jesus is that in every situation his response reveals one and only one motive, the desire to do the will of the Father. In his daily life, he realizes the ideal he sets forth in his teachings, and the motive which enables him to accomplish this is devotion to God. In this ideal he sets before men a seemingly impossible task, but if the dominant desire in the individual be that of performing this task, the Father in heaven will give the good things—aspirations, motives, resolutions, spiritual energies, all that later is connoted in Christian literature as divine grace, and thus the performance of the task becomes possible. Jesus sees no limit to human development if the individual be rightly related to God: "Ye therefore shall be perfect, even as your heavenly Father is perfect."

Jesus gives the highest valuation to man and sets before him the highest moral ideal. To him the tragedy of all tragedies is to turn from this ideal. Absolute disaster is certain to follow. Jesus thinks often in pictures. Into the vale of Hinnom, near Jerusalem, is thrown the refuse of the city; the fires are kept burning always to prevent the spread of pestilence. The Greek name of the place is Gehenna. Jesus says that whoever violates the principle of reverence for personality in calling his brother by a contemptuous name is "in danger of the Gehenna of fire." Those who do not avail themselves of the privilege of ministering to the needy shall be thrust "into the eternal fire, prepared for the devil and his angels." The Rich Man, whose only recorded sin is that he ignored the claims of the beggar at his gate, is in the future life punished by "being in torments." "The unprofitable servant," who simply fails to invest the talent entrusted to him by his master, is flung "into the outer darkness; there shall be weeping and gnashing of teeth." Every one who does not live in accordance with the teaching of Jesus is likened to a foolish man who builds his house on the sand. When the storm breaks, disaster follows.

Sin, according to the contemporaries of Jesus, is the violation of a regulation set forth in the Mosaic law or derived therefrom; sin, according to Jesus, is an inward lawlessness, growing out of the absence of the organizing and dominating principle of love to God and fellow man. Righteousness to him is more than obedience to a statutory religion; it is a passion for goodness, whose dynamic is devotion to God. "To miss the mark" is the New Testament definition of sin, and the mark can be attained only through the presence in the life of the individual of a dominant purpose to do the will of God.

The moral ideal, according to Jesus, is the character of God. The only motive in the human heart that can produce morality of this ideal type is an unselfish love, inspired by trust in God, that completely masters the individual life. Moral failure or sin prevails in every one, for man by his own strength cannot attain this ideal. To make possible such an attainment is the mission of Jesus. It is not sufficient that he illustrates this ideal in his own life and becomes thereby an example and a moral standard. He must make available some divine reinforcement by which man, hitherto defeated in the realization of his moral endeavors, may conquer the evil tendencies within and order his conduct in harmony with the ideal Jesus reveals. To this end everything Jesus says and does is addressed.

One-seventh of the material in the four Gospels is devoted to the record of the last twenty hours of the earthly life of Jesus. Under the shadow of the cross, the thoughts of Jesus might naturally be directed solely toward his approaching death. Such is not the case. Incident after incident is related in which he is seeking the moral betterment of those about him. He is concerned for others, not himself, and this is expressed in a solicitude for their well-being, most often for their moral well-being. A contention arises that fateful Thursday evening among his disciples as to which one is the greatest. Jesus reproves them and later washes their feet as an example of humility. He suffers his betrayer to take an honorable place at the table, and warns him as to the consequences of his treachery. He seeks to prepare his disciples for the shock of his arrest and crucifixion. He tells Peter that, though he will be disloyal, he has prayed for him. Only in the Garden of Gethsemane does he allow his mind to dwell wholly upon the cup of his sufferings. Betrayed, he pleads that his disciples be let alone. He heals Malchus, whose ear had been cut off by Peter's sword. As he is being taken to the cross, he begs the women of Jerusalem not to weep for him. He prays for those who engage in the crucifixion. He assures the malefactor, whose moral sense condemns the injustice done to Jesus, that they will be together in Paradise. He arranges for his mother to have a home with the Beloved Disciple. The day is filled with little, loving ministries and tender and serious expressions of anxiety in behalf of those about him, that they shall not fail to do their best. He suffers when they are shown to be weak, mean, dull of understanding, and disloyal to the ideal he is giving them.

The most insistent effort in which Jesus engages throughout his earthly ministry is to help others to be good. He illustrates perfectly the principle that to be rightly related to God is to be unconscious of self and keenly conscious of the needs and the claims of other selves. His ministry is to awaken in men a devotion to God and so to strengthen this devotion that it shall have a controlling power in every moment and incident of the personal life.

3. The religious consciousness is the highest level in human experience, and on this level Jesus lived and interpreted all the relationships of life. No other founder of a religion has ever made

such claims or such demands: "Neither doth any man know the Father save the Son, and he to whomsoever the Son willeth to reveal him. Come unto me, all ye that labor and are heavy laden, and I will give you rest." He asserts a knowledge of God unique and complete, and he commands all men everywhere to give to him voluntarily the complete control of their lives.

The closer one studies the Gospels, the more he is convinced that the note of authority in the teachings of Jesus is traceable to the deep conviction that all that he does is in harmony with the will of God, and that in all he says he is voicing the thought of God. The Synoptics are in complete harmony with John in the portrayal of this striking quality. The note of authority, which never fails to startle and deeply impress his hearers, unquestionably rests upon his consciousness of God. He is fully convinced as to his divine ambassadorship in revealing God's forgiving love for all repentant sinners.

To Jesus, God is the Ultimate Reality, present in a friendly universe; the Divine Providence, caring for the welfare of men; the Unseen, Universal Presence, to be worshiped in spirit and in truth; the Lord of Heaven and Earth, whose reign should be acknowledged and whose will should be done; the Source and the Inspiration of all holy living, human goodness in its highest form being the response to the goodness of God; the Father who, in Jesus, "the only begotten Son," reveals his life-giving truth, his perfect righteousness, and his infinite love to the end that his eternal unchanging purpose may be realized in the spiritual enfranchisement of mankind; so that those who receive the Son shall possess "the right to become the children of God." To enable men to enjoy this right is the mission of Jesus.

The Incarnation is the doctrine or teaching that, within the life of Jesus God is manifested. Every one who believes this is under a moral obligation to obey the commands of Jesus as the commandments of God. Whoever rejects the Incarnation, if he be logical in his thinking, must dismiss Jesus as an authoritative guide in both morals and religion.

Jesus speaks with authority in fields where no man has the right to speak unless he bears the credentials of God. Jesus does more; he makes demands and actually exercises authority to which he has no right unless he is the Spokesman of God. However he may be explained as a member of the Godhead, he is either the Mediator between God and man, and between man and God, or the Christian experience, as recorded in literature and expressed in the saintly living of multiplied millions, is a delusion. The impressive, inescapable fact is that Jesus asserts that he is in the world to create this experience in the lives of men: "The Son of man came to seek and to save that which is lost"; "I came that they may have life, and may have it abundantly." This is the dominant purpose in the mind of Christ; and to it we now give attention.

Absolute loyalty is the demand Jesus makes upon everyone. Devotion to a Person underlies the Christian experience. The transfer of the control of the inner life completely to Jesus is the primary requirement in discipleship, to be followed by the expression of this sovereign allegiance in every word and act. In the process the individual is saved from his sins and is given a divine reinforcement to develop a Christlike character. This is the strait and narrow gate through which his followers enter into life. Whosoever thus confesses Jesus, he will also confess before the Father in heaven.

As Jesus is limited by a human body, he also is limited by a human vocabulary, human thought-patterns, and human group minds, the contemporary Pharisaic mind being the most influential. A study of these confining factors would involve a prolonged discussion of such words and phrases as "Messiah" and the Messianic consciousness of Jesus; "Kingdom," with its various contemporary conceptions, contrasted with the one Jesus holds; "the Torah" or Law and its interpretation by Jesus in opposition to the view held by the Pharisaic group-mind; "the Son of Man" and its meaning when used by Jesus, and many other current terms. Jesus unquestionably gives to old conceptions new emphasis and introduces conceptions altogether original. The literature dealing with these problems is extensive and constantly increasing; to these books the interested student is referred.

Jesus describes the life to which he calls men as a striving to express in the round of daily living the principles which inhere in God. His temptations exhibit in himself the striving, and the complete success of his striving toward this selfsame end. Jesus seek more than doing right; he seeks in each situation the actualization of the perfect deed. Greatness is linked to lowliness of spirit and expresses itself in the service of all. The strain of this humble ministry to which he dedicates all his powers leads to exhausting toil. In the effort to woo and win men away from the love of sinning to the life of trustful, loving obedience to God, Jesus realizes the inescapable necessity of his suffering for them. This suffering, foretold by the Hebrew prophets, is seen to be a fulfilment of the Father's will and is an essential element in the expression of the love of God in Christ Jesus. "Behooved it not the Christ," says Jesus after his resurrection, "to suffer these things and to enter into his glory?"

Love toils and suffers for the welfare of those who are loved, and the love of God, expressing itself in the life of Jesus, toils and suffers, until the life itself is poured out unto death. The message of Jesus is that there is no limit to the forgiving and redemptive love of God and that this love is always effective in the saving of the people from their sins, except in those who, self-willed and unrepentant, do not respond to the appeal of divine love. Reverence for the human personality on the part of God prevents the use of divine power to compel the allegiance of men. If a man refuses to give to Jesus voluntarily the control of his life, that man must suffer the consequences of his choice.

The lowest level on which man lives is found in the adjustment he makes to his physical environment, the outer world. Jesus thinks of this outer world, which we call the physical universe, as beautiful, changeful, orderly and exhibiting a divine providence for the needs of men. In the realm of personal relationship he posits the principle of reverence for personality as basic, and affirms that love, the desire to bless others, is the only rightful motive to action. The holy and perfect character of God is the standard and guide for all moral acts. "Religion is the life of God in the soul of man," an experience perfectly realized and expressed in the earthly life of Jesus, an experience attainable in lesser degree by anyone who voluntarily devotes himself to "the culture of the consciousness of Christ"; for in this endeavor he is responding to the demand of Jesus, "Follow me."

IV

The Apostolic Mind

"We ought to obey God rather than men."—PETER and his fellow Apostles.

THE COURSE of Christian History may be studied descriptively, giving the succession of events, the growth of institutions, the development of doctrine, and the action and reaction of the Christian movement upon civilization. The purpose of the present study is interpretative rather than descriptive. The actual course of Christian history is marked by conflict without and within organized Christianity. Large areas and extended periods lie in obscurity, because the historical records are either scanty or altogether lost. Other periods remain to be more fully investigated and studied in order that a truer understanding may be gained. However, the interest of the student, who does not wish to specialize in the field of Church History, centers not in the data so much as in the drift of the Christian movement, and his demand can be met only by giving a satisfying answer to the following question: "If the mind of Christ be the norm, why has Christianity so often assumed forms and exhibited a character out of harmony with the norm?"

The theory is propounded and defended that in the Apostolic Mind are found the elements which in succeeding periods have been unduly emphasized, creating thereby an ascendant Christian group-mind, out of balance to a greater or less degree with Christian truth. This is due in every instance to the response which the Christians of that particular period make to the preponderant group-mind which, existing outside of organized Christianity, forms its intellectual climate, and in a large measure molds its contemporary economic and cultural environment. The three elements entering into this environment previously noted, are: The prevailing language, the characteristic thought-patterns, and the ascendant group-mind.

50

The changing environments of historic Christianity have demanded adjustments, and in making these adjustments organized Christianity has changed its emphasis, has accepted new centers of control, and has modified—sometimes radically—its interpretation of the Christian faith. An adequate study of Church History seeks to discover what the world has done to Christianity as well as what Christianity has done in the world.

The divisions into which the study falls cannot be arranged in a definite chronological scheme. Each general period shades away into other periods, and any group-mind within organized Christianity, whenever it gains an ascendancy, continues to influence and in a measure to control the thinking of at least a considerable group in succeeding generations of Christian believers. It is desirable at this point that an outline of descriptive Church History be presented as a historical setting to our study.

The divisions, as usually stated in the manuals of Church History, are: 1. From the birth of Christ to the end of the Apostolic Age (A.D. 100); 2. From the end of the Apostolic Age to the conversion of Constantine (C.A.D. 312); 3. From the conversion of Constantine to the founding of the Holy Roman Empire by Charlemagne (A.D. 800); 4. From the coronation of Charlemagne to the outbreak of the Protestant Reformation (A.D. 1517); 5. From the outbreak of the Protestant Reformation to the Peace of Westphalia (A.D. 1648); 6. The Era of Modern Denominationalism (since A.D. 1648). Such an outline as this is necessary to a descriptive history of Christianity.

Our chosen method does not lend itself to such definite chronological distinctions. The growth of a group-mind is usually a slow process, and the projection of its influence upon succeeding times continues long after it has been partially or wholly succeeded by another competing group-mind. The elements which form the Apostolic Mind furnish the basis of differentiation: 1. The inherited religious beliefs of Judaism; 2. The acceptance of Jesus of Nazareth as the risen and ascended Christ, who as man's only Saviour should be heralded to Jew and Gentile alike; 3. The growth of a Christian community, grounded upon a personal experience of God's forgiving grace; inspired by a missionary purpose; organized for promoting the spread of the Gospel, the maintenance of the highest standards in Christian living, and the fullest expression of active Christian love in caring for the needy brethren wherever they are found; 4. The appreciation of spiritual gifts and the conviction that no one is truly a Christian who has not received the Holy Spirit; 5. The belief that the complete control of the present and the future centers in God who, through Christ in his Second Coming, will judge the world and reward his saints.

These five fundamental conceptions have been successively emphasized in Christian history, and these periods of emphasis furnish the natural divisions for the epoch-making stages in the development of organized Christianity, each of which is characterized by a new language, new thought-patterns, and a new ascendant group-mind.

If a linguistic nomenclature be used, these epochs may be described as: 1. The Aramaic; 2. The Greek; 3. The Latin; 4. The Teutonic; 5. The English. Should characteristic thought-patterns furnish the titles, the list would be as follows: 1. The Legalistic; 2. The Philosophic; 3. The Imperialistic; 4. The Nationalistic, and 5. The Scientific.

The first epoch may be considered as nearing its close with the end of the first century; the second extends over the succeeding three centuries and continues as a mighty influence in the intellectual life of Christianity; the third is coextensive with Roman Catholicism; the fourth ushers in the Protestant Reformation and stretches well through the nineteenth century; the fifth covers the comparatively brief but fruitful period since the rise of modern science.

These epochs, interpreted from the viewpoint of ascendant group-minds, are divided into triads: the first portraying the group-mind that environs contemporary Christianity; the second, portraying the response made by Christian thinkers to the environing group-mind as it introduces new interpretations and possible departures from the Christian truth, and the third, portraying the group-mind within organized Christianity, resulting from the impact of its social environment, which undertakes to bind the thinking of all Christians to the teachings and the interpretations, the principles and the laws, which have the endorsement of this Christian but biased group-mind.

Adopting somewhat arbitrarily the language generally used during each epoch as the important characteristic, we may give to these five epochs the following titles: 1. The Aramaic Triad; 2. The Greek Triad; 3. The Latin Triad; 4. The Teutonic Triad; 5. The English Triad. In each of these there are three group-minds. Attention is called to the fact that although in each group-mind there may be found a collection of ideas so arranged that they form a harmonious group or system, yet within the group holding to these views there are, especially in the earlier stages of its development, differences of opinion, debate, and sharp controversy.

The Aramaic Triad is divided into: 1. The Mind of Christ as revealed in the Gospels and the Epistles; 2. The Apostolic Mind, the interpretation of the Mind of Christ as reflected in the thinking of the Apostles and others in the New Testament; 3. The Judaizing Mind, the powerful group within the Christian body, strongly nationalistic and Pharisaic in their sympathies, who seek to impose upon Jewish and Gentile believers alike the requirements of the Mosaic code, thus restricting the Christian movement to that of a sect within Judaism. The period ends with the disappearance of Judiac Christianity, early in the fourth century, but the defeat of the Judaizers is practically completed by A.D. 100.

The Greek Triad embraces: 1. The Gentile Mind, which environs the Christians wherever they extend their missionary efforts beyond the Jewish people; 2. The Hellenistic Mind, developing within the Christian body as men possessing Greek culture undertake to interpret the Christian faith to their contemporaries, placing the emphasis upon the intellectual aspects of Christianity; 3. The Theological Mind, represented by the scholarly group of distinguished Christian thinkers, who, defining doctrines and formulating creeds, seek, by the use of all available means, to enforce right thinking or orthodoxy throughout organized Christianity. The period of the Theological Mind, which formulates the Christian doctrines of the Godhead, extends from the beginning of the second to the close of the fifth centuries. The development of theology, in its wider sense, continues; but its connection is no longer limited to Greek terminology and philosophical thought-patterns.

The Latin Triad embraces: 1. The Roman Mind, which, politically environing Christianity at its very beginning, later becomes the determining factor in the development of its ecclesiastical government and law; 2. The Sacerdotal Mind, which, influenced in no small degree by the competing Mystery Religions, endows the forms and symbols of the Apostolic Period with divine powers, setting forth the theory that salvation is impossible outside of the Church, and, fixing the number of the Christian sacraments at seven, makes each sacrament a supernatural operation and the essential and necessary vehicle of divine grace; 3. The Ecclesiastical Mind, represented by the founders and supporters of the Papacy, which gives to the Roman Catholic Church the highest valuation as a divine institution and reaches a logical and final expression in the doctrine of papal infallibility (A.D. 1870), as now taught and promulgated by that Church.

The Teutonic Triad embraces: 1. The Mystical Mind, so interpreted as to include the intellectual trends within the Roman Catholic Church as well as the secular medieval thought which affect the freer, spiritual movements that seek expression during the Middle Ages, especial emphasis being given to the mystical view that in the Christian experience a union of the human soul and Ultimate Reality is realized and that direct intercourse with God is attained through a personal faith in Jesus Christ; 2. The Protestant Mind, which, believing that the acceptance of the message of the Gospel produces the saving Christian experience, seeks to re-establish upon the teachings of the New Testament the doctrines which grow out of salvation by faith in Jesus Christ, and finds its historic expression in the Protestant Reformation that formally begins A.D. 1517; 3. The Nationalistic Mind, creating contemporaneously with the Protestant Movement territorial sovereignties, whose rulers claim the right to exercise absolute authority, and which leads to the union of State and Church and the establishment of National Churches, controlled and supported by the State.

Modern history is the record of the spread of democratic principles, the growth of popular education, the rise of industrial civilization, and the dissemination of evangelical teachings, each of which has been a factor in transforming the absolute authority once exercised by rulers into constitutional governments that now recognize and enforce popular rights. In this era, the English-speaking peoples are the recognized leaders.

The English Triad embraces: 1. The Emancipating Mind, the fusion of all groups of thought in Europe as well as throughout the English-speaking world, that seek freedom from every form of unjust coercion, including a variety of movements, intellectual, political, economic and religious, each striving for some phase of human freedom; 2. The Denominational Mind which has its origin in the assumption that each individual possesses the right to interpret the teachings of the Bible and to affiliate with those who accept like interpretations in order that these views may be corporately maintained and actively propagated; 3. The Scientific Mind, a movement which, addressing itself first to a descriptive knowledge of the measurable aspects of the physical universe, has turned its attention in recent times to the study of all human relationships and has created the social sciences, including the investigation of the total measurable phenomena of religion. The supporters of Christianity are forced thereby to consider a reconstruction of the historic creeds, incident to the effort to harmonize science and religion or to contend that many of the scientific conclusions, especially those in the immediate field of religion, are erroneous.

The Apostolic Mind is the reproduction of the mind of Christ by his followers in the Apostolic Age. The material to be studied is the books of the New Testament, not excluding the Gospels, for they are interpretative as well as descriptive and in the interpretative sections reflect the Apostolic Mind. The new elements in the Apostolic Mind are the fact and the implications of the death and resurrection of Jesus, the outpouring of the Holy Spirit, and the concentration of interest and effort upon the proclamation of personal salvation through faith in Jesus Christ as Lord. The old elements are: first, the acceptance of Moses and the prophets as an authoritative revelation, with Judaism recognized as either a living part of or a precursor to the Christian faith, thus creating the religious background of all Jewish Christians and influencing greatly the Gentiles who become Christians; second, the apocalyptic hopes of the Jews, modified by the teachings of Jesus, resulting in the widespread belief by his followers that he would speedily return.

The primary expression of the Apostolic Mind may be found in the preaching of the Gospel, the content of which has been given in part, if not in its entirety, by the writers of the Acts and the Epistles. This Apostolic Message "on the one hand, was so simple that it could be summed up in a few brief sentences and understood in a single crisis of the inner life; on the other hand, it was so versatile and rich that it vivified all thought and stimulated every emotion. . . . Clear and transparent, it was also profound and full of mystery. It had statutes and yet it rose superior to any law. It was a doctrine and yet no doctrine, a philosophy and yet something different from philosophy." [5]

The preaching of Jesus centered in the announcement of the Kingdom of God; the preaching of the Apostles and their co-laborers, in the Lordship of Jesus Christ. The Apostolic Message was pre-eminently the Gospel of salvation, Jesus Christ being, by his resurrection from the dead, the divinely attested Saviour. As the Messiah or Christ, he was given the name that is above every name, save that of God the Father; and this exaltation was in consequence of his voluntary death. While the immediate causes of his crucifixion were traceable historically to sinful men, the motive which led Jesus to accept such a humiliating "exodus" was the purpose to do everything possible to convict men of sin and to save them that believe from sin; in so doing, the Apostles held that he acted in harmony with "the determinate counsel and foreknowledge of God." Writing less than twenty-five years after Pentecost to the Corinthians, Paul says, "I delivered unto you first of all that which I also received, how that Christ died for our sins according to the scriptures and that he was buried and that he rose again on the third day." Earlier, Paul had summed up the Christian message in these words: "Believe on the Lord Jesus Christ and thou shalt be saved."

Whatever modern scholars may say about the post-resurrection appearance of Jesus being merely apparitions, his disciples saw him and believed the evidences of their senses, confirmed by the testimony of their fellow disciples. Their loyalty had faltered with his arrest, and apparently their faith in him had been transformed when he died upon the cross into a wistful but bitter memory of a once cherished hope. Nothing but the actual resurrection of Jesus can reasonably account for the complete change of feeling and for the consuming enthusiasm with which they proclaimed him as their risen Lord.

With their faith restored, deepened, brightened and transfigured, they accepted as their task the bringing of all the hostile forces on earth of every kind and character into subjection to Jesus Christ as Lord. Wherever these disciples of the New Testament period went, they told, taught, and preached that trust in Jesus as the risen Lord wrought deliverance from the dominion of sin, from the fear of death and from the tyranny of demons. They proclaimed a salvation which, when experienced by the believer, manifested itself in a superhuman passion for holy living and in a sacrificial devotion to the welfare of others, culminating in the confident assurance of a future eternal blessedness, to be entered upon either with the return of the Lord Jesus to earth or with the believer's departure from this life.

The New Testament is the Apostolic Mind engaged in describing, interpreting, evaluating and glorifying Jesus Christ. The dominant desire of its writers is to know him better, "whom to know is life eternal," and to share this knowledge with others. They delight in describing themselves as slaves, "the bondservants of Jesus Christ." Despite hardships, sufferings and persecutions, exultation is the prevailing mood and joy is the ascendant emotion. They are a happy people, finding an exquisite satisfaction in seeking the good of others. They are gladdened by the possession of the Spirit of Christ. They use various terms, "the Spirit," "the Holy Spirit," "the Spirit of God," "the love of Christ," "the Comforter," "the Spirit of truth," to describe the divine spiritual reinforcement which strengthens, comforts, leads, quickens, guides, teaches and inspires them. Their efforts are directed toward holy living, in order that they may be worthy of their "high calling in Christ Jesus." They seek to live "the crucified life," becoming thereby insensitive and unresponsive to the evil in the world about them. This high idealism is linked to a practical-minded sanity.

Emotionalism rarely runs wild. Discipline, directed toward the maintenance of a high Christian character, is often severe but is always inspired by love for the wayward and by an unswerving loyalty to the ideals of Christ. Conscious of a union with Christ and filled with the Spirit, the Apostolic Mind has as its dominant desire the showing forth of the excellencies of him who has called his followers "out of darkness into his marvelous light."

"Paul never knew Jesus during his lifetime, but it was he who best understood him." [6] A recent scholarly writer has listed the moral precepts of Paul under the following significant headings: "1. Separate yourselves from all that would defile; 2. Be stedfast in all the conduct of life, 3. Through love serve one another; 4. Rejoice in the Lord always; again, I will say, rejoice." [7] So important is regeneration, the moment when by faith the soul is united to Christ and the high moral life which results from this experience becomes possible, that "the entire labor of the Christian mission might be described as a moral enterprise, as the awakening and strengthening of the moral sense." [8] However, it cannot be emphasized too strongly that Christian morality originates in and is sustained by a religious motivation. Indeed, Jesus never thought of human goodness as being as it ought to be, except as a voluntary response to the goodness of God.

The Apostolic Mind is interested in the Old Testament, as an authoritative source from which there may be gained evidence, typical and prophetic, to prove the Messiahship of Jesus. The supreme objectives of the Apostolic Mind are to glorify Christ, to develop in his followers a Christlike character, manifesting itself in loving ministries and devotion to the Christ ideal, and to carry "the good news," "the Gospel of Jesus Christ, the Son of God," into all the world. The religious, the ethical, and the missionary objectives are everywhere dominant.

The materials for the organizing of a theological system are present in the preaching of the period and in the writings of the New Testament. Some practical issues involving theology are discussed. Belief in the Lord Jesus Christ is the simple creed. Theology will arise later, when intellectualism has gained ascendancy over spiritual fervor and the followers of Jesus think more clearly but love him less.

V

The Judaizing Mind

"Except ye be circumcised after the manner of Moses, ye cannot be saved."—THE JUDAIZERS.

THE BACKGROUND of a religion in process of propagation is the language, the thought-patterns, the inherited tendencies, the moral standards, and the prevailing, contemporary religious convictions and hopes, as these are expressed in sacred literature, ordered worship and religious education. A study of its background is necessary to a correct understanding of the origination of any historic religion. The beginning of every great religion, if it be either ethical or redemptive, centers in one who claims to reveal religious truth and who is able to win disciples through their acceptance of his teachings as true, and therefore binding and authoritative.

The culture with which a missionary religion comes into contact is the aggregate of knowledge, sentiment, and purpose which a race or a linguistic group possesses for the continuance and the extension of its civilization. The ascendant purpose within the social order, to which the religion must adjust itself, furnishes the goal of secular corporate endeavor, and plays no small part in determining the type and the character of the organization which the religion assumes; for this ascendant purpose, visible in contemporary government, in education, and in the promotion of general prosperity, furnishes, through its methods and agencies, patterns of successful organization that the religion often readily adopts, changing their secular functions to meet its special needs.

The genius of an age or a people is the vital union of its spirit, attitude and ideals; as such it tends to control and to give character to that in which it abides. The successful propagation of a religion depends in no small degree upon its meeting the need which this genius, as thus defined, creates within a people.

Every one, however limited in knowledge, has some kind of a

philosophy; and in this philosophy is a world-view, a conception of the universe which pictures the relation of Ultimate Reality to those who are living in this ever-changing world. Every religion develops, if it does not possess it at its beginning, a cosmology.

Christianity is a historical religion which has its genesis in the teaching of Jesus of Nazareth and in the interpretation of his life and ministry, following his death and resurrection. Jesus Christ is the Author and the Finisher, the Alpha and the Omega, of the Christian faith. Early Christianity is loyalty to Jesus, fertilized by the Holy Spirit on Jewish soil.

There is a continuity of Christian thought and its crucial periods correspond to the successive linguistic cultures within which Christianity has sought and found a place of commanding influence. The five basic conceptions in the Apostolic Mind, as stated in the preceding chapter, are inherited Jewish beliefs, salvation through faith in Jesus Christ, the organization of church life, the enjoyment of the fellowship of the Holy Spirit and the hope of an emancipation from all earthly ills through Christ at his Second Coming or, after death, through being forever with the Lord. Successively, each of these conceptions became a central and crucial issue as Christianitiy passed from an old to a new dominating cultural environment.

The Judaism of the first Christian century formed the historic background of early Christianity and it was natural, if not inevitable, that the first serious conflict should arise out of the effort to define accurately the relation of faith in Jesus as Messiah and Saviour to contemporary Jewish beliefs. Thus emerged the Judaizing Mind.

The preaching of the Apostolic Period and the writings of the New Testament present Jesus of Nazareth as the risen and exalted Christ, the Lord of Life and man's only Saviour. As Christianity invades the Græco-Roman world, it encounters the demand that a rational explanation be given to the gospel message. The culture which environs Christianity is no longer Jewish, but Hellenistic. The reaction to this culture tends toward an over-intellectualization of the Christian movement, and undue emphasis is placed upon right thinking or orthodoxy. Loyalty to Jesus Christ, exhibited by a way of living in which the individual reveals that Christ controls his life, gives way to loyalty to a metaphysical interpretation of Jesus Christ in his relation to the Godhead. The theological formulations of this period grow out of the study of Jesus, the risen and exalted Christ, the Son of God and man's only Saviour as given in the New Testament, but they are expressed in philosophical terms by Christian thinkers skilled in the Hellenistic methods of thought. Theology in its classic forms is the product of the impact of Greek philosophy upon Christian thinking.

The third element in Apostolic thought is the Christian community, united by a common personal experience of God's forgiving grace, inspired by a missionary purpose which finds its expression in a united effort for the promotion of the spread of the Gospel, the maintenance of the highest standards in Christian living, and the fullest exercise of Christian love in caring for the needy brethren wherever they are found. The ascendant purpose is directed toward the realization of the following objects through co-operative Christian action: Christian character, Christian missions, and Christian charity.

All social endeavor, which seeks to become a permanent force in human society, is compelled to use institutional agencies. Religion is no exception. Jesus refers to the Church only once, possibly twice, yet Pentecost finds the Christian Church at least partially organized and actively at work. The existing social agencies, from the Jewish synagogues to the Gentile guilds, and the provincial government of the Roman Empire, influence the growing ecclesiastical organization. In the end, however, the Roman Mind guides and directs the union and determines the institutional forms of the Churches of Christ, despite the fact that these Churches in the New Testament period govern themselves as spiritual democracies, seeking in all their decisions to be guided solely by the Holy Spirit. Under the influence of the Roman Mind, the sovereignty of spiritual leadership is limited, in the interest of a catholic solidarity and an ecclesiastical efficiency, to Church officials; it being assumed that these and these only are led by the Spirit. The Roman Catholic Church, which is founded upon a belief in the sovereignty of its hierarchy and in its seven sacraments as miracle-working or magical religious acts, is the visible expression of the impact of the Roman Mind upon Christianity.

The fourth element in the Apostolic Mind is the appreciation of spiritual gifts and the conviction that no one is truly a Christian who has not received the Holy Spirit. This belief is the basis of Christian mysticism in all the centuries since Pentecost. Christian mystics are those who hold the Christian experience to be primary and essential. The Christian life for them is the uninterrupted culture of the consciousness of Christ by every individual believer. They deny that the gift of the Holy Spirit is limited in its sovereign power to ecclesiastics and they vigorously assert that it is the rightful possession of all true believers in Christ Jesus.

Mysticism accounts for the origin and the immediate and wonderful momentum of the Protestant Reformation. It plays an important part in the development of the Protestant Mind, which had molded so largely the faith of most of the Christian bodies, known today as the evangelical denominations. These evangelical groups concentrate their efforts upon preaching the Gospel, assuring all men that personal salvation is attainable through and only through faith in Jesus Christ.

The Nationalistic Mind guiding the decisions of Protestant rulers, leads them to assert their authority in the realm of religion. Each such ruler officially approves the establishment of a State church, gives to it support and protection, and aids in suppressing dissent either by persecution or by the withdrawal of civil favors. The Protestant State churches, to a greater or less degree, emphasize the scriptural teachings as to the value of spiritual gifts and recognize no one as enjoying full church membership, until it is assumed that he has received the Holy Spirit through the rite of confirmation or because of a personal testimony to such an experience of grace. The evangelical principle is destined to be given a much greater emphasis by those evangelical bodies which arise outside the State Churches. They will be discussed in the chapter on the Denominational Mind.

The last element is the belief that the complete control of the present and the future centers in God, who, through Christ at his Second Coming, will judge the world and reward his saints. This is the early Christian world-view and its background is the current Judaistic apocalyptic program. The essence of this Christian world-view is that the future, embracing the final destiny of man, depends upon the purpose and the climactic act of God, and that this act will be for the world a cataclysmic tragedy, but for his favored ones, an everlasting blessedness.

In our study, the Emancipating Mind precedes the Denominational Mind, which is followed by the Scientific Mind. Largely humanistic in spirit, the Emancipating Mind has found in the scientific method a satisfying procedure for the establishment of tested knowledge. Possessing no instruments for the testing of the supernatural, the Scientific Mind, in its philosophical moods, postulates a world-view in which the supernatural has no place.

A close kinship exists between the ardent premillenarianists and the materialistic scientists, for both make their world-view basic to all their thinking and they differ only in their definitions as to the control of the world that each views. The one posits a God inspired by a redemptive purpose; the other posits infinite energy under law. For the latter, the ultimate destiny of man is dust; the ultimate destiny of the physical universe, a cinder heap. The acceptance of this latter view, which is the distinguishing characteristic of the present-day anti-supernatural Scientific Mind, is fatal not only to Christianity but to all religion.

―――――――

Having sketched in broad outline the course of Christian thought, our attention is now directed to the study of the inherited presuppositions of the Jewish believers in Jesus as the Messiah, foretold by the Hebrew prophets, and the part these presuppositions played in molding their conception of the relation of the Christian movement to the Gentile world.

The two main principles of the Jewish religion are the assertion of the undivided unity of God and the paramount duty of obedience to his declared will, while the rite of circumcision and the observance of the Sabbath are the indispensable requisites of any profession of Judaism, affording two most clear and explicit proofs of loyalty to its ground principles. In the days of Jesus, the religious center of the local community is the synagogue, and of World Jewry, the Temple. The source of revelation is the Torah, the entire body of divine teaching, focused in the Pentateuch and irradiating the whole realm of life, feeling, thought, and action.

Scattered throughout the world, the Jews of the Dispersion form distinct moral and religious groups, whose "morose separation" evokes resentment on the part of their Gentile neighbors, because they refuse to participate in the amusements and the social interests of the Græco-Roman world. Their numbers, however, are impressive. It is estimated that when the Christian era began, seventy out of every one thousand men in the Roman Empire were Jews. Their strict adherence to their moral and religious convictions gives to them a strength and a social influence far greater than their numbers indicate. Believing intensely in an education, religious both in content and in objective, the highest honors in every Jewish community are paid to those whose knowledge of the Old Testament writings and of the accepted definitions of the correct manner in obeying the divine will, called the Halakah, is the most thorough and complete. These learned men were the scribes, the lawyers, practically all Pharisees, to whom reference is so often made in the Gospels.

Pharisaism had its beginnings in the revolution of the Maccabees, 167 B.C., which re-established the Jewish state and united with it the Jewish religion. The overthrow of the Jewish state, 63 B.C., did not result in the destruction of the Jewish national consciousness; for the succeeding generations with increased zeal maintained the folkways, the customs, and the regulations taught by the rabbis, honored the Mosaic Law and observed with meticulous care all of their religious festivals and ceremonies. Jesus, in his teachings, came into direct conflict with the leaders of this program. The attack of the Pharisees, however, is made, not so much upon the teachings of Jesus as upon his practices. Breaking the Sabbath (Mark 3:1-6; Matthew 12:1-14); associating with evil men, publicans, and sinners (Matthew 11:19, Luke 7:34); violating the traditions of the elders (Matthew 15:1-2, Mark 7:1-9), and assuming the right of God in the forgiving of sins (Mark 2:10-12) are the chief grounds of their growing antagonism. The Pharisees base their religion upon obedience to the Law; Jesus bases his religion upon the love of God, inspiring obedience to the divine principle

regnant in the character of God, as the ultimate source of all that
is eternally true in the Mosaic Law.

Jesus came into direct conflict with the Jewish established order.
To its leaders he was a dangerous revolutionary, threatening to
undermine their whole religious system. He repudiated the entire
body of their teaching as given in the Halakah, and did not hesi-
tate to criticize the Torah, the Mosaic Law itself, upon which the
Halakah was based. The Pharisees demanded loyalty to a revealed
law; Jesus, loyalty to himself as the heavenly Mediator who knew
and did the will of God. Judaism was and is obedience to Law;
Christianity was and is loyalty to a personal Mediator. The Incarnation of Jesus Christ is the crux of the Christian faith.

The earliest Christians were nearly all Jews, and at the first they
had apparently no thought of breaking with their ancestral faith.
Day by day, they adhered strictly to the requirements of the
Mosaic Law and continued to observe the Jewish customs with
devoted loyalty. Previous to the death of Jesus, his disciples hoped
that he would effect some form of national deliverance. After his
resurrection and ascension, the earlier hope was transferred to
heaven, whence they expected the exalted Christ to return in
power to set up his apocalyptic Kingdom.

The Christian body in Jerusalem was divided into two linguistic
groups: the Aramaic-speaking Jews, most of them Palestinian natives; and the Greek-speaking Jews of the Dispersion, called the
Hellenists, residing temporarily or permanently in the Holy City.
The implications of the universal character of the Christian faith
in the teachings, and still more in the death and resurrection, of
Jesus were apprehended first by these Hellenistic Jewish Christians.

The courageous espousal and the public proclamation of these
implications by Stephen led to his trial before the Sanhedrin,
meeting in the Temple, under the charge of his having said that
"Jesus of Nazareth shall destroy this place and shall change the
customs which Moses delivered unto us." In his defense, he asserted that the Jews, throughout their long and checkered history,
had been notorious for their unfaithfulness to the God of Israel, to
the Mosaic Law, and to the religion of the Temple, and that the
final proof of this sustained rebellious attitude had been recently
exhibited in the killing of the Righteous One, whom they had

betrayed and murdered. Without waiting for an orderly adjournment of the trial, the mob dragged Stephen forth and stoned him to death, Saul of Tarsus looking on approvingly. The irrepressible conflict between Judaism and Christianity had begun.

The persecutors of those who "were of the Way," Saul of Tarsus being the leader, seem to have recognized that a cleavage already existed within the company of believers; for Peter and the native Aramaic-speaking Christians were allowed to remain in the city, while the sympathizers of Stephen, probably all of them Hellenistic Jews, were driven in every direction. The chief event during the persecution was the conversion of Saul of Tarsus, "the chosen vessel," to bear the name of Jesus "before the Gentiles and kings, and the children of Israel." The driving of the more liberal Hellenistic believers away from Jerusalem, left the native Aramaic membership in full control of the Jerusalem church. Previous to the stoning of Stephen, "a great company of the priests were obedient to the faith." Many of the Pharisees had accepted the Messiahship of Jesus. James, the head of the Jerusalem Church, set an example by adhering closely to the customs and regulations of the Jewish religion. The conservative Judaistic element had won the ascendancy in Jerusalem.

Peter, on a missionary tour which takes him to Joppa, beholds a vision. Immediately after, he receives an invitation from Cornelius, a Roman centurion residing in Cæsarea, himself not a Jewish proselyte but a God-fearing Gentile, to come to him at once. Under the preaching of Peter, Cornelius and all with him are converted; the Holy Spirit comes upon them, and at Peter's command they are baptized. The conservative Judaizing group in Jerusalem sharply criticize Peter upon his return, and he defends his action by telling all that occurred, closing with the words: "If then God gave unto them the like gift as he did also unto us, when we believed on the Lord Jesus Christ, who was I, that I could withstand God?" The recital silences the Judaizers, at least for a time.

Time passes. The news reaches Jerusalem from Antioch that large numbers of Gentiles are being admitted into the Antiochene Church. The generous-hearted Barnabas is sent by the Jerusalem brethren to investigate. Upon his arrival he is gladdened by the convincing proofs of the presence of the grace of God in the hearts of these Gentile believers. He leads in preaching the Gospel, and many more accept Jesus Christ as Lord. He goes to Tarsus for Saul, better known later as Paul the Apostle to the Gentiles. Here the disciples are first called Christians. There are now three distinct groups within the rapidly expanding Christian fellowship: the Aramaic-speaking Jews, the Greek-speaking Jews, and the Greek-speaking Gentiles. From the first group come the Judaizers, maintaining that the Gentiles must be Judaized as well as Christianized and that the Christian experience in and of itself alone does not assure salvation.

The Judaizers, as these representatives of the Judaizing Mind have been called, believed and dogmatically affirmed that the Gentiles could not be saved without becoming Jews. A company of these Judaizers, on their own initiative, went to Antioch from Jerusalem and bluntly declared to the Gentile membership of the Church, "Except ye be circumsized after the custom of Moses, ye cannot be saved" (Acts 15:1). Christianity faced its first great crisis: Should it become a sect within Judaism or should it find its true mission as a world-wide redemptive religion?

The scene changes to Jerusalem. Barnabas and Paul, who have returned from a missionary tour through Asia Minor, in which many Gentiles were converted, are appointed by the Church in Antioch to attend a conference in Jerusalem, arranged to consider the issue raised by the Judaizers. When they finish their report to the conference of the conversion of the Gentiles (and this is made before the assembled membership of the Jerusalem Church) the Judaizers, formerly identified with the Pharisaic party, state their position: "It is needful to circumcise them and to charge them to keep the Mosaic law." The debate is on. Peter, reciting his experience in preaching to the Gentiles, bases salvation upon "the grace of the Lord Jesus." Barnabas and Paul rehearse the signs and wonders which God has wrought among the Gentiles through them. James, the president of the conference, expresses the judgment that they no longer trouble these Gentile Christians, but that they indicate in writing a course of action for them to follow. The conference agrees to this. The communication commends Barnabas and Paul, disapproves the unauthorized conduct of the

Judaizers, and concludes as follows: "For it seemed good to the Holy Spirit and to us to lay upon you no greater burden than these necessary things; that ye abstain from things sacrificed to idols and from blood and from things strangled and from fornication; from which if ye keep yourselves, it shall be well with you. Fare ye well." This Harnack calls "a summary of Jewish ethical catechetics."

The decision is a staggering defeat for the Judaizers. The fires of Judaistic prejudice smolder for a while and then burst into flame. The Judaizers renew their attack, contending that the Jerusalem conference has not settled the question of the social relations of Jewish and Gentile Christians. Coming again to Antioch, they find Peter eating with the Gentiles. Claiming to speak with the authority of James, they so overawe him that he discontinues this form of social intercourse with the Gentile Christians, and, surprising as it is, Barnabas does so also. Paul is aroused to passionate protest. He condemns the course Peter had taken. No man is saved by obedience to Mosaic requirements or Jewish customs, "the works of the law," but by "faith in Jesus Christ." "If righteousness is through the law, then Christ died for nought." Paul's boldness wins back both Peter and Barnabas.

The controversy with the Judaizers forces Paul to concentrate his thought upon the Christian salvation—its source, its ground, the method of its appropriation, and its redeeming and transforming power. The Epistle to the Romans is a measured, rounded, and carefully wrought out discussion of the theme. In a masterly, constructive fashion, he is answering, without naming, the Judaizers. The Epistle to the Galatians is a fervid defense of the freedom of the Christian man, based upon his interpretation of the Christian salvation. The grace of God is the one source of the Christian salvation (1:3; 2:21; 5:4); the Cross of Christ is its sole revealed ground (1:4; 2:19; 21: 3:13; 6:14); faith in the gospel of Christ is its all-sufficient means (2:16-20; 3:2, 5-9, 23-26; 5:5); the Holy Spirit is its effecting power (3:2-5; 4:6-7; 5:5, 16-25). Therefore, all Gentile believers are completely emancipated from the Jewish law and enjoy the full status of the sons of God.

The stars in their courses are fighting for Paul. The uncircumcised Gentiles are, in ever-increasing numbers, accepting the

Gospel. Because of Paul's passionate preaching of the cross and his interpretation of the Christian faith in his epistles as a salvation grounded in the grace of God and realized by man through faith in a crucified Saviour, the Judaizers meet defeat in Galatia, Syria, Asia, Macedonia, and Achaia. They are powerful in Jerusalem, the Mother Church, whose members, "all zealous for the law," now number many thousands. They circulate misleading reports as to Paul's position, charging him with teaching "all the Jews who are among the Gentiles to forsake Moses, telling them not to circumcise their children, neither to walk after the customs." Paul returns to Jerusalem, his enemies' stronghold, tries to prove to them his loyalty to Jewish law and customs in nonessential matters by participating in the worship and sacrifices of the Temple. Recognized by visiting Ephesian Jews, he is mobbed, saved by Roman soldiers, and for five long years he undergoes imprisonment in Cæsarea and in Rome. Seven years after his release from imprisonment, Jerusalem is destroyed. Paul has already suffered as a martyr, but he had lived long enough to see the victory over the Judaizers practically complete.

VI

The Gentile Mind

"The Greeks seek after wisdom."—PAUL.

THE GENTILE MIND is the social, intellectual, moral, and religious environment which enfolds the early Christian movement as it passes out of its original Jewish surroundings. Greek is the prevailing language, and the predominant thought-patterns are the product of Hellenistic culture, imposed upon the peoples who make up the Græco-Roman world.

Apostolic Christianity spreads eastward as well as westward. The first group listed on the day of Pentecost, "Parthians and Medes and Elamites and the dwellers in Mesopotamia," inhabitants of Asiatic lands beyond the boundaries of the Roman Empire, doubtless carried eastward the story of the Messiahship of Jesus. Tradition says that most of the apostles labored in the East—in Scythia, Parthia, Mesopotamia, and India. The vast number of Aramaic-speaking Jews in Babylonia offered an inviting field for apostolic missionary labor. Whatever success attended these efforts was probably transitory; for wherever the Jewish rabbinical schools were influential Christianity failed to convince any very large number of Jews that Jesus was the expected Messiah; and nowhere in all Jewry were these schools, during the period succeeding the Apostolic Age, so powerful or so ably manned as in Babylonia. Whatever record of Christian achievement there was then in existence in the East was wiped out by the Islamic avalanche, which in the seventh century overwhelmed all competing faiths.

The Gentile Mind, for the purposes of this study, is the background, the culture, the social order, the genius, and the world-view affecting the Christian religion within the Græco-Roman world. The extreme limits of the Hellenistic Age are its beginning in 336 B.C., when Alexander the Great ascended the throne, and its ending A.D. 529, when Justinian closed the schools of the heathen philosophers. The Græco-Roman Period starts with the founding of the Roman Empire, 31 B.C., and closes A.D. 529. The human activities of this period are embraced in the expression "the Græco-Roman world."

The background of the Gentile Mind was that inheritance from a far distant past which each of its racial, linguistic and provincial groups cherished and preserved as possessing value. While the entire population of the Roman Empire had been brought under imperial rule, only those who lived in the towns and the cities felt the influence of and responded gladly to Hellenistic culture. However the Græco-Roman world was preponderantly urban. The country, save as an important economic factor, played no significant part in its life. Great land-owners, whose estates were called *latifundia*, might spend the summer months at their country villas, but their places of residence were in town or city. Only the slaves, the overseers and the poor farmers remained in the country all the time. Rome was not only in population, but in every other respect, the greatest city in a world of towns and cities.

The rural Gentile Mind therefore remained practically unchanged, retaining its inherited language, culture and religion. The religious beliefs and customs of the country people may be traced to a primitive tribal state, with its objects of worship amalgamated to some small degree with the religions which the changing national life had imposed upon these rural communities. The early primitive cults therefore largely controlled their religious life. "The creeds and rites of the old time continued to be observed by ignorant persons, by peasants on farms and in villages, and by those who were naturally conservative, to whom any change from the traditional order involved the probability of some sort of bad luck. They continued to be observed also by cultivated persons by whom they were associated with art and letters, with the refinements of society and with the long past." [9]

The religion of ancient Rome, beginning as a family and agricultural cult in early Italic groups and later influenced by a composite race, the Etruscans, to give greater importance to divination, had become with the passing centuries a religion of patriotism, useful in promoting loyalty in the homeland. Conquered countries were encouraged to preserve their own religions. Foreign gods were given an honored place in Rome. Enriched by many Greek and Oriental as well as Roman myths, religion expressed itself in liturgies, processions, shrines, images, and temples and permeated all social and public life. The Emperor, as the embodiment of the Empire, was the official head of the religious system, and he himself was recognized as divine. All peoples, whatever their own religion, were expected throughout the Empire, when called upon, to burn incense before the statue of the Emperor as a declaration of unswerving allegiance.

The Græco-Roman world is a blending of the East and the West, fertilized by Greek culture on Roman soil. The religious backgrounds of the peoples who compose the Empire are as diverse as the tribes and the nations Rome had conquered. Good roads, constant travel, growing commerce, extensive correspondence, the frequent journeyings of statesmen, scholars, and religious missionaries from land to land, tend to acquaint the inhabitants of the towns and cities with all the religions within the Empire. The Dispersion of the Jews has its Syrian parallel in Syria's stellar religion; its Babylonian parallel in Babylonia's astralism; its Persian parallel in Mithraism, and its Egyptian parallel in the worship of Serapis and Isis. The spread of Greek culture, with its religious as well as its philosophical interpretations, is accompanied by a wave of temple building, resulting in the worship of Greek and Roman divinities practically co-extensive with the urban life of the Empire. All these and other elements, including the amalgamation of Greek and Roman pantheism, combine to produce a syncretistic ferment, out of which arises a blending and fusing of religious ideas and usages in the congeries of peoples. All faiths are flung into the melting pot. The old religions endeavor to adjust themselves to the new situation, not always successfully. The old national boundaries have disappeared, and the dynasties that protected and supported the national religions have been destroyed. The religious leaders realize that the perpetuity of their cult depends upon the propagation of their beliefs without reference to nationality or race. The conflict of religions within the Roman Empire becomes intense, active proselyting being carried on in practically all the towns and cities of the Græco-Roman world.

Alexander the Great "paved the way for the intellectual empire of the Greek and the political empire of the Roman." Hellenic culture, the aggregate of knowledge, sentiment, and purpose which the Greeks possessed was imposed upon all the lands which Alexander conquered. When Philip and Alexander led the Macedonians in the adoption of the classic speech of Athens, which in later years became the Koiné, the lingua franca of the Græco-Roman world, they provided the best possible vehicle for carrying Greek culture into all lands. Soon "Greek was spoken everywhere throughout Asia and for the first time in the world's history the inhabitants of the civilized part of the earth had a common tongue in which they could communicate their ideas to each other. . . . It was a better medium for the transmission of metaphysical theories than the founder of any world religion had ever had at his disposal or since." [10]

The Greek language, flexible and expressive, is admirably adapted to the development of poetic imagery, literary form, and logical thought. The literature of Greece falls into two main periods: first, the Ancient, extending from the beginning, A.D. 529, when the schools of heathen philosophy are closed; second, the Byzantine, 529 to 1453, the fall of Constantinople. The Ancient Period is subdivided into first, the early Ancient, from the tenth century B.C. to 500 B.C.; second, the Attic, including the fifth and fourth centuries B.C.; third, the Decadence, 300 B.C. to A.D. 529, divided by the founding of the Roman Empire (31 B.C.) into the Alexandrian and the Græco-Roman.

The center of Greek culture was Athens, and its most brilliant period, the Attic, extented from 500 B.C. to 300 B.C. The Early Ancient Period had developed epic poetry, of which Homer was the chief representative. The Attic Period produced within two centuries the greatest galaxy of poets, artists, orators, and thinkers the world has ever known. Among these were the tragic poets, Æschylus, Sophocles, and Euripides; the comic poets, Aristophanes, Antiphanes, Alexis, Philemon, and Menander; the historians, Herodotus, Thucydides, and Xenophon; the philosophers, Socrates, Plato, and Aristotle; the orators, Demosthenes, Æschines, Lysias, Hyperides, Lycurgus, and Phocion. The list could be greatly extended.

It was the culture of the Attic Period that Alexander, by his conquests, by his building of Hellenistic cities in conquered lands, and by his command that the colonized Greeks intermarry with the natives of the lands into which they had migrated, disseminated throughout the known non-Grecian world. Alexandria in Egypt, which was named for him, became the chief center of the original Attic culture, modified by its non-Grecian contacts, and to this culture has been given the name of Hellenistic. Here Ptolemy Philadelphius established the museum, a vast group of buildings, halls, and gardens in which was the Alexandrian Library, said to have contained 700,000 volumes. Later, Alexandria was recognized as the intellectual capital of the Græco-Roman world. But this Egyptian city did not stand alone in the promotion of Hellenistic culture. Pergamus, Antioch, Syracuse, Tarsus, Pella, Cos, Rhodes, Soli, and others had their universities, their noted scholars, and their many earnest students. New philosophies arose, the disciples of whom were called Cynics, Stoics, Sceptics, Epicureans.

Never was written so much Greek as during this Alexandrian period. Works on grammar, philology, rhetoric, mathematics, physics, astronomy, medicine, and kindred subjects appeared. It was an age, less profound, less original, and far less brilliant than the Attic, but it was intellectually more studious, with interests more widely diffused and with a passion for the propagation of the Greek language, the Greek thought-patterns, and the whole of Greek culture, the equal of which the world has rarely, if ever known. Politically, Rome conquered Greece and the whole Hellenistic world, but culturally Greece conquered Rome. The Attic Age brought to full fruition, the Alexandrian Age disseminated, the Græco-Roman Age employed and enjoyed Greek culture.

Three other phases of the Gentile Mind, connected directly or indirectly with the conquests of Alexander, must be noticed briefly. The deification of monarchs was common in the ancient Orient. Egypt declared her pharaohs and Persia her kings to be divine. Alexander seized upon this device and demanded of his own countrymen as well as of the conquered peoples that divine honors be paid to him. The worship of the Roman Emperor was one of the results of the deification of Alexander. The divine rights of kings would not have gained such an ascendancy in Europe had Alexander not adopted the Oriental idea of the divinity of rulers.

Theocrasia is the fusing of one god with the god of another people by affirming that the god worshiped by the one people is identical in fact with the one worshiped by another people under a different name. Alexander at Susa formally wedded the East and the West. He treated all—Persians, Egyptians, Macedonians and Greeks—as equals. Therefore, their divinities were placed upon a common level. The succeeding three centuries carried far this process of religious syncretism. "The Persian Mithra cult was at least partially Egyptianized; the Egyptian Isiac cult largely Hellenized. Stoicism exerted an immense modifying influence upon Gnosticism. The Hermetic literature is such a blend that scholars are not agreed as to the relative proportion of Egyptian, Babylonian, Stoic, Platonic, Neo-Pythagorean, and even Christian ingredients." [11]

The Greek mind was ever hospitable to intellectual novelties. Contact with new religious ideas led individuals to accept them readily and to associate themselves for the observance of the worship of the foreign god or gods. The nucleus of the body usually consisted of natives of the country in which the religion prevailed, now residing in some other part of the post-Alexandrian, Hellenistic world. Such organizations as these soon appeared in every important city. "Thus we see for the first time in history bodies of men and women banded together, irrespective of nationality or social rank, for the purpose of religious observances, and religion becoming recognized as the affair of the individual rather than of the State, while each member of the association was directly interested in its extension." [12]

Egypt, Babylonia, Crete, Phœnicia, Greece, and Rome produced great civilizations, and all but one, Babylonia, touched the shores of the Mediterranéan. The last of these civilizations, the Græco-Roman, was a social order permeated by Greek culture, governed by Roman law, uniting under imperial rule peoples who lived upon the three continents, Europe, Asia, and Africa. The Roman Empire stretched eastward from the Atlantic to the boundaries of Parthia in Asia, and southward from the Rhine and the

Danube to the wastes of the Sahara in Africa. The estimates of its population have ranged from forty-two to sixty millions. Many dialects persisted in the remoter districts and among the lower classes; but the leading languages were the Greek and the Latin, the former prevailing in the East and the latter in the West. All educated people, East and West, spoke Greek.

Pax Romana is preserved throughout this vast area by an army of less than 300,000 men, three fleets in the Mediterranean, another in the Black Sea, and flotillas on the Rhine and the Danube. The martial element has been unduly emphasized by historians, and not until recent years have the administrative and engineering elements received proper recognition. Epictetus thus pictures these tranquil Augustan days: "Cæsar seems to provide us with profound peace; there are no wars, nor battles any more, no great bands of robbers or pirates; we are able to travel by land at every season and to sail from sunrise to sunset." [13]

Preserving the semblance of the Republic of Rome by recognizing the traditional sovereignty of Senatus populusque Romanus, and retaining the theory that the Senate had a share in the government, the Roman Empire had become a centralized government, with the right to rule entrusted to the emperor. The territory of the Empire was divided into four prefectures: Gaul, Italy, Illyricum, and the Orient. These were subdivided into fourteen dioceses, each of which was composed of a certain number of provinces. The civil governor of the province was responsible to the vicar of the diocese, and he, in turn, was subordinate to the prætorian prefect, being charged also with the administration of justice and the raising of taxes. The smallest unit of government was the municipality. This centralization of power developed during the early years of the Empire.

Efficiency in government, the better administration of justice, and the establishment of the supremacy of Roman law (the last being Rome's most important contribution to subsequent civilization) were the ends sought by the Roman authorities. The imperial government was interested in the material development of the provinces, and, in order to make them more profitable, agriculture, road-building, colonization, and municipal improvements were actively promoted. "Augustus and the best and ablest of his successors patiently built up, for the Empire, consisting in part of small-town territories with traditions of particularism and in part of wide spaces tenanted by tribes of many races and cultures, a framework within which men could, on the whole, work out their own salvation, could be drawn together in mutual understanding and could acquire a wholly new patriotism linked with the great traditions of Rome and a new spirit of public service." [14]

The social gradations were as follows: slaves, of whom there were an enormous number; freedmen, manumitted slaves still dependent upon former masters; freemen, possessing the right to vote but not to hold office; citizens, a middle class between the slaves and the nobles, enjoying full citizenship rights, most of them extremely poor; nobles, varying in rank and title, some of the wealthier of whom either made generous gifts for the beautifying and upbuilding of their cities or spent their riches in extravagance and unrestrained dissipation. Many of the slaves were men of the finest education who, under the direction of their owners, engaged in intellectual labors. All workers, "not only such craftsmen as locksmiths, dyers, carpenters and bricklayers, but also readers, copyists, librarians, school-teachers, and architects, were either slaves or foreigners." [15] The economic order rested upon slavery.

One social feature must be mentioned, the *collegia* or guilds. Although the membership was limited to persons locally engaged in a particular trade or profession, they were neither labor unions nor benevolent societies. The nearest approach to the latter conception were the *collegia tenuiorum*, the poor men's burial clubs. Apparently they existed to satisfy the hunger for social contacts and fellowships. As Dill says: "Probably no age, not even our own, ever felt a greater craving for some form of social life wider than the family and narrower than the state. . . . These colleges became homes for the homeless, a little fatherland or patria for those without a country." [16]

Into this social order Christianity came with its message of spiritual equality before God, with its satisfying fellowships grounded upon a super-human love and with its programs of loving ministries, in which the care of the needy was given a primary place.

The popular conception of the Græco-Roman world, derived in part from the writings of the Roman satirists and in part from the denunciations of the age by contemporary Christian writers, has been that the Gentiles, having lost faith in the old gods, gave themselves with unbridled licentousness to indulgence in every form of gross and sensual immorality. It was a period in which vast wealth was concentrated in the hands of the few, in which direst poverty was the unhappy lot of most Roman citizens, while cruel and oppressive slavery was the fate of multitudes of men and women. Where such economic conditions have existed, immorality has always abounded. The portrayal of our present age, based upon extracts from newspapers, from magazines whose popularity rests upon their sex appeal, and from so-called realistic literature, would furnish from the moral point of view a companion picture to the debauchery of decadent Rome.

Because of the painstaking efforts of modern scholars, another far more appreciative interpretation of the Græco-Roman world has been given to us. One distinguished writer says: "There has probably been no time in the history of mankind when all classes were more given up to thoughts of religion, or when they strained more fervently after high ethical ideals." [17] The truth includes both interpretations. The practical-minded Roman had a secular interest in religion: it was useful in governing people. The inquiring Greek had an intellectual interest in religion: it offered solutions for the profoundest problems that philosophy raised. The ignorant masses had a superstitious interest in religion: it was the means by which they hoped to secure some magical benefit. All believed that mankind had commerce with a supernatural world, that spiritual beings, divinities, angels, demons, and devils could help or harm, and that in religion must be found the refuge, the security, the benefit which the individual craved, since these could not be gotten from human sources. When all of its evils have been properly evaluated, it remains a brooding, wistful, questing age, whose mood became articulate in the cry, "What must I do to be saved?" The contemporary answers given to this appeal for salvation will be studied in the succeeding chapter.

The world-view of all peoples within and without the Roman Empire was geocentric. The tribes had their creation stories. From a more ancient past Egypt, Babylonia, and Persia contributed accounts of the beginnings of the earth, the gods, and mankind, in which a conflict of gods, or the union of a male and a female deity, with the ocean or chaos as the background, were the common elements. The Egyptians believed that land and water evolved out of the primeval chaos of the universal ocean when "not yet was the heaven, not yet the earth, men were not, not yet born were the gods, not yet was death." [18] The Babylonians held that the ocean was the primordial element out of which the universe was generated. The Persians, thoroughly dualistic, held that the world was the result of the activities of two conflicting creators, Ormuzd, creating excellent lands, and Ahriman, bringing plagues, both physical and moral. The Hebrews declared that God "created the heaven and the earth." The idea of an original chaos is indicated in the words: "And the earth was without form and void and darkness was upon the face of the deep." These ideas as to the origin of the universe filtered into the thinking of the Græco-Roman world.

Hesiod, the first of the Greek writers to discuss cosmogony, says, "From Chaos was generated Erebos and black night, and from night again were generated Ether and Day, whom she brought forth, having conceived from the embrace of Erebos." [19] Homer represents Oceana as the Father of all the gods and Tethys, the Earth, as the Mother, while behind these Nature-powers, more august if not more powerful, is the goddess Night. The Romans associate Janus with creation. Ovid, writing about the time of the birth of Jesus, says that seething chaos precedes the orderly world; fire, air, and earth encircled by water appear; then deity completes the creative process, introducing life with all of its gradations, the last being man. Here is a mingling of myth and Greek philosophy.

The world-view, as held by each of the leading Greek philosophies, is essential to a proper understanding of the Gentile Mind. Thales (640-548 B.C.) and his fellow Ionian philosophers were interested in the origin and the causes of the universe. All gave natural explanations to mysterious events and cosmic complexities, but they did not agree as to the single material first principle. Thales said it was water or moisture; Anaximander, "the infinite mass of matter out of which all things arise," and Anaximenes, air. The followers of Pythagoras (c. 580-500 B.C.) held that "everything in the world is ordered according to numerical relations." They also believed in demons, the transmigration of the soul, and future retribution. Heracleitus (c. 535-475 B.C.) taught that matter was "organically alive," that fire was the primary element, guided by Intelligence or the Logos. "The Logos viewed on its corporeal side was Fire, and Fire viewed on its spiritual side was the Logos." He held to the universality of the impermanent, but he endowed his First Cause with the attribute of reason. Anaxagoras (c. 500-428 B.C.) declared the real cause of the movement by which the world was formed to be Nous or Reason.

Socrates, Plato and Aristotle brought Greek philosophy, on the one hand, to a scientific climax, and on the other, to a new and higher appreciation of the mind of man. Plato taught that God formed the world out of a material which could not be completely molded to His will and this intractability he called Necessity. The world has a Soul and a body, and the World-Soul has the attributes of Motion and Intelligence. God, as pure thought, can have no contact with matter, but the World-Soul provides the medium for the divine impress to be made upon matter. Aristotle interpreted the Divine Life as "an energy of self-contemplation." God does not create. "God moves the world as the beloved object moves the lover." He is pure energy. "Divine providence coincides completely for Aristotle with the operation of natural causes." Entelechy, the theory of Aristotle, is the belief that everything is guided from within by its own native structure and purpose. God is "the prime mover, unmoved."

It is hardly possible to exaggerate the influence which Greek philosophy has exerted upon succeeding times. Its impact upon the Græco-Roman world however was lessened by the secular element in Roman thought and by the growing popularity of new Oriental cults.

The masses of the Græco-Roman period viewed the world as the realm of capricious gods and goddesses; human life as controlled largely if not entirely by the movements of the stars, demons and fate; and death as the inescapable doom of every one. It was an age of transition marked by a searching, or rather a groping, for the living God.

VII

The Hellenistic Mind

"The influx of Hellenism, of the Greek spirit and the union of the Gospel with it, form the greatest fact in the history of the Church in the second century, and when the fact was once established as a foundation, it continued through the following centuries."—ADOLPH HARNACK.

HELLENISM is the cultural union of the East and the West. The fusion of all important Græco-Oriental elements is practically completed within the Alexandrian Period, 300 B.C. to 31 B.C. Thus Hellenism forms the historic cultural background of the Græco-Roman world. The Hellenistic Mind, as viewed in this study, is the blending of the Græco-Oriental or Gentile Mind with the Post-Apostolic Christian Mind, fertilized by the Mystery religions and by contemporary philosophical thought on Gentile Christian soil. This blending leads, on the one hand, to "the Hellenizing of the primitive faith" by the endowment of Christian rites or forms with causal qualities; on the other hand, by substituting for trust in a person, Jesus Christ, an intellectual conviction as to the ground on which the trust logically rests.

The Hellenistic Mind, acting within the Christian movement, is the precursor and is later the creator of the Sacramentarian-Theological Mind, which interprets the simple Christian ordinances, Baptism and the Lord's Supper, as possessing physical efficacy or magical power, and authoritatively sets forth in Greek philosophical terms the Christian doctrines of God as related to the historical revelation made through Jesus Christ. Salvation thus interpreted depends upon baptism and orthodoxy, that is, upon the recognition of the magical element in baptism as a sacrament and upon the acceptance of an ecclesiastically approved creed.

By the beginning of the second century, the Christian movement has won a complete victory over the Judaizing Mind that had earnestly endeavored to limit Christianity to the position of a

81

sect within the Jewish national religion. Christianity has now detached itself from its original Judaistic bonds. The Apostolic Age
lies behind us. A new and a radically different environment meets
the Christian missionary as he pushes westward. For four centuries, the Greek language, Greek thought-patterns, and the Hellenistic Mind will influence and largely determine the development of Christian thought and practice.

When the period ends, Christianity will be no longer *religio
illicita*, but all other religions will be illegal. Heathen sacrifices will
be forbidden under severe penalties by the Roman Emperor. The
extensive temple estates, whose incomes once increased the revenues of the polytheistic priesthood, will have been confiscated.
Priests and vestals will receive no more stipends from the public
treasury, and no heathen college or confraternity will be permitted
to accept a legacy. The legal protection and the economic support of non-Christian religions will cease altogether.

Harnack represents organized Christianity, now called the Catholic or Universal Church, as reviewing the preceding four centuries,
and speaks thus of the part she has played: "I have had to fight—
my body is full of scars and my clothes are covered with dust; but
I have won my battles and built my house; I have beaten back
polytheism; I have disabled and almost annihilated that monstrous
abortion, political religion; I have resisted the enticements of a
subtle religious philosophy and I victoriously encountered it with
God, the almighty Creator of all things; lastly, I have reared a
great building, a fortress with towers and bulwarks, where I guard
my treasure and protect the weak." [20]

The external factors which aided the spread of Christianity
were: the Roman Empire; the Greek *Koiné*; the Jewish synagogues,
furnishing strategic centers from which to appeal to the Gentile
community; the breakdown of national religions; the rise of individualism, lessening man's subordination to the State; the wide
distribution of Oriental cults and of Mystery religions, emphasizing personal salvation and promising a blessed immortality, and,
last, the development of a spirit whose chief interest focuses upon
religion, accompanied by a hospitality never known before to the
foreign interpreters of Oriental faiths which, they claim, have
arisen out of a far-distant past.

The Christian missionaries adjusted their preaching so as to secure the largest benefit from these favorable conditions. As Harnack points out, they proclaimed the Gospel of salvation through a gracious divine Saviour, of love and practical, helpful charities, of the Spirit of power, moral earnestness, and holiness; they told of a New Israel, a New People, a Third Race, the sons of God, for whom the whole cosmic process has waited in eager expectancy; they bore a volume of sacred writings, whose authority was attested by that ancient people, the Jews, and in which the sufferings of the Saviour Jesus Christ were foretold, and they denounced polytheism, idolatry, and all the immoral practices and degrading superstitions which characterized contemporary paganism. As the result of such preaching, multitudes of Gentiles became Christians.

Christianity first appeared in the Græco-Roman world as communities which were originally "unions for a holy life, on the ground of a common hope which rested upon the belief that the God who had spoken by the prophets had sent His Son, Jesus Christ, and through him revealed eternal life, and would shortly make it manifest. Christianity had its roots in certain facts and utterances, and the foundation of the Christian union was the common hope, the holy life of the Spirit according to the law of God, and the holding fast to those facts and utterances." [21] Early Christianity had a definite historical origin; a definite religious experience, which was made the prerequisite to church membership; a definite purpose, the establishing of the will of God as revealed through Jesus Christ in the hearts and the institutions of men. Early Gentile Christianity was a historical, spiritual, missionary, universal religion.

The Romans conquered the Greeks, but Hellenism, the contemporary Greek culture, later conquered Rome. The record of history is that Christianity subdued the whole Græco-Roman world; but in the process early Christianity was so completely Hellenized that its historical origin became obscured in theological and allegorical speculations; its required religious experience was ignored and then forgotten as baptism became a saving sacrament, and its missionary method of persuading men was supplanted by the use of the armed forces of the State and the exercise of the proscriptive powers of the Church.

Christianity escaped Judaism only to become so infected by Hellenism that its outward character was changed; its appeal was so adjusted as to benefit from the prevailing conditions which favored and fostered the contemporary Mystery Religions, while its method for the salvation of mankind was transformed from a personal faith in Jesus Christ to the submitting by the individual to ecclesiastically regulated forms and ceremonies, like in causal character to the forms and ceremonies of the Mystery Religions. The name given by the Greek-speaking Christians to these forms and ceremonies was the Mysteries; by the Latin-speaking Christians, the Sacraments. Transformed into a Mystery Religion, Christianity, with the support of Roman Emperors, conquered the Græco-Roman world, but at the cost of becoming partially paganized. The Christian movement became institutionalized in a corporate body called the Holy Catholic Church, Christian in its historic succession and in its conviction as to the human-divine Lordship of Jesus Christ, but Hellenistic in the method by which Christian salvation was attained and Hellenistic in the philosophical phraseology used in defining Christian orthodox beliefs.

Hellenism introduced sacramentarianism as the ground of salvation and of all other spiritual benefits, and it also gave to the intellectual aspects of religion the ascendancy over spiritual religion by its emphasis upon dogma and orthodoxy. For a proper understanding of present-day Christianity, the second century needs to be closely studied; for the sacramentarian conception of Christianity had its rise within this period, a conception which still controls the thought of the majority of those who claim in the twentieth century to be Christians.

The background of our study is pre-Christian Hellenism. Its particular thought-patterns, the groups and systems of ideas so generally held as not to evoke opposition, must be briefly noted. The centralization of power is recognized as essential to the success and the efficiency of any kind of government. Except for the Jews, certain Greek and Roman philosophers, and later the Christians, polytheism is universal, but the interest in the old national gods and in the native divinities is waning rapidly. Political religion extends throughout the Empire. The belief that matter is evil is widespread, if not universal. All kinds of superstitions flourish. The existence of a world of spirits, good and bad, few seriously doubt. Asceticism is highly approved both by Orientals and by Greeks. Though the belief in the magical value of religious rites originally came from the East, no other religious conception is more widely or more fervently accepted. The presence of such beliefs furnishes an ideal soil for the growth of the Mystery Religions.

The New Testament, since it is written in the Greek *Koiné*, is the earliest linguistic expression of the influence of Hellenism upon Christianity. The Christian writings of the second century still extant, those of Polycarp, extracts from Papias, the Ascension of Isaiah, the Acts of John, Melito of Sardis, the Martyrdom of Polycarp, the Acts of Peter, composed by Christians living in the province of Asia; the Didache or the Teachings of the Twelve, Ignatius, the Original Clementine Romance, Theophilus of Antioch, all written by Christians in Syria; First Clement, the Shepherd of Hermas, Justin Martyr, Tatian, "the Muratorian Canon," originating in Rome; Barnabas, Second Clement and others, the touching letter of the churches of Lyons and Vienna and the writings of Irenæus, coming from Gaul, and the Acts of the Scillitan Martyrs, from Africa, indicate the literary variety and the wide geographical range of the early Post-Apostolic literature. The earliest writings show but little knowledge of current Greek philosophy and are written primarily for the instruction of the Christian saints. They have an important bearing however upon the development of church government and they unmistakably indicate the early and rapid growth of the episcopacy.

The Apologists, converts who came into the Christian fellowship, possess a high degree of Hellenistic culture; these form the second group of Christian writers, and inaugurate the second stage of the Post-Apostolic literature. They defend the Christians against the charges of atheism, licentiousness and cannibalism, and they interpret the relation which Christianity, as the final universal religion, sustains to Judaism and to Greek philosophy. Aristides, a Greek philosopher residing in Athens; Justin Martyr, Samaritan by birth, who successively has been a Stoic, a Peripatetic, a Pythagorean, a Platonist, and is now a Christian; Tatian, a sophist, familiar with classical literature; Athenagoras, like Aristides an Athenian philosopher; and Theophilus of Antioch, the bishop of that city—all seek to defend the Christians and to show how easily Christianity and Hellenistic culture may be harmonized. They claim to have found in the Christian experience the satisfaction for every need, created by the spirit and the culture of their age.

The third literary stage is called the Polemical Period, the principal works being written by Irenæus and Hippolytus. To these might be added the Latin writers Tertullian and Cyprian, who devote themselves to the championing of the Christian faith and to the making of attacks upon Christian Gnosticism, a religious philosophy which, appropriating the Christian revelation, interprets it in harmony with current Gnostic presuppositions. Hellenistic thought-patterns and technical philosophical terms begin to appear frequently in the Christian writings. Theology, as a system of Christian thought, originates in the study of the facts of the Christian revelation and expression, being inspired by the Hellenistic spirit, prevalent during the second and third centuries.

The tendency of all powerful movements is ever in the direction of a permanent institutional expression, and this expression is determined, in part, by the social order which environs the movement. Christianity appears in the Apostolic Period as a religion of spiritual power, transforming and uplifting the inner life, releasing in the individual spiritual energies which find their expressions in an exalted enthusiasm, a sacrificial devotion to Jesus Christ and to all who love Him, an active missionary endeavor, and a moral character motivated by holy love. On this ground, Christianity has been, in this work, repeatedly described as a movement. Its local congregations, made up of believers in Christ, belong to the Christian movement which Jesus described as "my church" or "my called-out," and which Paul calls "the body of Christ" and "the bride of Christ." These local congregations, wherever the membership is overwhelmingly Jewish, reflect the synagogue organizations in the choosing of elders who lead the services of worship, who preach and teach and perform duties which may be described as pastoral. Deacons represent a later development. Whenever and wherever these local congregations become preponderantly Gentile, the religious and the semi-religious societies of the Græco-Roman world, which recognize the Hellenistic principle "that in the rule of one man was to be found the natural order of things and the only security for a well-ordered State," consciously or unconsciously exert a strong influence over these small Christian groups. Meeting in private houses, in secret places or in public halls, they adopt, first in cities where they soon become a no inconsiderable number in the aggregate, the monarchical idea as the most desirable plan of Church government. Thus arises the concentration of authority in the hands of a single minister, to whom is given the title of bishop or overseer. Ignatius of Antioch (A.D. 115) makes his claim as a monarchical bishop to the exercise of such ecclesiastical authority; and while the claim that the bishops have succeeded to all the authority exercised by the Apostles is not taught in the New Testament, it is not long before the bishops are declared to be the true successors of the Apostles and are exercising apparently greater powers than the Apostles ever enjoyed.

The genius of an age, the vital union of spirit, attitude and ideals, tends to mold and to give outward character to every movement arising within that particular age. No period offers a finer illustration of this statement than the one we are now studying. The genius of the Græco-Roman world, viewed religiously, may be summed up in the phrase "the yearning for salvation." This is admittedly a new point of view and diametrically opposed to the picture given in the past by most church historians. The thorough investigation of the Græco-Roman world during the early centuries of the Christian Era, made in recent years by competent and unprejudiced scholars, establishes the fact that the age is deeply religious and that men everywhere, eager for salvation, are welcoming the Mystery Religions. Indeed, it may be said that the genius of this age finds a natural expression in the fostering of these religions. This leads to the enquiry: "What are the Mystery Religions?"

Originating in some primitive cult which has survived the imposition of the national religions, the Mystery Religions appeared, in the period under study, as private religious associations that made a universal appeal by offering salvation to all who would participate in their rites of initiation. Angus defines a Mystery Religion as "a religion of symbolism which, through myth and allegory, iconic representations, blazing lights and dense darkness, liturgies and sacramental acts and suggestion, quickened the intuitions of the heart and provoked in the initiate a mystical experience conducing to *palingenesia* (regeneration), the object of every initiation." [22]

As religious of redemption, they "professed to remove estrangement between man and God, to procure forgiveness of sins, to furnish mediation," [23] giving a satisfying gnosis (knowledge) of God, through the sacramental drama which refined and exalted the phychic life and gave to it an almost supernatural intensity, such as the ancient world had never before known.

Appealing directly to the individual, whatever his birth or social status, these Mystery Religions professed to assure a personal salvation in the present and in the world to come, and on this ground they were seeking recognition as cults worthy of universal acceptation. "Pre-eminent among these cults were the Orphic and Pythagorean fraternities; those of the Great Mother and Attis; the Egyptian Lord Serapis and Queen Isis; the Syrian Baals and Adonis; the Samothracian Kabiri; the Persian Mithra; the Greek Eleusinia; the Gnostic fraternities; the Phrygian Sabazius; the *Dea Syria* and her satellites; Dionysos; the theosophical Hermeticists. These and similar Mystery-cults were the most popular means of satisfying the ardent desire for *soteria* (salvation) and of maintaining the democratic spirit in religion." [24] These religions attracted and held the interested attention of the largest number of "the religiously-minded men."

On the one hand, these religions prepared the way for Christianity, and, on the other, they became, especially Mithraism, its most active rivals. Membership in all the Mystery Religions depended upon the participation in special rites of initiation. While the individual, by applying for membership, expressed a personal faith in the religion, the benefits of salvation were attained only through the initiatory ceremonies. In the Mystery Religions, "the baptismal rite in particular, whether by water or by blood, was regarded as marking the crucial moment in a genuinely regenerative process." [25]

Coming out of the Orient, Christianity was classified generally by the inhabitants of the Roman Empire as another Mystery Religion. The defense made by the Christians deepened this impression. Justin Martyr, Barnabas, and Hermas regarded baptism as "the culmination of the process of regeneration in which remission of sins actually takes place"; but a few years later, Tertullian (b. A.D. 150-160) exclaimed: "Blessed is our sacrament of water in that by washing away the sins of our early blindness, we are liberated into eternal life."

Under the influence of the Mystery Religions, the Christian movement with its two simple outward rites, baptism and the Lord's Supper, became increasingly sacramentarianized and "by the third century it could already rival the most imposing cults in all paganism, with its solemn and precise ritual, its priests, its sacrifices and its holy ceremonies." [26] Thus Christianity, responsive to the Hellenistic Mind, which seemed incapable of conceiving of religious rites other than as mysterious and magical, hastened "to equip itself with such rites as were deemed to be requisite to enjoyment of communion with God. Contemporary magic was refined into sacramental efficacy. The robes of the Mystery-priest were worn and the privileges of the Mystery-hierphant appropriated by the Christian priest. The pontiffs of the Mysteries anticipated the Christian hierarchy in seeking political power and in using religious associations for other than religious purposes. Christianity soon claimed magical potencies for its rites similar to those claimed by its most catholic competitors. The God of the Mysteries, like the Deity of the larger sections of Christendom today, was approached properly and most securely through social acts of immense but mysterious intrinsic value, enhanced by the official character of the ministrants." "It was the whole mentality of the ancient world, which Christians shared with pagans, which forced this missionary religion to equip itself with what were regarded as the essentials or tokens of a religion in that age: miracle, secrecy and sacrament." [27]

Harnack probably exaggerates when he asserts that by the fourth century "Hellenism as a whole and in every phase of its development was established in the Church," but it is a fact, well attested in history, that as a formative and persisting influence these Græco-Oriental elements that enter into the Hellenistic Mind have been and still are present and in evidence, to a less or greater degree,

among all non-evangelical Christians. Greek and Roman Catholicism, conceived in the womb of Hellenism, retain the Christian
name and defend the primary Christian doctrines, but they exhibit
many of the characteristics of the mother.

There are certain distinctive phases of the world-view of the
Christians of this period which must be noted. They shared many
of the unquestionably erroneous beliefs of their day, adopted not a
few of the pagan conceptions, forms and practices; yet they preserved a loyalty to the essentials of the Christian faith: monothe-
ism, the divinity and saviourhood of Jesus Christ, the authority of
the teachings of the Apostles and of the writings which now
compose the New Testament. They refused to compromise on
any terms with polytheism, immorality, or philosophies which
lessened the divine pre-eminence of their Lord.

These Christians lived as citizens of a heavenly kingdom and
their virtues commanded the admiration of their bitterest critics.
They practiced the precepts of Jesus and gladly provided for all
of their number who were in need. They destroyed all social distinctions in the realization of Christian brotherhood. The picture
Aristides gives of the Christian life is true to facts. As Glover
says, "The Christian outlived the pagan, out-died him and out-
thought him." They believed themselves to be members of a new
order of humanity, and, inspired by a devotion to Jesus Christ, they
declared that in themselves was being fulfilled the purpose of
God, the Maker of Heaven and earth, so that joyfully they welcomed martyrdom, confident that after death a life of eternal
blessedness awaited all the witnessing followers of Christ. They
felt themselves to be the goal of the whole cosmic process, that
God had created the world as the arena in which Christians should
share in the fulfillment of the divine purpose and that therefore
all things were working together for their good. They were a happy
people, sojourning in this present world; but they looked for
something better in the future life; they described themselves as
pilgrims, journeying toward "a city which hath foundations whose
maker and builder is God."

VIII

The Theological Mind

*"The Christian Church and its doctrines were developed within the Roman world and Greek culture. * * * * The separation of Judaism having taken place, it was necessary that the spirit of another people should take its place."*—ADOLPH HARNACK.

THEOLOGY, as a system of doctrine, is the direct result of the impact of the Greek way of thinking upon the Christian movement as it passes through the process of becoming institutionalized, for a visible ecclesiastical authority is necessary to give to credal statements binding value. The growth of church government parallels the development of the historic creeds; the former is fertilized by the Roman Mind, the latter by the Greek Mind. The Theological Mind finds its expression in the systematic treatment and in the intellectual interpretation of the Christian revelation, fertilized by contemporary Greek philosophy on Post-Apostolic Christian soil.

Before accepting any revelation, the Hebrew Mind sought the proof of its possessing divine credentials, evidenced by the presence of the power of God: "Jews ask for signs." The Greek Mind desired a revelation in harmony with all known truth capable of being rationally understood, and containing within itself evidence of its divine origin: "Greeks seek after wisdom." Within this period the Jewish mental attitude gave place to the Greek, resulting in the development of the Christian doctrine of God, based upon the Christian revelation and expressed in Greek philosophical terms.

Faith is basic to the Christian experience. In the Greek translation of the Old Testament, the Greek word meaning faith or belief is used "chiefly in the sense of trust and primarily trust in a person," but in Greek philosophy the same word means an intellectual conviction rather than a moral trust. On entering the Græco-Roman world, Christianity is forced to adapt itself to this new intellectual climate.

While the New Testament, as we now have it, was not, in the early part of the second century, collected into a single volume, its most important books—the four Gospels, Acts, the Epistles of Paul, First Peter, First John, and probably Revelation—were being circulated and read in the churches, as possessing apostolic authority. These documents became the more valuable as the generation of those who had known the Apostles personally passed away. By the end of the second century, according to Tertullian, "the writings of evangelists and apostles" have been united into one volume, along with "the law and the prophets"; and the teachings of the New Testament were being used to prove the errors of the heretics, as well as to encourage and to edify the saints.

The acceptance of the New Testament writings rested, not upon the approval of a body representing all the Christian churches then in existence, but upon the conviction that God being true, the statements which He makes through his prophets and ministers are also true. Both the Old and the New Testaments emanated, according to Iranæus (147-207 A.D.), from "the one and the same God and were granted for the salvation of the human race in a form appropriate to the times." [28] In the conflict with those philosophically inclined Christians, such as Marcion (C.100-165 A.D.), who in the interest of propagating the belief in a good God who could not allow man to be tricked by the devil, rejected the Old Testament and denied that Jehovah, though the Creator of the world, was the God of redemption (thus teaching a crass ditheism), the conservative Christian leaders appealed to the writings of the Apostles and those closely identified with them as the authoritative work of men divinely inspired. "No greater creative act can be mentioned in the whole history of the Church than the formation of the apostolic collection and the assigning of it to a position of equal rank with the Old Testament." [29]

Apostolic Christianity was trust in the crucified and risen Jesus as Lord and Saviour and as the Christ who fulfilled the Messianic hopes of Israel, followed by loving obedience to his teachings and by a loyalty and an appreciation which gave to him the highest conceivable place under God. Saving faith was simply trusting Jesus; Christian character, loving and serving Jesus; the Christian hope, the expectation to be with Jesus. The primacy of the Christian experience, the centrality of Jesus Christ in that experience, the validity and the authority of the Hebrew Scriptures that foretold the sufferings of the Christ, the exhibiting of loyalty to him in conduct by loving sacrificial service in the keeping of his precepts, and in thought by giving to him the pre-eminence in all things under God, the enduement of the Holy Spirit linked with the hope of the speedy return of Jesus Christ, formed the beliefs, molded the character and made these early Christians "more than conquerors."

Greek philosophy, in the second, third and fourth centuries, had become the exegesis of received doctrines, and the philosophers of the period were professors, each disseminating the ideas of the founder of that particular school to which the instructor belonged. So successful were they, that metaphysical conceptions occupied in the popular mind relatively the same place that scientific ideas and laws hold in our day. These conceptions, made familiar by their frequent use, were a part of the intellectual equipment of all educated men and women.

Christianity offered to the ethical forces of the age, which were seeking higher and surer levels, a satisfying and inspiring motivation, and by its gospel of a Mediator between God and mankind made, in competition with the Mystery Religions, a more powerful appeal to the cultivated people of the Græco-Roman world. Simple, unaffected Christianity continued to be a religion of stern moral discipline and of unelaborated faith in Jesus Christ, but within the rapidly growing group of educated Christians the discussion turned more and more to the relation of knowledge (gnosis) to Christian faith. Conflict followed, and as a result "the extreme wing of each contending party dropped from the main body." The old-fashioned Christians, maintaining and exaggerating the older Judaistic ideas—the Nazarenes, the Pharisaic and Essenic Ebionites—gradually detached themselves from organized Christianity, the Holy Church; while the Christian Gnostics found themselves assailed as heretics. The struggle ended in a series of compromises, formally stated in the early Christian creeds. Both the Judaic and the Gnostic forms of Christianity were condemned, but the Hellenistic spirit, with its passion for definition, its delight in speculation and its belief in the incomparable worth of knowledge, found a permanent lodgment in Christianity, gained and still retains an ascendancy over trust in God and over the endeavor to live a holy life, whenever orthodoxy has been and is made the primary basis of Christian fellowship.

Apostolic Christianity was a way of living with Judaism as its background; Gnosticism, with which post-Apostolic Christianity came into conflict, was a way of thinking, with Hellenism as its background. The Christian Gnostics "attempted to capture Christianity for Hellenic culture and Hellenic culture for Christianity" and "they gave up the Old Testament in order to facilitate the conclusion of the covenant between the two powers and make it possible to assert the absoluteness of Christianity." [30] They sought to weave the Christian revelation into a philosophy of religion. Interpreting Christianity as a system of doctrine, they were the first to attempt to become Christian theologians.

Christian Gnosticism maintained knowledge, not faith, to be the key to a complete salvation. Gnosticism was a point of view natural to the Hellenistic Mind; for Greek culture and civilization were based upon knowledge. Sharp divisions developed within the Christian Gnostic movement, but the following doctrines were generally held: Christianity, the only true and absolute religion, is a revealed system of doctrine, communicated by initiations, like in character to the Mystery Religions; Christ, not the Old Testament Messiah, by his appearing wrought redemption, the true and full understanding of which is limited to the esoteric or Gnostic group; the Supreme God is not the Creator, but Jehovah, the God of the Jews, is; the Old Testament is rejected; matter is eternal, is evil, and possesses a physical potency; Christ is one of the emanations, or the fullness of all these emanations, from the Supreme God. Though they interpreted Christ as the Logos, the divine Word or Reason, they reduced his Incarnation to an illusion by their insistence that all matter is evil and the handiwork of Satan.

Marcion, Basilides, Valentinus, Saturnius, and other Gnostic Christian leaders founded systems and gained many followers. Marcion accepted only a part of the New Testament, the ten earliest epistles of Paul and the Gospel of Luke. A man of wealth, he came to Rome, defended his doctrines of faith, divine grace, the new covenant, and the ascetic life, denounced the Old Testament, and denied that the Christ was in any way related to the God of Israel. A rupture in the Church of Rome followed. A Marcionite body was formed and the movement spread far and wide. The Gnostic Christians by their teachings created a need and a demand for doctrinal statements in opposition to Gnosticism which would be in harmony with apostolic tradition and the writings of the New Testament.

History shows that the theological formulas, called the creeds of Christianity, were all forged in the fires of religious controversy. As given in the Acts, the simple declaration of the convert, just prior to baptism, was that he trusted in Jesus Christ as his Lord, and following this, he was baptized in or into the name of Jesus Christ. The Baptismal Confession was soon expanded to the following: "I believe in God, in Jesus Christ, and in the Holy Spirit." Before the close of the second century, the recital by the convert of the Apostolic Rule of Faith, which preceded baptism, varied as to its exact terms in different countries. Tertullian thus summarizes the one used by the Church of Rome: "She recognizes one God, Creator of the universe; and Jesus Christ, born of the Virgin Mary, the Son of the Creator God; and the resurrection of the flesh; she mingles the Law and the Prophets with the evangelical and apostolic writings, and thence she imbibes the faith." This statement of belief suggests in every line that it was written in opposition to the teachings of the Gnostic Christians: God is the Creator, Jesus Christ is his Son, whose real humanity is declared by his birth, the physical body is to be raised in the resurrection, while the books of the New Testament are placed upon an equality with the Mosaic Law and the Prophets.

A century later the summary of Tertullian is amplified into a form which closely approximates the so-called Apostles' Creed of the early fifth century: "I believe in God Almighty and in Christ Jesus, His only Son our Lord, who was born of the Holy Spirit and the Virgin Mary, crucified under Pontius Pilate and buried, and the third day rose again from the dead, ascended into heaven and is seated on the right hand of the Father, whence he is coming to judge living and dead, and in the Holy Spirit; Holy Church, forgiveness of sins, resurrection of the flesh, life everlasting." It is readily seen that the Apostles' Creed in its original, as well as in its present form, is an anti-Gnostic document, practically every phrase in it being a statement of belief directly opposed to Gnostic teachings. The introduction of "Holy Church," later "the Holy Catholic Church," is significant and indicates the growth of the belief in ecclesiastical authority.

The Christian Gnostics sought to Hellenize Christianity by imposing their Greek philosophy upon the Christian revelation. The Apologists sought to give to the Christian revelation its historical setting in Judaism and to show how it could be interpreted in harmony with the truths of Greek philosophy. The Controversialists—Irenæus, Hippolytus, Tertullian, Cyprian and others—assailed polytheism, pagan morals, the Christian Gnostics, and others whom they claimed to hold heretical views. The denial of the incarnation of Christ as real, made by the Christian Gnostics, led to the discussion of the Person of Jesus Christ and his relation to God the Father; and this became the dominant issue within the Christian world during the third and fourth centuries. Neither the Apologists nor the Controversialists made any attempt to provide a systematic exposition of Christianity as a whole. This endeavor had its beginnings in Alexandria under Clement, born about A.D. 160, and under Origen, born a quarter of a century later, who sought to incorporate into the Christian faith the best in Hellenistic culture, especially in the Platonic and the Stoic philosophies.

The Alexandrian school of catechists, under the leadership of Clement and Origen, "overthrew polytheism by scientific means whilst at the same time preserving everything of any value in Greek science and culture. These Alexandrians wrote for the educated people of the whole earth. They made Christianity a part of the civilization of the world." [31] Platonism, with an admixture of Stoicism and Pythagoreanism, was the prevailing philosophy. The Gnostics were interested in the Christian revelation only to give to it a place in their philosophical scheme; Clement, Origen, and those associated with them as loyal Christians were interested in Greek philosophy solely for Christian ends. The Christianizing of the world of human knowledge through education, producing a distinctly Christian culture, may be said to have had its beginnings in Alexandria. Clement posited the source of all knowledge in Jesus Christ. "Just as every family goes back to the Creator, so does the teaching of all good things go back to the Lord." As the Mosaic Law was the schoolmaster or pedagogue for the Hebrews "to bring them to Christ," so also was philosophy for the Greeks. "Thus the whole story of the world—cosmology, psychology and ethics alike—is centered in the benevolent action of the Logos, whose Incarnation is the final manifestation of truth and goodness, for whose Advent the world has been prepared by trial and discipline." [32]

Origen, who succeeded Clement, has been called "the father of theological science, and the founder of ecclesiastical dogma." His teaching and writing, covering the first half of the third century, mark an epoch in the intellectual life of Christianity. As Harnack says, "Orthodox theology of all creeds has never advanced beyond the circle mapped out by his mind." [33] He welded together Christianity and the science and the culture of the age. His method of interpreting the Scriptures in a threefold sense; his treatment of sin, forgiveness, the atonement, and the holiness of God; his emphasis upon the cleansing flames of purgatory and upon the eternal generation of the Son, reveal the influence of current philosophical thought. Living in a cultured literary age, naturally he sought to give to the Christian faith a scholastic form, and to a remarkable degree he succeeded. He created a system of thought in which Christian faith is reconciled with Greek philosophy, and in so doing he dealt Gnosticism its death blow.

The simple rule of faith, by the beginning of the third century, was being transformed into a compendium of a Greek philosophical system, and paralleling this development the churches of Christ were being united into a religious commonwealth, called the Holy Church or the Holy Catholic Church. Within this growing organization, two standards of Christian morality were recognized, a spiritual and a secular. Montanism, founded about A.D. 135-160 by Montanus, Prisca, and Maximilla, all claiming to be Christian prophets bringing a later divine revelation, sought to stop "the continuous secularizing of the Christian life and to preserve the virginity of the Church as a holy Community." [34]

Their leaders inveighed against the laxity and the worldliness within the churches.

Tertullian, born about A.D. 150, was carried away by the austerity and the enthusiasm of the Montanists, and became in Africa their most powerful champion. The movement failed and the Montanists were stigmatized as heretics by the first Synod of Bishops meeting in Asia Minor. This marked the beginning of ecclesiastical effort to determine orthodoxy. To be a Christian no longer necessitated that a man should live as a saint and that he possess the Holy Spirit. To be a Christian meant that he should obey ecclesiastical authority, share in the benefits of the sacraments, and engage in penances and good works.

The spirit of true Christianity, whatever its intellectual environment, seeks to give to Jesus the highest place under God, and to this end uses the language and the thought-patterns of the age in which the issue arises. The whole history of theology and especially Christology, the doctrines which deal with the Person and the work of Christ, illustrate and confirm this statement. The discussion regarding the Trinity, involving the deity of the Son and the Spirit, consumes the time and engages the deepest thought of the theologians in the closing half of the third and the whole of the fourth centuries, while the Person of Christ is the leading issue in Greek Christian thought until the close of the seventh century. The doctrines of Man and of Sin, in their accepted formulations, are not developed upon Greek soil, but upon Latin, and belong to the fifth century.

Parallel with the sacramentarian process in the second and third centuries, which made baptism necessary to salvation, there entered another tendency which made orthodoxy or right doctrine also essential to salvation. The conflict with erroneous teachings began in Apostolic times, there being frequent references in the later books of the New Testament to false teachers and prophets. The Christian churches therefore sought to protect themselves from heresy by adding to the Baptismal Confession; and in resisting the errors of Gnosticism, they adopted the formula which, with various additions and changes, is now called the Apostles' Creed. With the rise of the belief that the acceptance of right doctrines was also necessary to salvation, the formulation of precise and accurate theological definitions, especially in the field of philosophical speculation where the pre-eminence of Christ was involved, became a matter of life and death.

The philosophical conception of Jesus Christ, the Son of God, as the Logos, or uttered Reason of the Eternal, was seized upon by John as expressing the relation of the Son to the Father in the thought-pattern of Greek philosophy. But the Logos had a different connotation for different philosophical groups. It meant one thing to the Platonists, another to the Stoics, still another to Philo and his Hellenistic Jewish following. The Stoics believed in the Logos or Reason as immanent in the universe, and there was no other God. The Platonists believed in the transcendant God, "God over all," and the Logos was therefore subordinate to God. Philo linked the Logos with the religious conceptions of Judaism. A Christian interpretation of the Logos became imperative.

The Edict of Milan by Constantine and Licinius in the winter A.D. 312-3 granted to all peoples "liberty of worship." Christianity soon became the favored religion and Constantine a Christian. Theological controversy was rife. Every city was interested in doctrinal discussions. More than once the empire was shaken to its center by these bitter debates. "Bloodshed was not infrequent, bishops were banished by imperial authority, mobs raided now this side now that, emperors supported first one side and then the other, in the varying fortunes of battle." [35] In A.D. 325 Emperor Constantine called the first general Council of the Church, meeting at Nicæa, to consider the relation of the Son to the Father.

The controversy over the deity of Christ was in a sense a conflict between the two leading Christian educational institutions, the School at Antioch and the School at Alexandria. Arius, a presbyter, at Antioch, preaching about A.D. 318, interpreted the Trinity in a way offensive to his bishop in Alexandria. For the next seven years there was turmoil. Three parties developed: 1. The Arians, recognizing Jesus as the Logos, the Son of God, held that he was created out of nothing, was therefore finite though the first created and in turn the creator of the universe; that the body of Jesus was material but his soul was the Logos and that he was worthy of all the worship given him; 2. The Semi-Arians or Eusebians, rejected the finitude of the Son and his sameness in essence with the Father, holding only to likeness as to essence; 3. The Athanasians held that the Son was the same in essence with the Father and distinct as to personality. The followers of Athanasius won at Nicæa and wrote into the creed the belief "in one Lord Jesus Christ, the Son of God, begotten of the Father, only-begotten, that is, of the substance of the Father, God of God, Light of Light, true God of true God, begotten not made, of one substance with the Father, through whom all things were made, both those in heaven and those on earth, who for us men and for our salvation came down and was made flesh."

A divided Council approved the Creed and for over half a century the churches from Arabia to Spain debated it. Five times Athanasius was driven into exile. "Synods and provincial councils were summoned by the different parties in which these condemned and excommunicated each other." [36] Finally, by the Council of Constantinople (A.D. 381) it was reaffirmed and strengthened. This document, now called the Nicene Creed, contains the following additional statement as the deity of the Holy Spirit: "And [we believe] in the Holy Spirit, the Lord and Giver of life, who proceedeth from the Father; who with the Father and the Son together is worshiped and glorified; who spake by the prophets."

The center of theological interest from A.D. 381 to A.D. 680 was the Person of Christ. Apollinarius, condemned at the Council of Constantinople A.D. 381, denied to Jesus a true human soul. Nestorius, condemned at the Council at Ephesus A.D. 431, dissolved the unity of the Person of Christ by teaching the union of two natures in Christ; Eutyches, approved by the turbulent Council at Ephesus A.D. 449, commonly called "the Council of Robbers" and condemned by the Council at Chalcedon (A.D. 451), which followed the advice of Leo, Bishop of Rome, taught that there was no distinction of natures in Christ and that his body was different in substance from ours. The Monophysites maintained that Christ had but one nature and the Monothelites that he had but one will, the latter views being condemned by the Council at Rome A.D. 649 and by the Council at Constantinople A.D. 680.

The direct influence of Hellenistic thought upon Christian

theology terminates with the settlement of the Christological controversy. Soon after, Antioch and Alexandria, seats of progressive Christian schools, are destroyed by the Moslems. The conflict with Hellenism is practically ended. Christianity has won and lost. Polytheism and paganism have suffered a lasting defeat. Hellenistic philosophy has failed in its effort to define Jesus Christ in terms less than deity. The Empire has become the defender and the aggressive champion of organized Christianity.

These great victories have been gained at a frightful cost. The sacramentarianism of the dying Mystery Religions has supplanted personal trust in Jesus Christ as the basis of salvation. Right teaching or orthodoxy, as formulated by ecclesiastical bodies, is essential to salvation and any one who dissents thereform is anathematized. Devotion to Christ as basic in the Christian religion has given place to submission to an institution, the Holy Catholic Church, whose bishops and clergy claim the possession of apostolic authority.

The supreme victory of Christianity within this period, the victory which evidences the preservation of its most vital truth, viz. the pre-eminence of Jesus Christ under God, was gained in the realm of philosophical speculation by the definition in Greek metaphysical terms of the divinity of Jesus Christ. Whatever was lost, the Lordship of Jesus remained. The story of his life and teachings was preserved in the New Testament, and the Gospel, while hampered by ecclesiastical authority, was not altogether suppressed, for there were the tens of thousands of devout Christian men and women who continued to tell to others the truths they had learned in their own Christian experience, and in them that heard and believed, the Christian experience as described in the New Testament was reproduced.

IX

The Roman Mind

*"These thine arts shall be, to engraft the law of peace, forbear the con-
quered and war down the proud."*—Vergil.

In the realm of religion four types of mind are to be found. If
one of these types gains the ascendancy for a considerable period the
effect is evidenced in the course of religious history. These types
are: 1. The Intellectualist, 2. The Institutionalist, 3. The Experientialist, 4. The Individualist. In Christianity, the Intellectualist
becomes the theologian whose supreme interest centers in orthodoxy; the Institutionalist, the ecclesiastic whose supreme interest
centers in an efficient government; the Experientialist, the mystic,
whose supreme interest centers in the enrichment of the Christian
experience; the Individualist, the self-determinationist, whose supreme interest centers in the preservation of religious liberty. The
first two, the Intellectualist and the Institutionalist, tend to unite,
for each is primarily concerned in the promotion of organized
Christianity, especially in its intellectual expression. The one needs
an ecclesiastical authority to enforce his definition of orthodoxy,
and the other needs orthodoxy as the basis of Christian truth upon
which the ecclesiastical organization may rest. A like affinity draws
together the Experientialist and the Individualist; the first needs
religious liberty in order that he may be free to develop unhindered
his Christian experience, while the Individualist welcomes the
support of one who does not identify religion with the authority
of the Creeds or of the Church.

The preceding three chapters, outlining the development of the
Christian religion within the Græco-Roman world, have dealt
with the influence of the Intellectualists, the philosophically-
minded, outside and within the Christian movement which resulted in the formulation of ecclesiastically approved and therefore

authoritative creeds. This approval was possible because during the selfsame period the Institutionalists, seeking another objective, were able to create and to endow with authority the ecclesiastical bodies that enforced the acceptance of orthodoxy.

Christianity, in its historical development, passes from one to another of the four moods of the Greek verb: the indicative, the imperative, the subjunctive, and the optative. Primitive Christianity was proclaimed in the indicative mood: "That which we have heard, that which we have seen with our eyes, that which we beheld and our hands handled concerning the Word of life, . . . declare we unto you, also, that ye may have fellowship with us." The period of the indicative mood passes as the bishops begin to claim the rights of spiritual monarchs and as, in synods and councils, they fix the forms of Christian faith and anathematize all who refuse to accept their dogmas. The Bishop of Rome asserts his primacy, claiming to be the vicar of Christ. Roman Catholicism is Christianity in the imperative mood.

From Montanus and Tertullian, through the Dark Ages there are voices dissenting from the dogmas of the Church, protesting against the unjust exercise of ecclesiastical power, doubting, and therefore hesitating, to accept the dogmas of the Roman Church. These all speak in the subjunctive mood. Preceding the Reformation there is a period of yearning, wistfulness, and hope—an optative mood—which ushers in a new cycle of Christian history.

The Reformation restored the indicative mood: "The just shall live by faith." Again, Christianity was interpreted as a personal experience of divine grace. Linguistic, national, and theological differences split the Reformation movement into denominational groups. The framing of confessions of faith, followed by social pressure, and in not a few instances by actual persecution, brought in once more the imperative mood.

The nineteenth century was pre-eminently the period of the subjunctive mood. The marvelous discoveries of the scientists awakened widespread doubt regarding the theological and the ecclesiastical claims of Christianity. We are nearing the end of the second cycle. Many believe that we are now living in the period of the optative mood. The oppressed throughout this stricken world, brought to despair by their helplessness in the presence of ruthless conquerors, are yearning for the satisfactions which religion alone can give.

Recurring to the general outline, previously given, we call attention to the fact that in the early centuries of our Christian era the Greek-speaking Intellectualists molded and formulated the doctrines of God and gave pre-eminence to orthodoxy; the Latin-speaking Institutionalists, successfully promulgated in the succeeding centuries the theory, which the Roman Church made its basic principle, that there was no salvation outside the fold of the Church; the Experientialists, gained the ascendancy during the Reformation and re-established evangelical Christianity; and in modern times the Individualists in many lands, Christian and non-Christian, won religious liberty, promoting the spirit of voluntariness in religion through the establishment of freedom of conscience. As we survey the whole course of Christian history we see that each of these types of mind—the Intellectualist, the Institutionalist, the Experientialist, and the Individualist—has had, during a more or less well-defined period, an influential, if not a controlling place, and has thereby changed the course of Christianity during the centuries.

The Intellectualist was the predominant type in the Græco-Roman world, especially where the Greek Koiné was the prevailing lauguage. However, the Institutionalist was also during the self-same period a potent factor in the development of church life, and he clearly perceived in the imperial government, in Roman law, and in the effective administration of the provinces, the advantages of a closely knit and centrally directed ecclesiastical organization. The Institutionalist supplanted the Intellectualist; the ecclesiastic, the theologian. Roman Catholicism is that part of the Christian movement which came under the control of the Institutionalists, and its checkered, seemingly contradictory and yet consistent and persistent course in history, its unexampled power in both temporal and spiritual affairs, can be explained and understood only in the light of the fact that the Institutionalists, who have directed and who now direct the destinies of the Roman Church, believe it to be the one divine institution whose authority, above every other object under heaven, must be preserved, strengthened, and extended until all the peoples of the earth shall acknowledge the supremacy of the Pope of Rome. The transformation of the Christian religion from loyalty to Jesus Christ to submission to an ecclesiastical authority centering in the Pope of Rome is the most impressive, astounding and damaging fact in Christian history, and to its study the succeeding three chapters are given.

The Roman Mind, which produced the Republic, the Empire, and the Roman Catholic Church, is the expression of Latin practical-mindedness, fertilized by Hellenistic culture on Græco-Roman soil. It is grounded upon the necessity of maintaining an ordered society, and finds its natural expression in organization, law, and orderly government, in the forensic treatment of all human and superhuman relationships, and in the utilitarian handling of all problems arising within the social order.

From the founding of Rome to the downfall of the Roman Empire the chief sphere of action for the Roman Mind was the political; since then it has been the religious. The Pope of Rome has a better historical claim to the line of succession from the king, the consul, and the emperor of Rome than from the Apostles Peter and Paul. The Roman Mind, however, has functioned more successfully in the spiritual or religious realm than it ever did in the temporal or political realm; and the fact is the more surprising, since the attitude of the Roman Mind from the beginning to the present time has been that religion should be used as a means to strengthen the institution, that institution being in the earlier period the Republic or the Empire, and in the later, the Roman Catholic Church.

The Roman Mind, which politically environs the whole Christian movement in the Græco-Roman world, and environs politically, linguistically and culturally wherever Latin is the prevailing language, becomes as a result of its ascendancy within the Christian movement the Sacerdotal Mind. By endowing the clergy, divided into several orders, with ecclesiastical rights and powers and the sacraments with spiritual grace and magical efficacy, the Sacerdotal Mind has used every situation which has arisen to strengthen the influence of the Bishop of Rome.

The background of the Roman Mind is revealed in the Latin language, with its abhorrence of abstract ideas and with its legalistic thought-patterns, and in the history of Rome, with its emphasis upon the practical and the administrative, the controlling principle of which is to deal with facts in their ethical or social bearings. Its culture comes from Greece, and Roman writers glory in their dependence upon Greek originals. Virility and dignity characterize Latin literature. The Golden Age produces Terence, Lucilius, Catullus, Lucretius, Cæsar, Sallus, Cicero, Varro, and the poets Vergil, Horace, Tibullus, and Ovid. The Silver Age follows with Persius, Petronius, Seneca, Celsus, Juvenal, Martial, Quintilian, Pliny the Elder, Tacitus, and Pliny the Younger. The ascendant purpose is political, an ordered society under Roman rule, and its guiding principle is reverence for tradition and for the sovereignty of the law. The Greek Mind within the Christian movement delights in subtle doctrinal disputation; the Roman Mind prefers a rule of faith, a fixed theological standard approved and endorsed by an authoritative Christian body.

The Roman people possessed a genius for organization. They were born Institutionalists, believing in corporate union, with a central authority for the enforcement of the law and the preservation of good order. The eastern section of the Roman Empire, Greek-speaking and under the influence of the Hellenistic Mind, sought the extension and the enrichment of religious knowledge; the western section, Latin-speaking and under the influence of the Roman Mind, sought to unite all the churches of the world into one catholic or universal Church under the Bishop of Rome, and in so doing illustrated the unchangeable spirit and the indomitable purpose of the ancient Romans.

Rome constructed no philosophy of her own, but received it ready-made from the Greeks. Stoicism, with its apathetic acceptance of defeat, conceived of the whole universe as a single, intelligible unity, pervaded by reason. Epicureanism, with its endeavor to forget defeat in the arms of prudent pleasure, thought of the word as composed of whirling atoms in illimitable space. These were the two leading world-views which the Roman Mind could accept as being in harmony with the observable facts of life; but comparatively little interest was taken in such speculative matters.

Christianity was interpreted by the Roman officials as an offshoot of Judaism, a licensed or legally tolerated religion. The external factors which aided the spread of the new religion, it will be recalled, were the Roman Empire; the Greek *Koiné*; the Jewish synagogues furnishing strategic centers from which to appeal to the Gentile communities; the breaking down of the national religions; the rise of individualism, lessening man's subordination to the state; the spread of Oriental cults emphasizing personal salvation and promising immortality; and the development of a spirit whose chief interest centered in religion, accompanied by a hospitality never so warmly accorded before to the messages of foreign religious teachers.

The Christian missionaries adjusted their preaching to these favorable conditions. As Harnack says in his summary, they proclaimed the Gospel of the Saviour and of salvation, of love and practical charities, of the Spirit of power, moral earnestness, and holiness; they told of a new Israel, a new people, a Third Race, the sons of God for whom the whole cosmic process had waited in eager expectancy; they bore a volume of Sacred Writings whose authority was attested by that ancient people, the Jews, in which the sufferings of the Saviour Jesus Christ were foretold; and they denounced polytheism, idolatry, and all the immoral practices and degrading superstitions which were characteristic of contemporary paganism.

That Christianity was not a phase of Judaism, and therefore not a legally tolerated religion, was not recognized by the Roman authorities until A.D. 64. Nero, desiring to find a scapegoat, charged the Christians with setting fire to Rome. Little was said at the trials regarding incendiarism, but they were found guilty of "hatred of the race" and were thereby placed in the position of outlaws, along with pirates and brigands. This unjust decision involved the whole Christian body from that time forward. However, this did not mean a continuous attack upon the Christians. After two years the Neronian persecution ceased. A quarter of a century later, Domitian renewed the assault, probably as part of his effort to restore the worship of the Emperor. The correspondence between Pliny, the governor of Bithynia, and the Emperor Trajan recorded the prevailing policy of the Roman government. To be a Christian was a crime, but the Roman officials were not to take the initiative in dealing with the matter.

A century and a half later, Rome celebrated the one thousandth anniversary of its founding, and this was followed by a vigorous campaign throughout the Empire to restore the ancient customs and worship. Every householder was ordered to apply in the following terms for an official certificate in the interest of his own protection: "I have always sacrificed to the gods and now in your presence I have in accordance with the regulations sacrificed, poured libations, tasted of the victims and I request that you certify to the same." This edict went into force January 1, A.D. 200. Twenty days later, Fabian, the Bishop of Rome, was put to death. An unknown number of the faithful suffered martyrdom. Within two years the persecution wore itself out. Emperor Gallienus, A.D. 260-8, restored to the Church authorities all confiscated property, such as cemeteries, churches, and the like, and gave to the Christian ministry full right to perform their duties.

Disturbed by the influence which the clergy were exercising in secular matters, Emperor Diocletian ordered on February 24, A.D. 303, "the suppression of all Christian assemblies, the destruction of churches and all copies of the Scriptures and the abjuration of Christianity by all officials and members of the civil service on pain of degradation. The edict was received with defiance. The Emperor issued a second edict, ordering the imprisonment of all the clergy." [37] A later edict required that all the subjects of the Empire should publicly offer sacrifices to the gods. A reign of terror ensued. Every form of torture was used to enforce recantation. A multitude of devoted Christians suffered imprisonment, torture, slavery, or death. Diocletian abdicated. Cleansed by suffering, the Christian churches in all lands grew stronger. The last persecution had failed.

Ten years pass. Constantine has become Emperor, and in the winter of A.D. 312-3 he issues the Edict of Milan, declaring that "liberty of worship shall not be denied to any one but that the mind and the will of every individual shall be free to manage divine affairs according to his own choice," and that "every person who cherishes the desire to observe the Christian religion shall freely and unconditionally proceed to observe the same without let or hindrance."

The Christian leaders of the fourth century, however, are not satisfied with the acquisition of religious liberty. They want and are able to secure special favors from the Emperor. Soon after, Constantine exempts the clergy from all political duties, frees all Church property from taxation, grants to the Church authorities the right to receive bequests and to transfer law suits from civil to Church courts, establishes Sunday as the day of rest, and authorizes the making of government grants for church building. He assumes a somewhat intolerant attitude toward paganism, a policy carried out with greater fervor by his son and successor, Constantius, who orders the closing of the pagan temples and forbids the attending of sacrifices and the worshiping of idols under penalty of death.

Julian, called the Apostate, gained the throne in 361 A.D. and reigned less than two years. He sought to establish "The Holy Church of Paganism," and he failed. Succeeding emperors aided organized Christianity by the proscription and the active persecution of paganism. They forbade magic, nocturnal sacrifices, and astrology, denied to apostate Christians the right to make a will or to give testimony in the courts, and finally outlawed paganism altogether. They banished the astrologers from Rome, abolished pagan holidays, appropriated all pagan temples with their income, transferred the property of the Donatists and other alleged heretical bodies to the legally recognized ecclesiastical organization, the Catholic Church, and prohibited under heavy penalties anyone making use of the temples for the purpose of heathen worship.

Justinian (A.D. 527-565), who collected the laws of his predecessors into the *Code*, the opinions of the juris-consults into the *Digest*, and prepared a manual of jurisprudence, the *Institutes*, to be studied in law schools, sought in religion, as in government, unity, consolidation, and central authority, and therefore severely penalized the heretics, who were described in the edict as "whoever is not a member of the Catholic Church and of our orthodox and holy faith." He also barred all pagans from office and approved the confiscation of their property.

The secret of the strength of the Roman Mind is found in its unique conception of authority. *Imperium*, the word used to describe this power, is an absolute and unlimited authority, derived in a far distant past from the gods, disobedience to which by anyone is treason. The head of the family, the master of the slave, the king, the magistrate, the emperor, possess *imperium*, though custom and precedent tend to modify it. Roman law, built upon tradition and legal principles, directs the rightful exercise of this sovereignty. "There is no language or literature into which legal conceptions enter so deeply as the Roman. The texture of Roman political history is interpenetrated by law to a degree which can hardly be paralleled." [38]

> "Others the breathing brass shall softlier mold,
> I doubt not, draw the lineaments of life
> From marble, at the bar plead better, trace
> With rod the courses of the sky, or tell
> The rise of stars; remember, Roman, thou,
> To rule the nations as their master; these
> Thine arts shall be, to engraft the law of peace,
> Forbear the conquered, and war down the proud." [39]

The Roman Mind politically environed the Christian movement from its beginning. The registration incident to the Roman census brought Mary and Joseph to Bethlehem, where the Saviour of mankind was born. A Roman procurator, Pontius Pilate, condemned Jesus to be crucified. Roman soldiers guarded the tomb in which his body was laid. The first of the Gentile "God-fearers" to accept the Christian faith was Cornelius, a Roman centurion. The enjoyment of the rights of a Roman citizen greatly aided Paul in the prosecution of his missionary labors, and he exhorted Christians to subject themselves "to the higher powers," on the ground that these powers were divinely ordained.

"The whole world lies in the power of the evil one," wrote John in his First Epistle, and to him "the whole world" was the heathen social system, manifesting itself in various human institutions, of which the State was the most important. In Revelation, he graphically described the Roman Empire as an irresistibly powerful Beast to whom the Dragon, Satan, had entrusted world-wide authority. Christianity, opposing all idolatry, refused to burn incense before the statue of the Roman emperor and the conflict was on.

The persecution of the Christians intensified their hostility to the Empire. With some exceptions, they refused to hold any

public offices, though they promptly paid their taxes and sub-
mitted meekly and unresistingly to the sufferings inflicted during
the periods of persecution. Prayers were offered for rulers as
divinely-appointed officials "in order that we may lead a tranquil
and quiet life." Justin Martyr declared to the Emperor that the
Christians "more than any [other] men are your helpers and allies
in [promoting] peace; seeing that we hold this view, that it is impossible for an evildoer or a covetous man or a conspirator or a
virtuous man to escape God's notice and that everyone goes to
eternal punishment or eternal salvation according to the merit of
his deeds." [40]

Rome is able to secure all the soldiers she needs without drafting
Christians. Mithraism, a saving cult, highly honoring the heroic, is
the popular religion in the imperial armies. "No Christian soldier
is known to have existed between A.D. 50 and 170." [41] Many soldiers, according to Tertullian, writing about the year 200, leave
the army upon their conversion. Tertullian, Hippolytus, Origen,
Celsus, and Cyprian, "testify to the strength of the Christian ob-
jection to military service." It is not until organized Christianity
undertakes to preserve orthodoxy and to maintain discipline by
the exercise of force that anti-militarism is abandoned and the
imperial point of view is adopted. The Synod of Arles (A.D. 314)
approves military service; Athanasius holds that it is praiseworthy
to slay enemies in war, and from this time forward pacifism has
few Christian champions.

It is a far cry from the cross, at the foot of which Roman soldiers
gambled for the possession of the seamless robe, to the cross which
hovers at the head of the Roman legions, who march forward,
trusting in this sign to conquer all the enemies of the Empire.
Those who bear this standard interpret it as meaning, not that the
genius of Rome has been Christianized but that the Roman Mind
in all its distinctive and essential attitudes and purposes has gained
the ascendancy inside Christianity. Contemporary Christian leaders
see, in the adoption of the cross as the imperial military emblem, a
victory for the Christian faith. The student, in the presence of
these opposing claims, turns to the history of Christianity for the
verdict, as it is given in the events of the succeeding centuries.

X

The Sacerdotal Mind

"Priesthood, broadly speaking, owes its origin to the universal need felt by mankind of superhuman assistance in the struggle of life."—GUNNAR LAUDTMAN.

Sacerdos, the Latin noun from which the adjective sacerdotal is derived, means priest. The Sacerdotal Mind has its origin in the universal sense of dependence upon the higher powers or Power, linked with the sense of a lesser dependence upon human mediators whose greater knowledge and position enable them to communicate in behalf of mankind with superhuman forces, divinities, or God. Whenever religion assumes such a relationship the need of the priest is felt. The concept of human mediatorship extends from the medicine man, the witch doctor, the shaman of primitive peoples to the Primate of the Church of England, the Pope of Rome and the universal priesthood of all believers in evangelical Christianity.

The Sacerdotal Mind, in the period under study, is the practically universal belief in the necessity of human mediators, fertilized by the Roman conception of an ordered society governed by law, on the soil of the Græco-Roman world which was in the process of becoming Christianized.

Those who are believed to possess greater ability than others in securing aid, protection and other benefits from the superhuman powers or Power, are called priests or magicians. Among primitives the two are often united in a single individual. Priests are the recognized mediators between men and the superior powers; magicians are believed to possess the trick of coercing these powers. As ritual observances and magical formulas become too complicated for the ordinary man to master, the need of the mediator is felt to be imperative.

Patriarchs and kings, especially in the early periods of a civilization, often serve as priests. As national life emerges, the priesthood tends to become a hereditary institution and frequently possesses sufficient power to influence, if not to control, the State. Priests and sorcerers as a rule come from the most intelligent elements of their people. "The scanty learning of savage races is almost exclusively confined to the priests." The changes of the weather, the habits of animals, the properties of herbs, the use of medicines, and other forms of knowledge increase their authority. They create confidence in their mediatorial powers through the performance of the seemingly miraculous, such as cutting themselves with knives in different parts of the body, throwing themselves into the fire, or allowing poisonous snakes to bite them. Almost universally they use a different language in their religious services and in communicating with one another. They stimulate fear by enveloping all that they do in deepest mystery.

The ancient civilizations, from Babylonia, Egypt, and Crete to India, Mexico, and Peru, possessed highly organized priesthoods. The Græco-Roman world, despite skepticism in certain literary centers as to the existence of the gods, could not conceive of approaching and of securing favors from these divinities except by the observance of proper rites and ceremonies, the performance of which required priests and priestesses.

The King, under the ancient Roman monarchical system, was both priest and ruler. The Republic made religion a branch of the government, assigning its technical phases to priestly organizations, subject to some control by the senate and the magistrates. The four leading priestly bodies were the pontifices, the augurs, the commission in charge of the Sibylline books, and the college which supervised the sacred banquets. The qualifications for membership were "free birth, Roman citizenship, unblemished civil record, and a physique free from infirmities." Priests received from the State funds necessary for the maintenance of the duties of their office, and if they so desired were exempted from all civil and military duties.

The Collegium Pontificum, originally composed of the king and five pontifices, was later increased to fifteen, with the following as ex officio members: the rex sacrorum, the flamines, each a priest attached to the worship of one of the important Roman divinities and thus an official representative of the priesthood of the particular god or goddess, and the six vestal virgins. The president of this body, called the Pontifex Maximus, held the highest, the most honorable and the most influential place in the religious life of the Roman Empire, and was, in some respects, the most important personage in the State. Julius Cæsar was for twenty years the Pontifex Maximus. Augustus assumed the office in 12 B.C., "thus combining in his own person the civil and religious supremacy." His example was followed by his imperial successors.

One of the basic convictions of the Roman Mind was that the favor of the gods depended upon the meticulous observance of the minutest detail of the ritual. The pontifices, experts in all these matters, were, in fact, theologians, professors of the sacred law, and the final authority upon all state religious questions. They were appealed to by private citizens as well as by the magistrates and the senate. Charged primarily with the administration of that part of the civil law which regulated the relations of the community and the deities officially recognized by the State, the Collegium Pontificum, the Roman supreme court, dealt not only with these distinctly religious matters but also with burials, wills, adoptions, and the performance of patrician marriages, thus exercising great authority in the private life of the citizens.

Two tendencies in the Collegium Pontificum were destined to influence profoundly the historic development of Christianity: first, by the strict regulation of the elaborate systemization of the Roman religious life, the habit of complete obedience and of unquestioning trust in the authority of religious officials became firmly fixed in the minds of men and paved the way for the later Christian hierarchy; second, in that the Collegium Pontificum extended its authority beyond the control of the Roman cults, a historic basis was laid which enabled the Roman Church to extend its system of government, with its exercise of *imperium*, the right to command, over the domain of the temporal as well as over the realm of the spiritual.

The spell of the priesthood lay upon the whole of the Græco-Roman world. For many centuries the priests of ancient Egypt officers of the State, the beneficiaries of the rich revenues of their several corporations, ranked next the Pharaoh in the powers they exercised, due in no small degree to their being the possessors and the guardians of Egyptian lore. The priests of Greece were, with rare exception, native-born citizens chosen "for their personal beauty or for the wealth which enabled them to give in honor of the gods magnificent pageants and other festivals." [42] The priesthood of the celebrated Eleusinian Mysteries was hereditary and highly paid, while the priests of the Hellenic gods were elected for only a brief term. The Greek priests possessed a high social position and more than average culture.

Jonathan Maccabeus (160-135 B.C.), the high priest, ruled the Jews and was succeeded in his religious and political office by John Hyrcanus (135-41 B.C.) who retained the position of ruler, with one interruption, until Judea became a Roman province. The priests of Judaism did not possess the thorough Hebraic culture of the Pharisees, but their position was more firmly established, and their influence upon the Gentile world was unquestionably greater.

The conquests of Alexander were followed by the breaking up of priestly colleges in Babylon, Persia, Egypt, and elsewhere, and resulted in the scattering throughout the Græco-Roman world of the knowledge of the curious arts which these Oriental priests possessed. The Magi, a Persian priestly caste, diviners and sacrificers under the kings who had ruled Persia preceding its conquest by Alexander, spread their religion in the form of Mithraism, stimulated the belief that the changes of the heavenly bodies influenced the affairs of men, and by the practice of magical arts, contributed much to the growing popular belief that light upon the mysteries of life could be gained from these representatives of ancient Oriental religions. Priests of the great goddess Cybele and her son Attis, priests of the Egyptian Isis in long linen robes, priests of Mithra, priests of the Syrian Baals, priests from nearly all lands became familiar figures in Rome and other cities of the Empire, and each group possessed sufficient learning and culture to interpret and to propagate its particular religion. New cults, with new liturgies, with mysterious and reputedly efficacious ceremonies, with priests giving all their time to the spreading of the faith, successfully encountered the religions of Greece and Rome, winning multitudes of adherents. This achievement is a convincing testimony to the intellectual attainments of the priests and missionaries of these new faiths.

The function of the priest is to perform on behalf of the community certain public ritual acts, particularly sacrifices, directed toward the objects or the Object of worship. The purpose of these acts, as participated in by the community, is a satisfying adjustment to the demands of the higher powers or God. The priest is the human mediator, expressing in solemn ceremony, usually a sacrifice, the dependent, yearning, and worshipful attitude of the people. The ritual acts evidence the conviction held by the worshipers that the higher powers or Power, the divinities or God, really exist, that the suppliants acknowledge their dependence and seek for blessings that they are not able themselves to supply, and that they empower the priest to act in their behalf. If these beliefs are well founded, the priests sustains to the worshipers a relationship whose value cannot be overestimated. He is the intermediary through whom divine blessings are made available. It is this confidence which lies at the basis of the world-wide and age-long authority of the priesthood. The power of the priest is measured by the faith the community has in him as a mediator. When the priesthood is strongly supported by tradition, by hereditary right, by the tribal or the national will, the chief purpose of the priest is to perform with zealous care every minute requirement of the ritual, and the knowledge he possesses of these matters gives to him an honored and unassailable position in the community. The tendency in long-established religions is to elaborate the ritual and to give to its meticulous performance a constantly increasing value. Two striking illustrations are the religion of ancient Rome and Brahmanism in India.

A different situation arises when the priesthood of one religion is competing with the priesthood of another religion for the confidence and the support of the same people. Among primitive peoples the tribal will gives the priest authority, but these tribes when invaded successfully by a missionary religion, especially Christianity, turn against their priests.

The tolerance of the Roman Empire led to the encouragement of the people in the provinces to continue their old customs, including the worship of their native divinities. The movement of increasing numbers of the population from one part of the Empire to another, linked with the opportunity of propagating any new faith, inspired missionary endeavors, which were carried on by priests and lay adherents, merchants, travelers, and soldiers. The priests of these new religions, nearly all Oriental in origin, thus were interested in more than the minutiæ of the ritual. They were preachers and champions of the new cults, engaged primarily in making new converts. To use a modern phrase, they were selling a new religion and they found the whole of the Græco-Roman world a promising territory. If these new Mystery Religions could, without compromise, conform to all the demands of the Roman State religion, they were free to proclaim their tenets and make their converts anywhere; and this they were able to do.

The underlying purpose of the priesthood is to gain for the priestly institution permanence and security. This is evident whether the priest believes in the validity and the efficacy of the rites he performs or not. If he is confident that through the sacred services, of which he is the authorized minister, benefits of a supernatural character are secured to him and to all those whom he represents, he desires above everything else that the priesthood, which is an essential factor in the enjoyment of these benefits, shall be made permanent and secure. If he be skeptical or even unbelieving, his participation in the rewards of the priestly office, which provides a livelihood and an honorable position, will intensify rather than lessen his interest in the maintenance of the institution.

The economic aspects of the business of religion, such as the sharing of the priest in the sacrifices and in the altar gifts made to the divinity, the benefits which accrue to him and to his fellow priests because of the investments in property, temples, images, and the whole paraphernalia of worship, his participation in the stipends from the State and in bequests made by deceased worshipers, the ownership of income-producing estates by the order of which he is a member, all of value in preserving the priesthood as an institution, have throughout the whole course of religious history tended to make the priesthoods of mankind greedy for financial independence and anxious to maintain unquestioned and unrivaled authority. Whenever a competing religion has threatened the revenues and the unique privilege of a monopolistic priesthood, all available means for a successful defense have been put to use. Religious persecutions have been always inspired, if not actually led, by priests. The need of economic support and the exercise of physical force for the protection of the priesthood and of the religion it represents, naturally lead to the strengthening of the alliance between the State and the organized religion, whatever its name or character.

The vital union of spirit, attitude, and ideals in the Sacerdotal Mind forms its genius. Formal reverence is universal among all the priesthoods of a worshiping humanity, and there is good reason to believe that this usually has been and is the expression of a sincere spirit. The power of the priesthood, dominant in practically all the religions to which man has given allegiance, could not have been maintained so long and so completely had the priests generally been hypocrites and frauds. The Sacerdotal Mind produces in the worshipers the conviction that the ritual is valuable and necessary, sustains and strengthens the belief that the priests are the fully equipped mediators between them and the objects of adoration, and leads to the assurance that the proper performance of these religious acts will actually secure for them the divine blessings they desire. The people accept the responsibility for furnishing the gifts and the sacrifices; the priests, the observance of the ritual in the form pleasing to the higher powers or Power; and they both rely upon the divinities or God to protect and to bestow superhuman favors. The people, so long as their faith is not impaired, depend more and more upon the priesthood; the priests enrich and enlarge the ritual, assume greater authority, and often become domineering and avaricious, concentrating their efforts upon making impregnable the institution of which they are a part.

Priests are always Institutionalists, whose chief concern is the promotion of the religion they serve by the strengthening of the authority of the priestly class. The assertion, the propagation, and the maintenance of the superiority of the priesthood over the laity have evoked greater activity within all organized religions than any other phase of co-operative effort except worship itself.

The priesthood is the most nearly universal institution in which mankind, groping for divine aid, has trusted. By doing so, this believing world has created and made effective a most powerful agency for the enslavement of the race to superstition, to bigotry and to moral and religious error.

There is another side to the picture. The priesthood promoted and preserved tribal and national solidarity, encouraged and perpetuated culture, strengthened the powers of rulers and thereby fostered peace and good order, gave a religious interpretation to material blessings and to crushing calamities, exercised the most effective conservative influence in human society, cherished and idealized the history of the group and popularized religion itself through feasts, processions, sacrifices, and every kind of ritual. It deepened the feelings of serenity and joy by awakening in the hearts of men the conviction that the divinities or God welcomed their homage, approved of their eating a part of the victim offered in sacrifice, overlooked their sins, and would in the future as in the past bestow divine favors upon them.

The world-view of the priesthood has ever been religious and varies with the cosmology of tradition or revelation. Belief in the future life is found wherever the organized priesthood exists. Ordered worship is not only pleasing to the object adored but benefits all who participate in it. The conception of Ultimate Reality, however dim, vague, and mysterious, is interpreted religiously; within the mysterious, or the imperfectly known, reside the objects or Object of worship and they or He control the universe. Polytheism tends toward the grouping and the graduation of the divinities, with one as presiding and supreme. The realm of mystery is interpreted as mediatorial, with the priests as the divinely chosen mediators, who demand from the worshipers respect, intellectual submission, and sometimes worship itself. In the ritual the priesthood possesses "a tremendous spiritual machine whose movement is essential to salvation, but no one but the priest knows how to make it go." The world-view of the individual worshiper, horizoned by his imperfect understanding of the ritual and by the creation stories handed down by tradition, becomes a concept so confused and so complicated that he concludes that the consideration of such a matter is too high for him; hence the ritual becomes for him the sum total of his philosophy as well as his religion.

The priesthood presents one of the most baffling problems of socialized religion. Organization is impossible without recognized leaders. Worship by any group, however informal it may be, needs intelligent guidance, and in the simplest religious service someone presides. If there be a rite, there must also be an officiant who in the performance of the rite fulfills a priestly function. Civilized life is always accompanied by a division of labor, special groups being assigned definite duties and responsibilities. This applies equally to sacred and secular activities. If ordered worship be something in which groups of people should participate, a chosen leader, set apart for this service, seems to be both logical and necessary. If he renders a valuable service, he has earned the right to some remuneration. He cannot function without the endowment and the exercise of some authority. Whence is this authority derived?

There is practical unanimity in the answer to this question from all the religions of the world: The authority is given directly, or once was given to the founder of the priestly succession, by the higher powers, or God. He who breaks the stillness of the Quaker meeting does so upon the conviction on his part and upon the assumption on the part of those who listen that God has inspired him to speak some truth which he formulates in his own words. He believes that his right to participate in the worship has come to him directly from God. The Sacerdotal Mind is naturally very skeptical as to the truthfulness of such a claim when made by a layman; but granting it to be true, he would interpret the utterance as a prophetic utterance and not a priestly act.

The prophet is chiefly concerned for the right, the priest for the rite; the one enthrones character, the other worship; the one appreciates the individual and seeks his spiritual betterment, the other appreciates the institution of organized religion and seeks in every way to make it the stronger. The Sacerdotal and the Prophetic Minds have competing interests and divergent interpretations as to the truly vital elements in religion. Briefly stated, the prophet holds that religion must meet the deepest needs and serve in promoting the moral and spiritual welfare of the individual man; the priest holds that the individual man must meet the needs and serve in promoting the welfare of the institutions of organized religion, especially the priesthood. In the conflict between the prophets and the priests the prophets usually are put to death. Jesus is not crucified until the priests join his enemies and clamor for his destruction.

Wherever men unite because of common interests which inspire them to secure ends unattainable through individual action, institutions are the chosen agencies for the realization of the corporate purpose. Religion is no exception. Mediatorship is a function of every organized religion. The priestly conception is inevitable. The issue for Christianity is twofold: 1. Is the mediator, often called the priest, one who functions or one who officiates? 2. Did Jesus in saying to the disciples on the evening of the resurrection day, "As the Father hath sent me, even so send I you," limit this commission to an official priesthood, or did he include all faithful disciples in all the future generations? The deepest cleavage within Christianity has been the result of this issue: an official Christian priesthood, or a universal priesthood of all Christian believers. Uniformly, the Sacerdotal Mind has championed the official Christian priesthood.

XI

The Ecclesiastical Mind

"The situation, commonly regarded as the conquest of the Roman Empire was, quite as truly, a Romanization of Christianity."—SHAILER MATTHEWS.

THE SUCCESS of the Christian movement, grounded upon a personal faith in and an unrivaled devotion to Jesus as Christ and Lord, is attended by the voluntary co-operation of all believers which expresses itself in worship, in fellowship, and in loving ministries bestowed upon those in need. The scattering of "the disciples of the Lord," incident to the persecution which began with the death of Stephen, leads to the preaching of Jesus as the Christ in new centers and the organization of Christian bodies other than the Mother Church in Jerusalem. Missionary endeavor is soon inaugurated by the Church at Antioch. Toward the close of the first half of the first century, organizations called churches are coming into existence throughout the Roman Empire for the promotion of distinctly Christian ends.

Beliefs, rites, interpretations, and religious organizations are modified and molded by the social order in which they arise. The language, the thought-patterns, the generally accepted contemporary principles that control social institutions—in brief, the ascendant mind—are factors to be clearly investigated in the study of the institutional development of organized religion, and Christianity is no exception. It is comparatively easy for the critical student to point out the departures made by organized Christianity from the fundamental principles taught by Jesus and the Apostles; but it calls for greater research and a more sympathetic insight to understand the situation when the departure is made, and to interpret with clear understanding the motives which impel the Christian movement in a wrong direction. The discovery of the causes which lead to the emergence of these motives is vitally needed in any true interpretation of Christian history.

The Christian Church, as an institution within the Græco-Roman world, arose out of a social milieu in which may be distinguished the Jewish Mind as the background, the Gentile Mind, with its fusion of Hellenistic culture possessing both Greek and Oriental elements, and the Roman Mind, with its sacerdotal impress upon all religious organizations and its characteristic emphasis upon an ordered society. "Ecclesiastical" means "pertaining to the church." The Ecclesiastical Mind is the corporate intelligence which, fertilized by Roman practical-mindedness and skill in administration, fosters organization and promotes centralized authority within the rapidly expanding and gradually federating Christian bodies, scattered far and wide on the soil of the Græco-Roman world.

The word Church (ἐκκλγσία) is found in the Gospels twice and only in Matthew (16:18; 18:17), and of these passages only the first unquestionably refers to the Christian Church. The divergent interpretations of Matthew 16:16-19 have created the bitterest divisions and the deepest and most lasting cleavage in the whole course of Christian history. To the inquiry of Jesus: "But whom say ye that I am?" addressed to the Twelve, Peter answers, "Thou art the Christ the Son of the Living God." Jesus felicitates him and reveals and emphasizes the divine source of the experience which makes possible the confession: "Blessed art thou, Simon Bar-Jonah, for flesh and blood hath not revealed it unto thee but my Father who is in heaven. And I say unto thee that thou art Peter (πέτρος) and on this rock (πέτρα) I will build my church (ἐκκλγσία) and the gates of Hades shall not prevail against it. I will give unto thee the keys of the kingdom of heaven and whatsoever thou shalt bind on earth, shall be bound in heaven and whatsoever thou shalt loose on earth shall be loosed in heaven."

The Roman Catholic Church bases upon this scripture its claim that the Pope of Rome, as the successor of Peter, is the sole vicar of Christ on earth, that "all those who do not acknowledge the Roman Pontiff as their Head, do not belong to the Church of Jesus Christ," and that outside of the Church there is no salvation (extra ecclesiam nulla salus). The Roman ecclesiastics interpret "Church" as a visible, self-perpetuating society founded by Jesus Christ; "Catholic," meaning "universal," as indicating the world-wide scope of the authority of the body; "Roman" as indicating that the Bishop of Rome is the true head of the Church of Jesus Christ and as such is the divinely appointed center of unity and the authoritative voice of infallible truth, being so endowed by the Divine Redeemer.

A visible supernatural institution, possessing a divinely authenticated charter, entrusted with the performance of rites called sacraments which are essential to the salvation and the santification of all Christians, governed by a clergy which has promised and sworn "true obedience to the Bishop of Rome, successor to St. Peter, Prince of the Apostles and Vicar of Jesus Christ," the Roman Catholic Church stands as the most powerful group of professing Christians and in many respects the most effective institution on earth. It challenges alike the evangelical theologian and the Christian historian, the one to disprove its claims to a religious monopoly, and the other to describe and to indicate the causes and the prevailing motives which have led to the successful establishment of these assumptions on which the Roman Church rests.

The theologian is interested in the question of the position of Peter in the Apostolic churches; the historian, in the sequences of events which have led to the actual supremacy of the Roman pontiff within the organization of the Roman Catholic Church.

It is claimed by Roman authorities that the Roman Catholic Church fixed and determined the list of books in the New Testament which are canonical, the books which meet the standard as inspired Christian documents. What do these books teach regarding the Church and the authority which Peter exercised over the Early Church?

The tradition is well established that Peter aided Mark, who wrote the earliest of the four Gospels. This book contains no text which would suggest that Peter possessed a higher rank than the other Apostles. The record of his confession is limited to the words: "Thou art the Christ." Peter, James, and John belonged to an inner group and are present with Jesus at the healing of the daughter of Jairus, at the Transfiguration, and in Gethsemane. On one occasion James and John ask for the highest positions and Jesus declares that such authority is "not mine to give you," and lays down the principle that the "first among you shall be the servant of all." There is no reference to the Church in Mark or in the Epistles of Peter. "She that is in Babylon, elect together with you, saluteth you; and so doth Mark my son" (1 Peter 4:13), may be interpreted as meaning that the First Epistle of Peter was written from Rome, but in this letter there is not the slightest trace of the exercise of ecclesiastical authority on Peter's part. He writes simply as an inspired Apostle. All believers, according to Peter, form "a royal priesthood," and as "a holy priesthood" are to offer up spiritual sacrifices, "acceptable to God through Jesus Christ." Neither Mark nor Peter makes any claim for the possession by Peter of any authority other than that of any inspired teacher in the administration of the affairs of any church.

The account given by Matthew (16:13-20) is the principal, if not the sole, foundation for the Roman claim of the primacy of Peter. Jesus solemnly and impressively comments upon the confession which Peter has just made. He gives the primary place and the greatest emphasis, not to the binding and the loosing, not to the keys of the Kingdom, not to the Church, not even to the confession, but to the religious experience of Peter which preceded and made possible the confession: "Blessed art thou, Simon Bar-Jonah; because flesh and blood hath not revealed it to thee, but my Father who is in heaven." As God raises Jesus from the dead to confirm his Messiahship and Lordship, so He brings to bear upon the mind of Peter a divine disclosure which enables him to recognize Jesus as "the Christ, the Son of the living God." Jesus founds his Church, the Church of God, upon the capacity of man to receive and to express a divine revelation, and Peter is the first of the disciples in whom the revelation regarding the person and the work of Jesus Christ becomes articulate. This is the theme of Peter's sermon at Pentecost.

The presence of the Holy Spirit in the disciple is the prerequisite of his baptism and initiation into church membership. The universal priesthood of believers is grounded upon the possession of a religious experience like that which Peter had, in that its source is found in God. The witnessing disciple to whom the

Father has revealed that in Jesus access to Ultimate Reality is attained and a union of the human and the divine is actualized within the human personality, is the nucleus of the living social organism which Jesus called "my Church."

Peter, rash, impulsive, swayed by his emotions, frequently rebuked for his imprudent speech, is not the man to be entrusted with complete and autocratic authority. While he is the recognized leader of the disciples preceding and following Pentecost and his name is recorded frequently in the first twelve chapters of the Acts, he disappears altogether from the record save for a brief utterance in connection with the Jerusalem Council (Acts 15:6-11). Three definite ecclesiastical acts are recorded in the Acts of the Apostles: 1. The selection of the successor to Judas by the company of disciples, suggested by Peter; 2. The election of the Seven to care for the believing widows, suggested by the Twelve; 3. The letter to the Gentile Christians, sent by "the apostles and the elders with the whole church," the terms of which are declared by James, the head of the Mother Church in Jerusalem. In these actions there is not a suggestion of the primacy of Peter.

From the Jerusalem Conference on, Paul is the dominating figure in New Testament Christianity, and he expressly declares Peter's responsibility as an Apostle to be limited to the Jews, as his own is to the Gentiles. The primacy of Peter would never have been asserted had the Bishop of Rome not needed a New Testament basis for his claim to the headship of the Catholic Church. The evangelical theologian finds the theory that holds Peter to have been in any sense "the Prince of the Apostles" to be grounded upon a fallacious interpretation of the teachings of the New Testament.

Bellarmine (1542-1621), archbishop of Capria, framed the accepted definition of the Roman Catholic Church: "a body of men united together for the profession of the same Christian faith and by participation in the same sacraments under the governance of lawful pastors, more especially of the Roman Pontiff, the sole Vicar of Christ on earth." The characteristics of the Church, as interpreted by Roman theologians, are unity, catholicity, sanctity, coercive jurisdiction, and the superiority of the Church over the

State in the maintenance of the truth revealed by God. The Church is a threefold institution: 1. *Ecclesia triumphans*, the souls of the blessed in heaven; 2. *Ecclesia militans*, the church militant; 3. *Ecclesia patiens*, the souls suffering in purgatory.

The theological statements formulated by the undivided Catholic Church previous to the separation of the Greek and the Roman Churches, July 16, 1054 A.D., embracing the Apostles', the Nicene, the Chalcedonian, and the Athanasian creeds, are accepted by practically all the liturgical Christian bodies and are highly esteemed by most of the evangelicals. In the acceptance of the Holy Scriptures as divinely inspired and therefore authoritative, and in adhering to the doctrines of the Godhead as formulated by the Councils representing a united Catholic Church, Roman, Greek, and Protestant Christians are in practical agreement. Most of the differences, if not all, grow out of the meaning and the value of the ordinances or sacraments and the powers and privileges of the Christian ministry or the clergy. Sacramentarianism and sacerdotalism, the most divisive elements in Christianity, are the foundations of Roman Catholicism.

False prophets, heretical teachers, scholars who set the Christian Gospel in a philosophical context that strips Jesus of his divinity, the necessity of preserving orderly worship and of enforcing needed discipline, the growing demand for an organized agency to direct the distribution of the gifts of believers among the poor and needy, the problems which grew out of gifts of money, the possession of property and the administration of things spiritual and material—these, not to mention more, made necessary in the New Testament Churches some form of government. Unprejudiced scholars are unable to find a divinely inspired and universally adopted church order of government. Variety in government is proved. Jewish Christian bodies are patterned more after the Jewish synagogue, and purely Gentile Christian bodies exhibit the influence of the social organizations about them. Elders and bishops are official designations that seem to be used interchangeably, though "bishop" soon became the title chosen for the recognized head of the church in the community. The highest rank is given to the Apostles, the word being used to include others than the Twelve. Next in honor are the prophets, men and women divinely inspired to speak for God; evangelists who go everywhere preaching the Word; are third, and pastors and teachers, whose chief duties are to instruct converts regarding the life and the precepts of Jesus Christ, are fourth in the New Testament list. In every locality the Church is a fusion of theocracy and democracy. The membership is limited to those who give some evidence of being Spirit-possessed, and when these act upon any matter, it is believed that the voice of the people is indeed the voice of God. If this ideal could have been maintained, no other government would have been needed.

The New Testament at this early period was not as yet available in its completed form as a rule for faith and practice. The closing books of the New Testament indicate a waning spiritual fervor and declare that there are evil men within the Christian bodies. The Apostles are passing; the prophets do not always agree, and the power of trusted local officials increases. The process is a perfectly natural one.

Ignatius, writing about the year 115, declares that "no church is named" without the three orders of bishop, presbyter, and deacon, and in his letter to the Church in Ephesus he says, "We ought to regard the bishop as the Lord himself." In still another letter Christians are exhorted to follow the bishop as Jesus Christ follows the Father, and the presbytery as if it were the Apostles.

Tertullian (c.160-235) expresses the current belief that the Twelve Apostles, including Matthias, having carried "the faith in Jesus Christ to the nations," gave to the churches they formed the true doctrine; that the doctrine, "derived from the tradition of the apostles," taught in Carthage, is true because it "differs in no respect" from that held by all the other apostolic churches. The Catholic Church is the totality of the churches planted by the Apostles, which preserve through episcopal succession the pure faith which the Apostles taught. The personality of Peter, Tertullian associates with the founding of the Church: "On Peter in person the Church was reared, that is, through him."

Cyprian, a fellow citizen of Tertullian in Carthage, a pagan lawyer of great wealth and social position, who did not become a Christian until he was nearly fifty years old, interpreted the Holy

Catholic Church in harmony with his Roman legalistic training.
To him, the Church is a divinely ordained, visible society, with
fixed laws, government, and privileges for its members according
to their rank, and all outside of it are outside of the benefits of the
grace of God. The government of the Church has been put by
God himself into the hands of "an aristocracy of equal bishops."
The primacy of Peter is recognized, but the Bishop of Rome is
not acknowledged as Peter's successor in the exercise of authority
over the other bishops. Cyprian is the father of the ecclesiastics, as
Origen is the father of the theologians.

The first recorded statement that the Church at Rome was
founded by Peter and Paul is made by Dionysius of Corinth
about the year 170, more than a century after the event. There
is no documentary proof, except in recorded tradition, that Peter
ever visited Rome. Clement, writing from Rome about the year
75, mentions the sufferings and death of Peter and Paul, but the
place and the manner of their martyrdom are not given. The
whole statement is vague. Irenæus (c. 130-c. 200) says that Peter
and Paul both preached at Rome and that "the blessed apostles
there founded and reared up this church and afterwards committed unto Linus the office of the episcopate."

The Church of Rome was probably founded by Jewish pilgrims
from Rome, attending the feast of Pentecost at Jerusalem, where
they were converted. When Paul wrote his letter to the Romans
about A.D. 57, the Church of Rome was then a flourishing and
influential Christian body. From the beginning of the third
century on, documentary statements affirming Peter's presence
in Rome multiply, many of them dealing with the legendary
account of the conflict of Peter with Simon the sorcerer. While
the other great centers of Christianity were spending their energies
in doctrinal disputations and engaging in conflict with alleged
heretics, Rome was displaying the highest organizing ability,
winning prestige and gaining for the Bishop of Rome a position
of increasing influence and power. The sixth canon of the Nicene
Council (A.D. 325) gave to the bishops of Alexandria, Antioch,
and Rome "a certain authority over the bishops of the great
divisions of the Empire of which these cities were centers."

Leo the Great (A.D. 440-461) secured from the Emperor Valentinian III an edict making the Pope of Rome the sovereign of the Church. The disobedience of a Gallic bishop was the occasion. The decree granted unlimited authority: "That not only no Gallic bishop, but no bishop of any other province, be permitted in contradiction to ancient custom to do anything without the authority of the venerable pope of the Eternal City; but on the contrary to them and to all men, let whatsoever the authority of the Apostolic See has ordained, does ordain or shall ordain, be as law; so that any bishop being summoned to the judgment seat of the Roman pontiff be thereunto compelled by the governor of the province." Gelasius, Pope from 492 to 496, enunciated the principle that the King rules over men in the world but in relation to the administration of divine ordinances he is the subject, not the ruler. Earlier, Ambrose, Bishop of Milan, had summoned the Emperor Theodosius to repentance for the massacre of seven thousand Thessalonians, affirming that since he was "within the Church, not above it," he could not "approach the table of the Lord" except as a humble, penitent supplicant. The Emperor reluctantly obeyed the bishop.

The fall of the Roman Empire, the spread of the Roman Catholic faith in western and northern Europe, the invasion of the East by Mohammed, the severing of the undivided Catholic Church into the Greek and the Roman Churches, the freeing of the election of popes from political interference, the Holy Roman Empire, the Crusades, the rise of the monastic orders, the founding of the great Catholic schools, the formulation of scholastic theology, the successful missionary activities led by members of the monastic orders, the establishment of sacerdotal celibacy, the development of the canon law into a codified legal system, the suppression through the Inquisition of all Christian movements that threatened papal power, the centralizing of absolute authority in the Pope, giving him autocratic power over the Councils of the Church—these are all important factors in the development of the authority of the Bishop of Rome during the Middle Ages. The Vatican Decree of papal infallibility, issued in 1870, completes the process of making the Roman Catholic Church an autocratic totalitarian institution, unique in human history. Pope

Innocent III (1198-1216) united in his person the natural and the supernatural realms, and was described as "royal high priest of the Christian Church, *verus imperator* of the Christian Empire, the first judge of Christendom."

Patterned after the ancient Roman Empire, international in its domain, the Roman Church, through the reigning Pope, was able during the Middle Ages to impose upon peoples, whoever might be their temporal ruler, a system of laws which took precedence over the law of the land; to deal with kings and emperors as an equal sovereign in temporal affairs, and to exercise absolute power in the spiritual realm by his use of the keys that could lock as well as open the door of salvation and eternal blessedness to all, king and subject alike. The apex of papal glory was reached in the early thirteenth century. The Reformation, the spread of democratic principles, the separation of Church and State, the growth of the scientific spirit have limited the range of papal authority; yet the Roman Catholic Church remains unchanged in spirit and purpose. The Pope of Rome is the most powerful ecclesiastic on earth.

The foundations of this mighty ecclesiastical structure are pre-Christian. Its conception of authority, the right to command, *imperium*, is a legacy from the Roman Empire. The positing of magical efficacy in the simple forms of New Testament Christianity is a legacy from the Mystery Religions. Its interpretation of the authority of the priesthood is a legacy from the ancient polytheistic cults. Its elevation of the Pope to the place of supreme autocratic power is a legacy from the ancient oriental despotisms.

The vital spiritual power of the Roman Catholic Church, exhibited in thousands of saintly lives, is devotion to Jesus Christ, to which is united the conviction that the Church is the one divine institution within whose fold salvation is found. Faith in the Church is united to, if it does not actually precede, faith in Christ. Apparently the masses, who, in the past as in the present, make up most of its membership, submit to the requirements of the Church, expecting the sacraments to save and to sanctify, and for these the power of the Church grows out of its possession and use of the sacramental system. The sacrament presupposes an officiant; hence the necessity of the priest. Upon the priestly office as a foundation the Ecclesiastical Mind has created and constructed the Roman Catholic Church, an interpretation of the Christian religion in the imperative mood, and this it has done through the perpetuation of the organizing spirit of ancient Rome.

XII

The Mystical Mind

"Mysticism is a type of religion which puts the emphasis on immediate experience of God, a direct and intimate consciousness of divine Reality. It naturally involves a reaction and even a revolt from ecclesiasticism, ritualism, abstract theology and all tendencies toward religious crystallization, in behalf of the direct testimony of the soul of man."—RUFUS M. JONES.

MYSTERY, universal in human experience, evokes normally in the individual two attitudes: "I know something of the enzoning mysteriousness within my mental life," and "while my knowledge of it is necessarily incomplete and therefore imperfect, this knowledge can be extended and therefore I will try to pierce it." To these must be added two opposing inferences which grow out of the interpretations thus given to the totality of the mysterious. Some say that "all that seems so mysterious to me is known and therefore the mysterious veils and yet mediates Ultimate Reality," while others take the position that "the mysterious in all human experience is inescapable, perpetual, expands as knowledge increases and therefore increasing fluxation may be affirmed but not Ultimate Reality."

The mystic, whether Christian or non-Christian, believes the former inference, acts upon it and affirms that through the acquirement of first-hand knowledge, he is able to testify with complete confidence and certainty that Ultimate Reality exists; that the contact, the impact and the intercourse which he describes are not the products of his own imagination, but are reliable data which prove that the mysterious not only veils but also mediates Ultimate Reality or God. Scientists, limiting their field to the description of the unceasing fluxation of our phenomenal world, cannot as scientists, take issue with the mystic, although they may endeavor to study, in accordance with some accepted scientific method, the data which the mystics provide.

It is otherwise with the philosophers, for all of them must be classified in theory as mystics or non-mystics, depending upon their definition of Ultimate Reality. The foremost interpreter of the Christian faith, in speaking to the Athenian philosophers, grounds the origin of mysticism in the purpose of God: "He made of one blood all nations of men for to dwell on all the face of the earth, and hath determined the times before appointed and the bounds of their habitation; that they should seek God, if haply they might feel after him and find him, though he is not far from every one of us, for in him we live and move and have our being; as certain also of your own poets have said: 'For we are also his off-spring.' "

The Mystical Mind has its origin in the universal quest of humanity for a satisfying relation with the superhuman or divine, fertilized by whatever revelation is accepted as true, and further enriched by the personal realization of the presence of the super-human or the divine in states of consciousness that vary from quiescent serenity to ecstasy.

Mysticism is the immediate consciousness of a personal relationship, involving intercourse with the superhuman or the divine. In its highest expressions, mysticism is fellowship with God and rests upon the conviction that the human personality is competent to receive and to become the vehicle for the expression of a divine revelation; that vital communion with God lies within the reach of the individual, and that the experience which grows out of this communion has its origin in a definite personal contact with Ulti-mate Reality or God, though its interpretation and expression be circumscribed by the individual's incapacity to report the experi-ence clearly, truthfully and completely.

The assumptions of Christian Mysticism are the competency of the individual soul to gain access to God without the aid of priests or other human mediators, the full acceptance of Jesus' revelation of the fatherhood of God and of His readiness, because of infinite love, to bless and reveal Himself to all who seek Him, and the reality and the incomparable worthfulness of the experi-ence which grows out of this communion with God, though hu-man limitations may render imperfect its expression to others.

Christian mysticism is grounded upon faith in man, faith in God, and faith in the Christian experience; and these in turn rest upon Jesus Christ as the true and perfect Mystic who in himself realized during his earthly ministry all that mysticism and the mystics have sought to attain: "I and my Father are one." Mysticism is "the type of religion which puts the emphasis on immediate awareness of relation with God, on direct and intimate consciousness of the Divine Presence. It is religion in its most acute, intense and living stage." [43]

An undue emphasis upon the intellectual element tends to make the Christian religion the acceptance of a creed; upon the institutional element, the submission to an ecclesiastical authority; upon the purely ethical element, the formation of a character; upon the emotional element, the enjoyment of an esthetic satisfaction. "The truly mystical may be summed up as simply a protest in favor of the whole man—the entire personality. It says that men can experience, and live, and feel and do much more than they can formulate, define, explain or even fully express. Living is more than thinking." [44]

Mysticism places the emphasis upon the Christian experience which is the outgrowth of the transfer of the control of one's life in its entirety to God as mediated in Jesus Christ, and affirms that in this experience the dualism of man and God is overcome by an inward reconciliation through which the divine gains the ascendancy over the human, and the goal of human endeavor becomes the fulfilment of the will and purpose of God. This is the norm of the Christian life as exemplified by Jesus Christ, as interpreted in the New Testament and as striven for by the early Christian saints. Christianity is a mystical religion—a religion which lives because its members experience the actual presence of God as they voluntarily transfer the control of their human freedom to God as revealed in Jesus Christ.

The Christian mystic is one who, accepting God and worshiping Him "sees all things in God," and so opposes those who deny the existence of God or who fail to make Him real. He interprets his mystical experience as a reproduction of the New Testament Christian experience in which the loving, joyful submission to Jesus Christ is described as an enslavement. The conscious releasing of spiritual aspirations and energies is declared to be the evidence of the presence of the Holy Spirit. The Christian mystic, using the phrase in its broadest sense, is any one and every one who has the religious experience of the New Testament followers of "the Way." As Moberly says, "All Christians profess belief in the Holy Ghost. Had all Christians understood and lived up to their belief, they would all have been mystics; or, in other words, there would have been no 'mysticism.' " [45]

The Christian experience is essentially and primarily a mystical experience, characterized by a confidence which amounts to a certainty, that the individual has sought and found peace with God through faith in Jesus Christ. One aspect of this confidence is the assurance of personal salvation. The first stage of discipleship is redemptive and is marked by the reorganization of the inner life about a new center of control, with Jesus Christ as Lord and Master. To this whole process is given the name of regeneration or the new birth.

Every disciple is called to be a saint, and the process by which saintliness is attained is named by the evangelical theologians, sanctification. While there is an obligation upon every Christian to seek to become a saint, there is the greatest variation in the performance of this supremely important religious duty. The challenge of Jesus which, when accepted, leads the disciple to deny to himself the exercise of any selfish control over his personal decisions; to take up daily his cross and to follow his Lord by ordering his life in obedience to the divine will; to express in lowly faithful service the spirit of his Master, reproducing in word and act his attitude toward all the problems of human life, has been met successfully by so limited a number of his followers that all such are not given the Biblical name of "saints," but are loosely denominated as mystics; their reported experiences are often discredited, and their intense devotion is too frequently attributed to mental malady.

Though the mystics have striven in every generation to become Christian saints in the truest sense, they have never been able, since the Apostolic Age, to control either the development of doctrine or the growth of church government; they have never enjoyed the complete ascendancy in the Christian ministry, and when they have fled from the world, seeking as hermits or monks to live the spiritual life, they have not been able to perpetuate their devotion to saintliness so that those who succeeded them as members of the orders they had founded, reproduce their passion to live as ever in the presence of God.

Yet in every generation the Christian mystics have been numerous, forming sometimes influential groups that protested against the worldliness of professing Christians. They always affirmed the accessibility of God and the factual character of the religious experience they reported. Some of them sought to improve the spiritual conditions within the ecclesiastical body, called the Holy Catholic Church; others toward the close of the Middle Ages endeavored to reform the Roman Catholic Church, while others, among whom the Anabaptists were prominent, undertook to build a new church upon the New Testament pattern. The mystic in every age has been the most important factor in the presentation of a spiritual Christianity and has been most effective when he possessed superior organizing ability. Paul, Augustine, Francis of Assissi, Luther, Calvin, Wesley and General Booth combined mysticism and Christian leadership.

The Mystical Mind, studied in relation to the course of Christian history, is the mental attitude which emphasizes the primary, essential element in the Christian religion as the realization on the individual's part of a satisfying, uplifting experience in which union with God is secured through faith in and devotion to Jesus Christ. This experience stimulates and promotes the development of the spiritual life by concentrating attention solely upon distinctly Christian ends. The objective of the Mystical Mind was and is to preserve and to perpetuate Christianity as a spiritual religion, grounded upon a conscious union of the believer and God, through the presence and the ascendancy of the Holy Spirit in the human heart, and to express this relation in holy living, in the teaching of Christian truth and in loving ministries that illustrate the altruistic spirit of Christ, seeking in the performance of these things, the co-operation of all others who are inspired by a like constraining motive.

The Mystical Mind prevails in the New Testament. Teaching, personal trust in Jesus Christ, the presence of the Holy Spirit in the believer precede and condition baptism. Paul and John are truly great mystics. The churches, as corporate spiritual entities, are guided by the Holy Spirit. Prophets and Apostles proclaim the will of God. The Gospel spreads as good news, told by all who have experienced its inspiring benefits. Practically all the early Christians are mystics, practicing good works, and giving themselves to the culture of the inner life. The goal of every endeavor is that "in all things God may be glorified through Jesus Christ."

"The greatest transformation which the new religion ever experienced—almost greater even than that which gave rise to the Gentile Church and thrust the Palestinian communities into the background—falls in the second century of our era. . . . The living faith seems to be transformed into a creed to be believed; devotion to Christ into Christology; the ardent hope for the coming of the 'Kingdom' into a doctrine of immortality and deification; prophecy, into technical exegesis and theological learning; the ministries of the Spirit into clerics; the brothers into laymen in a state of tutelage; miracles and miraculous cures disappear altogether or else are priestly devices; fervent prayers become solemn hymns and litanies; the 'Spirit' becomes law and compulsion." [46] The original enthusiasm, born of mysticism, has evaporated by the time that the Hellenistic Mind, chiefly concerned in the formulation of right doctrine and the Roman Mind, chiefly concerned for the solution of the problems incident to the government of the interrelated if not definitely united Christian Churches, together gain the ascendancy. Multitudes are coming into the Christian fellowship without the mystical experience, and therefore the basis of fellowship in the primitive churches, "the power of the experience of the Divine Presence" in their membership, gives place to another radically different conception, which represents the united thought and action of the Intellectualists and the Institutionalists.

Faith is no longer a mystical experience, the soul's response to God as revealed by Jesus Christ; it is the acceptance of a deposit of doctrine, delivered to the Apostles and entrusted to their successors, the bishops. Baptism, under the influence of conceptions derived from the Mystery Religions, becomes a magical rite, effecting the forgiveness of sins and the "restoration to the image of God," and is accompanied by an illumination and is, in fact, "the bath of regeneration and sanctification." Through baptism, properly administered, Christian salvation is assured to every one who submits to the rite. "Complete obscurity prevails as to the Church's adoption of the practice of child baptism, which, though it owes its origin to the idea of this ceremony being indispensible to salvation, is, nevertheless, a proof that the superstitious view of baptism had increased." [47]

The Lord's Supper in the New Testament is a solemn memorial meal, usually preceded by the Agape or love-feast, in which the offering of praise and thanksgiving takes the place of the bloody sacrifices with which the early Christians had been familiar. The Sacerdotal Mind emphasizes the sacrificial aspect and changes the name from the Lord's Supper to the Eucharist, with the bishop offering in behalf of the congregation the sacrifice of praise and thanksgiving, thereby fulfilling a priestly office and laying the foundation for the separation of the laity and the clergy. Later, the Lord's Supper, called the Mass, is authoritatively declared to be a sacrifice in which the same Christ, who upon the cross offered himself up, is actually present, the wine becoming his blood, the bread becoming his body. These two rites, baptism and the Lord's Supper, belonging to the New Testament period, become saving sacraments and are to be interpreted in the light of the prevailing mystery cults of Greece, Egypt, and the East. The validity of the sacraments depends upon their proper administration, and an exclusive Christian priesthood, properly ordained, becomes a logical necessity.

There is scanty room for mysticism in Christianity Hellenized into a creed and Romanized into an institution that exercises imperial authority; yet the stream of Christian mysticism, sometimes hidden from the observer's view, may be traced through the centuries from Pentecost to the present hour. In some instances the only record now available is penned by its bitter enemies; in others, the literature is extensive and illuminating.

Montanism, arising in the latter half of the second century, is an effort to give to the mystical prophet a higher position than the ecclesiastic, who seeks to exercise a priestly authority. Tertullian (c. A.D. 145-220), next to Augustine, the greatest of the African theologians, becomes a Montanist. He seeks to restore "the

Church of the Spirit," as opposed to "the Church which consists of a number of bishops." The movement ultimately dies, its literature is destroyed and its prophets are thrown to the beasts.

The rush of the unregenerated pagans into the Christian Churches, the increase of the number of those who, baptized in infancy, grow to maturity without the mystical experience, and the consequent lowering of the Christian life by the introduction of pagan beliefs and practices created, as Harnack says, "a Christianity of the second rank." "It consisted in worship of angels—demigods and demons, reverence for pictures, relics, amulets, a more or less impotent enthusiasm for the sternest asceticism—therefore not infrequently strictly dualistic conceptions—and a scrupulous observance of certain things held to be sacred, words, signs, rites, ceremonies, places and times. Catholicism, as it meets us in Gregory the Great (A.D. 590-604), and in the final decisions of the seventh Council, presents itself as the most intimate union of Christianity of the first order with that subterranean, thoroughly superstitious and polytheistic 'Christianity'; and the centuries from the third to the eighth mark the stages in the process of fusion which seems to have reached an advanced point even in the third and was yet reinforced from century to century to a most extraordinary extent." [48]

As Duchesne, the eminent Roman Catholic historian, says concerning the fourth century: "The mass of the community was Christian in the only way in which the mass could be, superficially and in name; the water of baptism had touched it, but the spirit of the Gospel had not penetrated its heart. . . . The Christians, who were really worthy of the name held aloof from public affairs and refrained even from entering the ranks of the clergy, whom they considered too much occupied in the things of the world. They lived in retirement, in town or country, engaged in religious meditation and the practice of an ascetic life." [49]

Self-denial and daily cross-bearing are, according to the teachings of Jesus, essential to the mystical life of the disciples. During the Neronian, Decian, and Diocletian persecutions devout Christians find opportunity for voluntary suffering by being loyal to the faith. The Montanists, Novatians, and Donatists, bodies of Christians who resist the growing encroachments of a centralized ecclesiastical authority, glorify asceticism. The Christian hermit life has its beginning in Egypt, about the middle of the third century, and soon spreads into Syria and other parts of the Empire. The younger monks meet for instruction given by some celebrated monastic, and the association, at first informal, leads to the organization of monastic orders, with rules for government and terms for admission. The mystic urge originates monasticism and, in turn, monasticism offers to mystics of this early day the opportunity of an escape from the world and a life devoted to the culture of spiritual values.

The mystical life of the individual, when brought into subjection to an institution—the monastic order with a government which regulates every detail of conduct, requiring the strictest obedience to authority—in some, exhibits piety of the highest degree, but in others, and impartial history indicates that in the Middle Ages they form the majority, saintliness is not at all in evidence. Avarice, intolerance, bigotry, sectarian zeal, sensuality, idleness, luxury, and utter moral worthlessness, rather than the Christian virtues, prevail. The mystical experience inspires the forming of the Early Christian Churches; but in a few centuries they are unified into an institution, in which the mystics are in a hopeless minority and exercise no control; the mystical experience inspires the life of self-denial which creates monasticism and within a few centuries these institutions, born of this spirit, have grown enormously rich, and their members are better known for their vices than their virtues.

Augustine (A.D. 354-430), the Bishop of Hippo in Africa, is the real father of Catholic mysticism." In him, as in no other Christian leader, is united "the religion of the spirit" and "the religion of authority." Converted at thirty-two, he sums up his earlier spiritual struggles in words that make a universal appeal: "Our hearts are restless till they rest in Thee." "Augustine's theology and his religious fervor denote a special resuscitation of the Pauline experience and doctrine of sin and grace, of guilt and justification, of divine predestination and human servitude. . . . What released him from the entanglements of the world, from selfishness and inner decay, and gave him strength, freedom and a consciousness of the Eternal, he calls, with Paul, grace. With him he feels too that grace is wholly the work of God, but that it is obtained through and by Christ, and possessed as forgiveness of sins and as the spirit of love." [50] If Augustine, the mystic, is completely divorced from Augustine the ecclesiastic, and he may be honored as one of the greatest interpreters of evangelical religion, giving to divine grace its rightful place.

The pseudo-Dionysius, the Areopagite, probably a Syrian monk of the sixth century, greatly influenced the mysticism of the Middle Ages. Bernard, Abbot of Clairvaux (1091-1153), Richard, dying about 1170, Hugh (1097-1141), Thomas Aquinas (1225-1274), the greatest of the medieval theologians and the chief authority of Roman Catholic doctrine; Meister Eckhart (1260-1329), laying the foundations at once of German philosophy and German mysticism; John Tauler (c. 1300-1361), friar-preacher of Strassburg, Henry Suso (c. 1300-1365), a German Dominican, John Ruysbroeck (1293-1381), a parish priest who became a recluse; Gerard Groot (1340-1384) the founder of the Brotherhood of the Common Life. Thomas á Kempis, (1380-1471) author of the *Imitation of Christ* and Richard Rolle (c. 1300-1349), an English hermit, form an incomplete list of the great mystics, devoted to the monastic life, obedient to the Roman Catholic hierarchy, who conscious of a personal union with God fearlessly interpreted their mystical experiences in the interest of promoting a deeper spiritual life. Eckhart alone suffered ecclesiastical condemnation. Among the notable women mystics were Hildegarde (1098-1179), Elizabeth of Shoenau (1138-1165) Gertrude (1256-1311), Julian of Norwich (1343-1443), Catherine of Siena (1347-1380) and Joan of Arc (1412-1431).

"There are as many unveilings of God (theophanies) as there are saintly souls," writes John Scotus Erigena, the great Irish philosopher and theologian, in the ninth century. He is called " great light in the dark ages." He teaches that "man is an epitome of the universe, a meeting place of the above and the below, point of union for the heavenly and the sensuous." Three centuries later, mysticism begins with renewed force to make itself felt in medieval life. Hugh of St. Victor is teaching that "faith has virtue only when it becomes effective through love." Eckhart is declaring that "what a man takes in by contemplation, he must pour out in love." A new social order is beginning. The capitalistic age is about to dawn. Towns and cities are growing. The Crusades have greatly stimulated the intellectual life. Scholasticism undertakes to unite philosophy and theology, and Aristotle is given the honored place that Plato held among the earlier Greek Christian theologians. Revelation is more important than reason. Thomas Aquinas writes his *Summa Theologica*, in which he combines the philosophy of Aristotle and the faith of Augustine. Free investigation and the spiritual life are being smothered, the one by scholasticism, the other by the Roman hierarchy.

The mystics keep alive the spirit of primitive Christianity. The feeling is widespread that the orthodox sacerdotalism, supported by the most powerful institution in the world, the Roman Catholic Church, has failed in its task. The priests and the monks are notoriously corrupt. The Church, proprietor of an enormous number of serfs, harshly exploits the lower classes. Social misery increases. The Cathari, convinced by what they see about them that Satan has created and rules the world, reject the authority of the Roman Church, live righteously and win by their fine, noble moral character the admiration of their ecclesiastical oppressors, only to be wiped out of existence by persistent persecution. The Valdensians accept the Bible as the only religious authority, place the emphasis upon conduct rather than creed, and though subjected to the most cruel and pitiless persecutions, in their spiritual descendants, still survive.

The sale of indulgences, the pardoning of past or future sins upon the basis of payments made to the Church, encourage and promote among Roman Catholics many forms of immorality. The Dominican friars are chosen to suppress unapproved mysticism and this they strive to do through the Inquisition. Wyclif is translating the Bible into English, developing a popular evangelism and inaugurating thereby the revolution that bears in Church history the name of the Reformation. With an open Bible, an open mind and an obedient heart, Christian mysticism will renew its strength and mount up with wings like the eagle.

XIII

The Protestant Mind

"Unless I am convinced by the Scriptures or by clear argument, I cannot and will not recant anything. For I am bound in conscience, and against conscience it is neither safe nor right to act. God help me."—MARTIN LUTHER.

THE ROMAN CATHOLIC CHURCH, Latin in speech, Roman in spirit and purpose, sacramentarian and sacerdotal in its interpretation of the Christian faith, committed to the conquest of all human institutions and to the mastery of the minds of all men, so that in faith and morals they submit to its ecclesiastical teaching and judgment as the will of God, is the great fact which dominates the history of the Middle Ages. Other agencies are present, but their manifestations are comparatively isolated or sporadic.

The social order is feudalistic. Its economic basis is the possession of great estates by a landed aristocracy, with the millions of Europe's workaday population—slaves, serfs, villeins, and free peasants—supplying the labor needed for the cultivation of the soil. The Latin language, which the Roman has imposed upon Western Europe, is modifying and molding the speech of the peoples, except those who live in Germany, Scandinavia, and Britain, and even in these countries Latin is the literary language of the State and of the Church. Vulgar Latin, later to develop into the Romance languages, is spoken in Italy, Castile, Portugal, Provence, Northern France, and the area of population which now bears the name of Rumania.

Toward the close of the Middle Ages, the cultural and economic center of gravity passes from the country as trade and manufactures increase and towns multiply. Guilds, associations of workmen in each separate craft, are organized. Markets, where people meet at fixed times for the sale and purchase of goods, are established. Fairs are held for business and for pleasure. Commerce is being extended to distant countries. A capitalistic age begins to dawn. Urban life makes for wealth, freedom, and culture. Feudalism gives way to nationalism.

However, as we trace human progress during the millennium we call the Middle Ages, the one pervading impulse, the only formulated program, the single concentrated effort present at every point, dominant in every age, striving for supremacy in every sphere of action, exhibit the spirit, the purpose, and the power of the Roman Catholic Church. In all the struggles for world domination the records of mankind offer no parallel comparable in character or reach to that of the Papacy, striving for the mastery of both the temporal and the spiritual realms. "This vast fabric of ecclesiastical supremacy presents one of the most curious problems which the world's history affords. A wide and absolute authority, deriving its force from moral power alone, marshaling no legions of its own in battle array, but permeating everything with its influence, walking unarmed through deadly strife, rising with renewed strength from every prostration, triumphing alike over the savage nature of the barbarian and the enervated apathy of the Roman tributary, blending discordant races and warring nations into one great brotherhood of subjection—such was the Papal hierarchy, a marvel and a mystery." [51]

The Reformation (1517-1648) was "the widespread and irresistible movement which marked the sixteenth century as one of the world's creative eras. That movement was political, economic, literary, scientific, artistic, and ecclesiastical. . . . When the movement had spent its first force, every institution in Christendom, every system of authority, was changed." [52]

From the closing part of the second century to the Reformation, the visible institution of the Christian movement, called the Church, passed through three stages in its political relationships:

1. The loosely related churches, forming, as Harnack says, "a league of individual communities spanning the Empire from end to end," *stand under the State;*

2. The growth of papal power, following the Teutonic invasions and the consequent downfall of the Roman Empire, assures to the Roman Catholic Church a place *alongside the State*, the latter now known as the Holy Roman Empire;

3. The popes, on the basis of their claim that they are the suc-

cessors of Peter, assert the right to rule over all princes and kings, and from the eleventh through the thirteenth centuries so successfully exercise this authority that the Roman Catholic Church is placed *above the State.*

"The Roman World Empire is continued in and through the Roman Catholic Church. In the dim solitude of the cloister, the monk is training the minds which are to mold the destinies of the period, while his roof is the refuge of the desolate and the stranger. In the tribunal, the priest is wrestling with the baron and is extending his more humane and equitable code over a jurisdiction subject to the caprices of feudal or customary law, as applied by a class of ignorant and arbitrary tyrants. In the royal palace, the hand of the ecclesiastic, visible or invisible, is guiding the helm of state, regulating the policy of nations and converting the brute force of chivalry into the supple instrument of its will. In Central Europe, lordly prelates, with the temporal power and possessions of the highest princes, joined to the exclusive pretensions of the Church, make war and peace, and are sovereign in all but name, owing no allegiance save to Emperors whom they elect and Popes whose cause they share. Far above all, the successor of St. Peter from his pontificial throne claims the whole of Europe as his empire and dictates terms to Kings who crouch under his reproof or are crushed in the vain effort of rebellion." [53]

The hierarchy of Rome, as a superstate, molds for weal and for woe the political life of the Middle Ages, exercising everywhere spiritual dominion. Its jurisdiction prevails over the natural dividing lines of language, nation, and race, and imposes upon all peoples within Christendom an authority so complete that Gregory VII, in the exercise of his lordship, writes William the Conqueror, "to yield unto me unconditional obedience." Too, he forces Emperor Henry IV to come to Canossa, where, outside the papal residence, barefooted in the snow, he waits as a penitent the summons of the Pope, at whose feet he will beg for papal forgiveness.

An institution, making such claims and exercising such power, needed vast revenues, and these the Church of the Middle Ages was able to procure. Its economic resources were limited only by the capacity of the peoples of Europe to produce wealth. Feudalism grew out of the nobility's emancipation of their estates from the royal administration, thus placing the owner between the kingship and the great mass of the people. Those lands had been secured by inheritance, royal grants, and the transfer to the nobleman of small freeholders' property, surrendered in return for protection from attack by other feudal lords. Feudalism arose as the masses became economically dependent upon the great landed aristocracy. The Medieval Roman Church, Christian in origin, Hellenized in its creedal statements, sacramentarianized by the Mystery Religions, Romanized in spirit, purpose and administrative polity, was transformed by the social and economic conditions of the Middle Ages into a profoundly feudalized institution, becoming in the process by far the greatest landowner in Europe.

The beginnings of episcopal power may be traced, in large measure, to the bishop's control of the Church's finances and property. Constantine the Great and his Christian successors vastly increased the revenues of the Catholic Church by grants, by transferring income-producing properties once belonging to the pagan priesthoods, and by legalizing and encouraging the leaving of legacies to the Church. The time soon came when "to die intestate was regarded as robbing the Church." In the Middle Ages, legacy hunting by the clergy became a scandal. In practically every country, the property of the Church was exempted from taxation, and this involved from one-third to one-half of all the real property in medieval Europe.

In addition to the revenues from its vast estates, the Church demanded and vigorously collected the tithe, or one-tenth of all that was made by the peasant, the artisan, and the merchant. "The farmer who deducted working expenses before tithing his crops damned himself thereby to hell." In addition to the tithe, many fees were collected, and in time "the practice of exacting fees was enormously extended."

The bishops who held the episcopal estates and the abbots who held the monastic estates were drawn almost entirely from the nobility. The tendency of the clergy to provide for their offspring by gifts of ecclesiastical property endangered the temporal possessions of the Church, and to prevent its continuance the celibacy of the clergy was made an ecclesiastical requirement.

The Church did not oppose the slave trade. It treated its serfs rigorously and long retarded their emancipation. The peasant rebellions of the twelfth and thirteenth centuries were almost always upon Church lands. Persecution was often inspired by greed. In the Albigensian Crusade, the property of the alleged heretic was promised to the informer. During the Inquisition in Italy, the usual division of the possessions of the convicted heretic was one-third to the informer, one-third to the Inquisitors, and one-third to the local magistrates. "Persecution became almost as much a financial speculation as a matter of faith."

Church offices were multiplied. Simony, the buying and selling of church offices and emoluments, a medieval form of ecclesiastical graft, widely prevailed. In the sale of indulgences "the Church capitalized its spiritual authority for revenue purposes," and sold an immunity from the punishment of God to any sinner who was able to meet the scale of prices, fixed by the ecclesiastical authorities. The theory was that the contrite sinner could substitute the payment of a sum of money to vouch for his sincerity, in lieu of some difficult or distasteful penitential act. This remission of the penalties of sin was extended to souls in purgatory, and vast sums were secured. "Money rolled into Rome." The Roman Church in the Middle Ages was "a governor, a landed proprietor, a rent collector, an imposer of taxes, a material producer, an employer of labor on an enormous scale, a merchantman, a tradesman, a banker and a mortgage broker, a custodian of morals, a maker of sumptuary laws, a school master, a compeller of conscience—all in one." [54]

In the light of its program to achieve world dominion, the Roman Catholic Church must be studied and interpreted as an institution seeking wealth, power, and complete authority in order that the will of God as declared by the Church might be successfully imposed upon all mankind. The thought-movements and the literature of the Middle Ages indicate the ascendancy of this purpose. The world-view of the masses is a mingling of every kind of pagan superstition with a Christian tradition in which are crowded many superstitious elements, so that credulity and fear unite and create in them the attitude of abject submission to the priest, whose delegated power in the sacraments offers the only hope of salvation and of eternal blessedness. The people fear the priest more than the prince, and their devotion to the Pope is usually stronger than their allegiance to the Emperor. From this point of view, the period of the Middle Ages is an intensely religious one.

A government imposing its rule over millions of people must create and administer law. In purely secular issues the Church follows the Roman civil law, largely as codified by Justinian; but in religious matters the canon law is supreme. This is based upon the Bible, upon the traditions of the Church, upon the decisions made by ecumenical and other councils, and upon decretals, letters sent by the Popes in response to requests for information, interpretations, or instruction. Toward the close of the fourteenth century the Corpus Juris Canonici, embodying Church law and large portions of medieval Roman civil law approved by the Church, is published. No member of the clergy could be tried for any crime, however flagrant, in any other than an ecclesiastical court.

Litigants by agreement might transfer their case to a Church court. Ecclesiastical jurisdiction dealt with all such crimes as perjury, oaths, sacrilege, adultery, and offenses against orphans and widows. The Church courts could condemn to the fires of hell, impose immediate penance—involving such punishment as fines, wearing a hair shirt, going on a pilgrimage—or excommunicate the offender, which meant the loss of his soul and his complete and immediate abandonment and ostracism by the community; while the interdict, the denial of all the privileges of the Church within a designated area, could be imposed upon all, peasant, lord, or king, who resisted the will of the Pope.

The universities, beginning with Bologna in the twelfth century, introduced the study of the Code and Pandects of Justinian and the Decretum of Gratian, the earliest textbook devoted to the canon law. Christian thought became legalistic, and doctrine "was recast under the categories of judge, accused, satisfaction, and penalties." Anselm's doctrine of the Atonement, in which the death of Christ is necessary to the satisfaction of the honor and the justice of God, illustrates the influence of Roman and canon law upon medieval theology.

The Crusades (1095-1291), ten in number, inspired, approved, and supported by the Church, were a series of campaigns by the armed forces of Christendom, made with the special objective of recovering the Holy Sepulcher from the hands of the infidel. They led to the undermining of feudalism, the enrichment of the papacy, the diffusion of the learning of the East, the building up of new commercial centers, and the growth of freedom of thought. The founding of the great medieval universities is one of the indirect results. Science received a powerful impulse.

Architecture, essentially a communal art, is the noblest creative expression of the Middle Ages. The Romanesque gives place to the Gothic, in which the soaring spirit of Christian faith finds a visible embodiment. The cathedrals of Europe, with their lofty towers, their beautiful sculptures and jeweled windows, and the masterpieces of Michelangelo, Raphael, and Da Vinci dealing with religious themes, preserve the best that the age is able to produce.

A new day is about to dawn. Feudalism is crumbling. Serfs are breaking away from servitude. Commerce is growing. The Renaissance, a rebirth of culture, is beginning in Italy and is destined to spread throughout northern and western Europe. In Petrarch and Boccaccio and later in Reuchlin and Erasmus, humanism, the appreciation of culture, becomes articulate. The rational spirit finds its realization in a political entity, the nation which, growing stronger and more stable, brings the feudal lords into complete subjection. A strong middle class is rising, the third estate. A new world is discovered by Columbus, Da Gama finds a sea route to India, and Magellan circumnavigates the globe.

The Popes of the Church, some of them guilty of vilest debauchery and the grossest immorality, lead in the further secularization of the Church. The papal court removes in 1309 to Avignon in France. Germany, England, and Bohemia protest. Two popes reign at the same time from 1378 to 1439, and during one year, three. Despite the saintliness of many faithful men and women in the monastic life, avarice and moral corruption are widespread throughout the religious orders. The clergy, in order to live in luxury, sell for money the appointments they control and squeeze the poor of Europe without mercy. Famines, crop failures, incessant warfare, and the Black Death (1347-1351) create social and economic unrest. In travail, a new era in Christianity is being born. The struggle between the altar and the pulpit, the priest and the preacher, begins.

The Protestant Mind, emerging as a reaction to the unhappy economic and religious conditions of the Middle Ages, fertilized by the New Learning whose spread is rapidly extended by the invention of printing, centers its thought and effort upon the reformation of the Roman Catholic Church. Basic in all its activities is the conviction, derived from the serious study of Apostolic life as given in the New Testament, that personal faith in Jesus Christ is essential to salvation.

The background of the Reformation includes the mystics of the Middle Ages: spiritually-minded groups such as the Friends of God in Germany; the Brethren of the Common Life in the Netherlands; the Waldensians in France, Spain, Italy, Switzerland and the Rhine Valley; the Reformers who precede the Reformation—Wiclif in England (1324-1384), Huss (1370-1415) in Bohemia, Savonarola (1452-1498) in Italy; and the thousands of saintly men and women who "counted not their lives dear to them" and died at the hands of Roman persecutors rather than be untrue to their religious convictions.

Race and language are also factors. Protestantism today is limited largely to peoples of Teutonic descent and speech. The early Teutons were devoted to personal liberty. Contact with Christianity of the Romanized type gradually tames these sons of the forest but does not change their spirit. In the Middle Ages, they submit to the awesome, mysterious, and supernatural institution, the Roman Catholic Church; but, resentful of ecclesiastical taxation, impatient of its autocratic rule, with the growth of Biblical knowledge and the critical spirit, and with the inspiring possession of a personal religious experience, they are ready and have the courage to overthrow the yoke of Rome. Law and centralized authority are so wrought into the structure of the Latin and its derivative languages that revolt against ecclesiastical authority has never been successful; but no such spell has ever fallen upon the linguistic families whose speech is Teutonic in origin.

These and other factors create a situation which waits only a voice to arouse multitudes to resolute action. A young monk, thirty-three years of age, on October 31, 1517, posts on the door of the castle Church in Wittenberg, ninety-five theses against the sale of indulgences, then being conducted by Tetzel, a representative of Pope Leo X. No one is more surprised at the effect produced than their author, Martin Luther. Thousands rally to his support. The Pope summons him to Rome and Luther refuses to go. A papal bull, issued by Leo X in 1520, gives the Augustinian monk sixty days to recant or be excommunicated. Luther makes a public bonfire of the bull and throws to the flames also a copy of the canon law. The act symbolizes rebellion against the whole Roman system.

Luther, beginning with the intention of reforming the Roman Catholic Church, finds himself a leader of a revolution. The year is crowded with literary labors, in which he attains the greatest heights as an author. *Christian Liberty, Good Works, Brief Explanation of the Ten Commandments, The Creed and the Lord's Prayer, Prelude on the Babylonian Captivity,* and *An Open Letter to the Christian Nobility of the German Nation* set northern Europe aflame and awaken widespread interest in England, France, and Italy. Scholars, princes, peasants, as well as the serious-minded who would reform the Church from within, rally to him.

The denial of the authority of the Roman hierarchy involves the rearing of another and better rule for Christian faith and practice, and this Luther finds in the Holy Scriptures. Cited to appear before the Diet of Worms, April 16, 1521, presided over by the Catholic Emperor, Charles V, he refuses to recant the views he has published: "Unless I am convinced by the Scriptures or by clear argument, I cannot and will not recant anything. For I am bound in conscience, and against conscience it is neither safe nor right to act; God help me." Though he leaves Worms unmolested, the Diet places him under a ban, prohibits the publication of his writings, suppresses his books and tracts, and orders his arrest.

The political history of the Reformation hinges upon the enforcement of the Edict of Worms. The Emperor, depending upon the local political units, the princes and the municipalities, for the enforcement of this Edict, finds it necessary to postpone action in order to prevent civil war. The Elector of Saxony provides for Luther an asylum, a tower in the Wartburg, where he completes in an incredibly brief period the great work of his life—the translation of the Greek text of the New Testament into German. This is published in September, 1522, and is followed ten years later by the entire Bible. In translating the Hebrew of the Old Testament Luther is aided by Melanchthon and others. Most local German governments are putting into operation the practical reforms Luther demands and are reorganizing Church life within their own territories, under the protection and the general direction of the local authorities.

The Diet at Speyer in 1526 establishes the principle of *Cujus regio, ejus religio*, thus permitting each separate government to adopt the reforms of Luther, should the reigning prince or governing municipality so desire. Three years later a second Diet, held at Speyer, annuls the principle. This calls forth a "protestation," signed by the princes of Saxony, Brandenburg, Brunswick, Lunenburg, Anhalt, Hesse, and by the representatives of fourteen cities, declaring that they will not carry out the new edict or tolerate the Mass in their dominions. Because of this political action regarding a religious issue, the signers are called Protestants and the movement they head is given the name of Protestantism.

The following year, these protesting rulers adopt the Augsburg Confession, prepared by Melanchthon in conference with Luther, as expressing the beliefs of the Lutheran Churches within the territory of which they are the political rulers and representatives. This theological document is the classical statement of Lutheran doctrine and remains to the present day the bond of union among all Lutheran Churches. More important in the religious development of the German people is the *Small Catechism* prepared by Luther in 1529, in which his view of essential Christianity is given in words a child can understand. Excepting the Bible, no single work produces during this period so lasting or so widespread an influence.

Luther is a conservative reformer and reorganizer, preferring to retain whatever in life, worship, and Church polity is not contrary to the Scriptures rather than restore the New Testament order. Harnack truly says, "The Reformation . . . as represented in the Christianity of Luther, is in many respects an old Catholic or even a medieval phenomenon, while if it be judged of in view of its religious kernel, this cannot be asserted of it, it being rather a restoration of Pauline Christianity in the spirit of a new age." [55] For him the Gospel is the power of God to everyone that believeth, that is, everyone that puts his trust in Jesus Christ as Lord and Saviour. "What the gospel is must be ascertained from Holy Scripture; the power of God cannot be construed by thought, it must be experienced; the *faith* in God as the Father of Jesus Christ, which answers to this power, cannot be enticed forth by reason or authority, it must become part of one's life; all that is not born of faith is alien to the Christian religion and therefore to Christian theology—all philosophy as well as all asceticism. Matthew 11:27 ("All things have been delivered unto me of my Father; and no one knoweth the Son, save the Father; neither doth any know the Father, save the Son, and he to whomsoever the Son willeth to reveal him.") is the basis of faith and of theology. In giving effect to these thoughts, Luther, the most conservative of men, shattered the ancient Church and set a goal for the history of dogma. That history has found its goal in a return to the Gospel." [56]

Luther takes over from the Roman Catholic Church "the Canon of the Scriptures as it was held before the Council of Trent, the Apostles' Creed, the Nicene Creed, the Athanasian Creed, the Chalcedonian Christology, the doctrines of sin, divine sovereignty, and election, atonement through the death of Christ, future rewards and punishments." He justifies infant baptism "as a means of grace in the strict sense," thereby separating personal faith and divine grace, concerning which Harnack says, "In this way, the most splendid jewel of evangelical Christianity became robbed of its practical power—became, that is, of no effect." [57] He declares "the real presence of the body and blood of Christ in the Eucharist to be the essential part of the Sacrament."

The Protestant Mind, functioning through Luther and those associated with him, organizes and leads a revolution against the Roman Catholic Church because of its unscriptural claims, its exercise of a fallaciously founded temporal and spiritual authority, and its system of good works and of miracle-working sacraments. Within the Teutonic linguistic areas the revolt against Latin theocracy is successful. A new social order, in which small states will grow into nations, supplants the feudalistic system and plays an important part in the subsequent development of Christian belief and practice. The Protestant Mind is the precursor of the nationalistic mind and is to a large degree the creator of the dominant thought-pattern of the era that follows, namely, the divine right of Kings. Luther gave to the secular power an authority and dignity almost, if not completely, divine: "The hand that wields the sword is not a human hand but the hand of God. It is God, not man, who hangs and breaks upon the wheel. It is God who wages war." It is not too much to say that, powerful as the influence of Luther was in the realm of religion, his doctrine of the State was mightier in Protestant lands than his doctrines of grace, and created a new phase of the age-long problem of the relation of organized government to organized religion.

XIX

The Nationalistic Mind

"Half of the Wars of Europe, half of the internal troubles that have vexed the European states, from the Monophysite controversies in the Roman Empire of the fifth century to the Kultur Kampf in the German Empire of the nineteenth, have arisen from theological differences or from the rival claims of Church and State."—LORD BRYCE.

THE LEGACY of the dying Roman Empire to the Middle Ages was the bestowal of the right to command upon an unnamed universal authority. Therefore an institution functioning as a world-state, was the only potical instrument medieval thought could conceive as meeting the needs of an ordered society. The Papacy and the Empire both laid claim to this legacy.

A common religion, the Roman Catholic Church; a common language in use by all educated men, the Latin; a common enemy during the Crusades, the infidel; a common social order, feudalism—these united medieval Europe; and the expression of the unity logically demanded an institution in which supreme authority should be vested—a world-state.

Though the medieval world was so closely bound together by common elements, two contrasting aspects were to be distinguished, the spiritual and the temporal, the ecclesiastical and the political. The Popes claimed to be sovereign in every sphere but were willing to entrust temporal power to the Emperor. Friction was inevitable. The strife between Pope and Emperor dominated the second half of the Middle Ages, both seeking to exercise universal and international jurisdiction.

Gregory the Great (590-604), one of the ablest of the Pontiffs gained temporal power at Rome and was successful in maintaining order and in protecting the Roman people. He drilled the Romans for military defense, issued orders to generals, appointed governors of Italian cities, and directed missionary efforts in Spain and England. The rise and rapid spread of Mohammedanism

(622-782) over western Asia, northern Africa, and Spain, and the break between the Roman Pontiff and the Patriarch in Constantinople which resulted in the division of the Catholic or Universal Church into the Roman Catholic and the Greek Catholic Churches, increased the need for a political institution coextensive with the jurisdiction of the Roman Pontiff to function in temporal matters and always in the interest of the Roman Catholic Church. Charles Martel (719-741), the King of the Franks and a stalwart defender of the Roman faith, stayed the Moslem advance at Tours and aided Boniface, the Apostle of the Germans, in establishing the supremacy of the Papacy in Germany and Gaul.

Pope Stephen II, threatened by the King of the Lombards, made a treaty with Pippin, the son of Charles Martel, in which he promised to confirm the house of Pippin perpetually in the kingship of the Franks, and Pippin agreed to become the defender of the Roman Catholic Church. The victories of Charlemagne, the son of Pippin, extended the Frankish Kingdom from northern Spain to the shores of the Baltic and from the Atlantic to the Oder river, and on Christmas day, A.D. 800, he was crowned by Pope Leo III in St. Peter's Church as Emperor. Thus the Papacy and the Holy Roman Empire were brought together, with the Emperor kneeling to receive his crown at the hands of the Pope. The enemies of the Pope were promptly banished from Rome by the Emperor. However, the partnership of the Papacy and the Frankish monarchy as a coequal union of the spiritual and the temporal powers of Christendom was maintained more as a theory than as a fact.

The Empire of Charlemagne falls to pieces and is succeeded by the Holy Roman Empire of the German Nation." Otto I (936-973), who had brought under the spiritual jurisdiction of the Roman Pontiff the Scandinavians, the Wends, the Poles, the Bohemians, and the Hungarians, is crowned by Pope John XII as Emperor. In theory, the Holy Roman Empire is a double sovereignty, founded upon the conception that "the Empire and the Papacy are co-ordinate instruments of the divine will for the government of mankind," the Emperor possessing absolute authority in matters temporal, the Pope in matters spiritual; the Emperor heeding the spiritual guidance of the Pope, and the Pope as the divinely ordained successor of Peter needing the temporal protection of the Emperor.

This equality of sovereignty in different spheres could not last. Pope Gregory VII (1073-1085) asserts that "the Roman Pontiff has the right to depose emperors. He may absolve subjects from fidelity to unjust princes," while Boniface VIII (1294-1303) declares "that it is altogether necessary to the salvation of every human creature to be subject to the Roman Pontiff." The powers of the Papacy and of the Empire from this time begin to diminish. The successor of Boniface VIII withdraws the papal court to Avignon in France; from 1375 to 1417 there are two popes. Worldliness, greed, immorality, and even debauchery in papal rulers weaken public confidence in the Papacy itself. With the rise of local sovereignties, whose rulers are able to command the allegiance of the nobility within their territories, the authority of the Emperor rapidly declines.

The seizure of Constantinople by the Ottoman Turks, May 29, 1453, marks the extension of a new era in the cultural, political, and religious life of Europe. The scholars, fleeing from the Moslem invaders westward, bring with them the early Christian, the Neo-Platonic, and the Classic Greek manuscripts, which contribute so much to the rise of the New Learning. The study of Greek flourishes in the areas of Europe where Latin has been so long supreme. The growth of commerce, the increase of urban population, the organization of the artisan groups, the falling revenues from the landed estates lead to the decline of the medieval system of feudalism. Latin, which has bound together the medieval world of learning and is the spoken language of the church liturgy and of the universities, no longer is the sole vehicle for literary expression. The laymen are entering the field of letters and by the use of the "vulgar tongues," the vernaculars of the common people are creating masterpieces.

The rulers of England, France, and Germany are endeavoring within their realms to curb papal power, to bring into loyal adherence and subjection the feudal lords, to destroy the ties that bind them to the fading Holy Roman Empire, and to establish the doctrines of territorial sovereignty and self-determination, as opposed to the claims of universal authority made by both Pope and Emperor. A new spirit stirs the hearts of men. Printing makes possible the wide dissemination of fresh, fertilizing ideas. New conceptions of the Christian religion awaken the deepest human emotions. All classes are thrilled by the feeling that a new day is dawning.

The outstanding movements within this period of ferment are the Renaissance, the Protestant Reformation, the Catholic Counter-Reformation, the so-called Religious Wars, and the rise of modern nations. The stimulating study of the classics and the awakening of the spirit of scientific investigation, the seething confusion of religious controversies, and the growth of new political institutions are important factors in molding the life of Europe.

The rise of modern nations is given the determinative place in the interpretation of the period, on the ground that the culture which had its origin in the Renaissance has transcended the boundaries of nations and the confining limits of languages and has become international. But the ecclesiastical expressions of Christianity, arising within the Reformation, are from their very beginning largely, if not completely, under the control of the forces—political, economic, and religious—that destroy feudalism, overthrow the absolute authority exercised by the Papacy, and create a new social order. Intellectually quickened by new modes of culture, Europe experiences an interaction of all these forces, which culminates in the formation of modern states, with their sovereigns asserting the principle of absolute authority, based upon the divine right of kings.

The evangelical interpretation of the Christian faith, with its emphasis upon divine grace and upon salvation through a personal trust in Jesus Christ, was denied the right to apply freely the principles taught in the New Testament and was forced to make such compromises as princes and kings deemed expedient. By these compromises the evangelical movement assumed institutional forms, whose continuance depended upon the favor of the ruler and the support given by the State. The union of the Papacy and the Empire was succeeded by the union of the national church and the national State.

The Nationalistic Mind gained the ascendancy over the Reformation itself and determined the form and type of the Christian religion that should be allowed and promoted within the bounds of the principality or the kingdom. In some instances the State favored the Roman Catholic, in others, the Protestant or evangelical faith; but in all countries everyone who could not conscientiously accept the State religion was oppressed and persecuted. By submitting to the authority of the State, the approved interpretation of Christianity was permitted to develop its own institutional life, subject always to the interests of the ruling dynasty.

The Nationalistic Mind is the fusion of groups of people through the possession of common memories and customs of the past, common ideas and interests in the present, and common hopes and purposes as they face the future, fertilized by a loyalty to their traditions, their public weal, and their national destiny. It is physically limited to the soil over which those who govern them exercise territorial sovereignty, and spiritually limited by the ideals and the moral principles expressed in the policies carried out and the laws enforced in the interest of justice and public welfare. The influence of the Nationalistic Mind has steadily grown during the past four centuries. Modern history is the story of nations, their expansion, their internal development, their international relations. National churches are in form and in many of their conceptions the religious by-products of the Nationalistic Mind.

The Reformation (1517-1648 A.D.) was a revival of evangelical religion in which the Bible was accepted as the authoritative rule of faith and practice; the Counter-Reformation (1521-1648 A.D.) was a revival of sacedotal religion in which the Pope was recognized as the infallible and authoritative head of the Roman Catholic Church, to whom should be given world-wide and undisputed submission and allegiance.

The Renaissance, the revival of classical learning which preceded and accompanied the Reformation, promoted art, literature and the critical spirit, and stimulated intellectual freedom. It began as a cosmopolitan movement; it ended in national literatures. The rise of a strong moneyed class, the Third Estate, incident to the growth of commerce, played an important part in building up the new form of political life, the sovereign state, the modern nation. The doctrine of the divine right of kings furnished the basis for the assertion of absolute power by the rulers of the states formed during this eventful period. The growth of nationalism was a necessary stage in the development of religious liberty.

Historians have chosen the Peace of Westphalia (1648) as the date on which the Reformation ends. This peace, described in the treaties as "a peace Christian, universal, and perpetual and a friendship true and sincere," was, in fact, the declaration by sovereign European states of their independence of both Emperor and Pope. The Emperor Ferdinand III was stripped of imperial power and remained a sovereign only in the domains of the House of Austria. The right of each ruler to protect and to foster the form of Christian faith—Catholic, Lutheran, or Calvinist—which he accepted, was confirmed. In vain did the Pope of Rome fulminate against the treaties as "perpetually null, vain, invalid, wicked, and . . . without force and effect." The agreements were reached by the representatives of sovereigns, who claimed and mutually recognized one another as possessing absolute power over the territory which each governed.

The term Protestantism had its origin in the protest of five German princes and fourteen cities made in 1529 against an order which the Diet passed upon the demand of the Emperor. The protest inaugurated a Revolution which was successful in the areas which lie outside the boundaries of the ancient Roman Empire. When it ended with the peace of Westphalia, Lutherans were placed under the protection and control of Lutheran princes, and Calvinists were enjoying like privileges under Calvinist rulers. The movements and the events which ended in making the treaty of Westphalia the fundamental law of Europe now engage our attention.

Five elemental forces struggle for the supremacy between 1517 and 1648: the German princes, restive under the Emperor and eager to restrict papal power within their realms; the Pope of Rome, supported by a powerful hierarchy; the Emperor, Charles V, head of the House of Hapsburg, committed to the suppression of heresy and to the maintenance of the authority of the Pope; the humanistic movement, which founds universities in Germany and produces scholarly critics of clerical abuses but prefers the slow processes of education rather than revolution as the method of ecclesiastical reform; and the peasants, whose conditions of living have become so unendurable that when their just and reasonable demands, based in large measure upon their acceptance and application of the teachings of Luther, are denied, they rise in revolt.

Luther chooses to ally himself and his cause with the German princes, who wreak a ferocious vengeance on the peasants. Though in the earlier days he stood for an unfettered religion, grounded upon justification through faith, he promoted the new ecclesiastical institutions of Protestantism and favored their control and support by the State. Most of the free cities and principalities in Germany adopted Lutheranism. Sweden, Denmark, and Norway followed, each creating its own independent Lutheran Church, as had been done in the many and various German states, all under State control. Poland for a time and Hungary in part were conquered by the Protestants, only to be lost. The Nationalistic Mind molded Lutheranism, wherever it spread through northern Europe, into a National Lutheran Church, controlled by State authority. These State Churches were bound together by the Book of Concord, adopted in 1580, containing the confession of faith which is recognized as the standard of doctrine for all the Lutheran clergy. Thus each State Church became and long remained a department of the government, with its office holders appointed by civil rulers.

Luther posited the authority of the Bible in denial of the authority of the Pope, salvation through faith in denial of salvation through the sacraments, and the priesthood of all believers in denial of the priesthood of the Roman Catholic Church. The first of these affirmed the objective principle, the second the subjective principle, and the third the social principle of the Reformation. The free exercise of all three of these principles was checked by the Nationalistic Mind.

The absolutism of kings and other rulers lessened the authority of the Bible. Infant baptism, a necessary concomitant, if the State Church should embrace as members all subjects within the realm, discredited the experience of divine grace which Luther held to be essential to salvation, by permitting the enjoyment of church membership without the exercise of personal faith. The alliance with the State created an ecclesiastic officialdom which retarded in

Lutheran lands the rise of political democracy. Luther needed the State to preserve the basic truth for which he stood, but this basic truth the succeeding centuries have shown to be more powerful than the German States that played the rôle of patrons. However, Hüss's failure in Bohemia one hundred years earlier to establish the same evangelical truth seemed to confirm the wisdom of Luther's course in seeking an alliance with the civil rulers; at any rate, the compromise which Luther accepted enabled him to stabilize the movement he led.

Ulrich Zwingli (1484-1531), humanist, reformer, and forerunner of Calvinism, acting in Switzerland, from Zurich as a center, led the attack upon the abuses of Romanism and enthroned the Bible as the standard of life and doctrine. Dying in battle, he was followed in his mission as teacher by John Calvin (1509-1564), a statesman, an organizer, and a theologian. Zwingli had carried forward his reform, subservient to the civil authorities.

Calvin united Church and State in a theocracy. "He combined moral earnestness, learning, analytical power, and practical organizing and administrative ability in a degree unapproached by any other Protestant leader." [58] He was easily the greatest polemical writer, the greatest ecclesiastical statesman, and the greatest systematic theologian of his age. Holding to the absolute authority of God, the Scriptures as the sole authority in faith and practice, human rights as God-bestowed and human government as a covenant between ruler and people, the mind of Calvin has exerted a religious and a political influence upon non-Lutheran Protestant lands probably surpassing that of any other thinker Europe has produced. In theology he developed a logical, scriptural, inflexible system of doctrine, grounded upon the sovereignty of God.

Resistance to tyrants was advocated by Lutheran and Roman Catholic thinkers, but the Calvinists provided a method of resistance that was at once definite, legal and practical; combined with it other theories and the sound experiences of self-governing churches and civil communities and finally worked it out into something of world-wide significance, responsible, representative, constitutional government.[59]

Zwinglianism, repudiating all that was not expressly warranted in the Scriptures, tended toward drastic revision of Roman ritual and polity and the establishment of congregational government. Calvin, believing that it was the duty of the Church to maintain by discipline a strict Christian life, and to preserve and propagate a system of doctrine derived from the Scriptures, sought to govern the community, including both members and non-members, in accordance with Biblical standards. The form of local government in Geneva made possible this politico-ecclesiastical program, in which the civil was subordinated to the ecclesiastical power and Calvin was able to maintain this relationship in Geneva from 1541 to his death in 1563.

Calvin, like Luther, was a prodigious creator of religious litera- ture. His *Institutes of the Christian Religion*, written when he was only twenty-seven, was the ablest, the profoundest, and the most consistent evangelical system of doctrine produced within the Reformation period. His *Catechism* became one of the chief symbolical works of the Reformed Churches, the name given to the Christian bodies adopting Calvinism in Europe. (In Great Britain, later, they were called Presbyterians.) In Geneva alone did Calvinistic principles gain complete ascendancy over civil af- fairs; elsewhere, save in Scotland and northern Netherlands, the followers of Calvin were in the minority.

The monarchs of the recently formed kingdoms were asserting and exercising absolute power over their realms. Religion, either in its Roman Catholic or in its Protestant form, was the crucial issue in politics. While Lutheranism was assuming the form of State Churches, under the fostering care and control of the con- glomerate governments of northern Germany and of the kings of Denmark, Sweden and Norway, Calvinism was permeating France, portions of western Germany, the Netherlands, Scotland, and parts of England. Many able minds were studying the fundamental principles of Calvinism as they affected ecclesiastical and civil life. Their published works, together with the distribution of Calvin's works, which ran into hundreds of editions, led to the discussion of the rights of evangelical minorities and to the study of new theories of government, especially the source of regal sovereignty.

The nations were becoming absolute monarchies, based upon the principle of territorial sovereignties, thereby freeing them- selves from an absolute papacy. Holding that human rights were bestowed by God, that the ruler of a people sustained the relation of a tutor to a pupil, that regal power was "nothing but a mutual covenant between king and people," that rulers received their power from the people and had the right to exercise this power only as they kept faith and observed their covenant or contract with the people, Calvinism espoused the theory that sovereignty was derived ultimately from the people and therefore rested upon God-given human rights.

In the struggle to limit the power of a sovereign who was imposing religious uniformity, the Calvinists in lands ruled by Roman Catholic kings became the exponents of political liberty. As Marsiglio of Padua (1270-1343), Nicholas of Cues (1401-1464), and others had proclaimed popular sovereignty in opposition to papal authority, declaring that "government springs solely from the consent of the governed," so François Hotman, Herbert Languet, Du Plessis-Mornay, and others, inspired by devotion to Calvinistic principles, assailed the doctrine of absolute, indivisible, and inalienable sovereignty which the kings now claimed to possess. John Locke, in his theory of government, became later the exponent in large measure of the Calvinistic teachings.

The principles of Calvin, coming into direct conflict with the Nationalistic Mind, which was committed to the theory that the ruler possessed *imperium*, the absolute right to command, found a living expression in the forms of government developed in the Netherlands under William of Orange, in the English Commonwealth under Cromwell, in Scotland under the Solemn League and Covenant, in the Puritan Commonwealths of New England, and has played no small part in the development of all modern representative and constitutional governments.

Calvinism permeated France, inspired the Huguenot movement which spread rapidly until the bloody massacre of St. Bartholomew's Day in 1572, and largely maintained its strength until the revocation of the Edict of Nantes in 1685 that drove 400,000 Huguenots into Holland, Germany, England, and, later, America. Calvinism inspired the revolt of the United Provinces of the Netherlands, under the leadership of William the Silent, against the despotic rule of Roman Catholic Spain. Dutch independence was practically won by 1581. From this time forward, Holland became, as Geneva had been during the days of Calvin, the refuge of all persecuted peoples.

John Knox (1505-1572), Scotch reformer possessing a fiery eloquence and an indomitable resolution, learned at the feet of Calvin in Geneva the doctrines of the Reformed faith. Mary Queen of Scots vainly sought to impose upon her people the recognition of papal authority. In 1560 the Scottish Parliament, amid scenes of unexampled enthusiasm, adopted a Calvinistic confession of faith, abolishing the mass and papal jurisdiction in Scotland. Again and again, the devotion of the Scottish people has been tested, but never have they swerved from their loyalty to the doctrines proclaimed by Knox. No people have surpassed them in appreciation of learning or in loyalty to high Christian ideals.

Through the action of the Reformation Parliament, 1529 to 1536, Henry VIII of England was able to sever the tie between England and Rome, to make himself "the supreme head" of the Church, and to abolish the monasteries throughout his realm. From the days of Wiclif the demand for reform had found expression only to be suppressed. The King desired a divorce from his wife, Queen Katharine, the aunt of Emperor Charles V, the champion of papal authority in Germany. The Pope hesitated and finally declined to annul the marriage. Henry, under the advice of Thomas Cromwell, determined to apply the principle of absolute regal authority, the theory of government generally held by kings, by making the Church a department of the State. By the Act of Supremacy, Parliament in 1534 declared the King of England to be "the only supreme head on earth of the Church of England." Little change was made in doctrine. Henry was never excommunicated by the Roman Church. The denial of trans-substantiation in the observance of the mass was made punishable by burning at the stake. Persecution of those who held evangelical views increased.

Calvinistic tendencies under Edward VI (1547-1553) are encouraged. The Forty-Two, later reduced to the Thirty-Nine Articles, adopted in 1552 as the Confession of Faith of the Church of England, recognize the Scripture as possessing absolute and exclusive authority, assert that salvation is attained by faith alone and accept the Calvinistic view of baptism and the Lord's Supper. The Book of Common Prayer is revised in harmony with the evangelical views. The reign of "Bloody Mary" (1553-1558) is marked by the restoration of Roman Catholicism and the burning of many of the notable Protestant leaders. Under Elizabeth (1558-1603) there is a steadily growing resistance to Romanism. The event which leaves the most lasting impression upon England during the sovereignty of James I (1603-1625) is the publication of the Authorized Version of the Bible, issued in 1611. Charles I (1625-1649), a Roman Catholic at heart, prohibits Calvinistic preaching but fails in his efforts to reign as an absolute monarch. When the Peace of Westphalia is made in 1648, England and Scotland are safely and permanently Protestant.

The Counter-Reformation, the movement which sought to Catholicize again the lands into which Protestantism had spread, while aggressively supporting the Papacy, co-operated with Catholic kings and princes and furthered their territorial ambitions. The absolute authority of the Pope in temporal matters was not made an issue with monarchs who lent their civil powers to the promotion of the aims of the Roman Catholic Church. Three factors contributed to the success of the Counter-Reformation:

1. The Council of Trent (1545-1563), which enacted some sorely needed reforms, formulated an authoritative statement of doctrine, and declared the Pope to be predominant;

2. The Society of Jesus, founded in 1540 by Ignatius Loyola, whose members, through the education of the sons of nobles and princes, through their active participation in political matters, not the least of which was intrigue in court life; through popular preaching, the use of the confessional, and the establishment of universities, were able, sometimes by persuasion, sometimes by inciting persecutions and wars for the extermination of Protestants, to regain much territory lost to the Protestants. They secured the co-operation of Catholic rulers, the House of Hapsburg leading, and reconfirmed Roman Catholicism in Austria, Bohemia, South Germany, Belgium, Poland, and France, but failed in England, Scotland, Northern Germany, and Sweden:

3. The Inquisition, which inflicted upon all who dissented from the Roman faith, particularly in Spain and Southern France,

cruelties and barbarities, shocked an age which had grown callous to suffering and intolerance.

The era closes with the Nationalistic Mind molding, guiding, controlling the institutional life of Lutheranism, Calvinism and Anglicism, through the support of State Churches in the countries accepting one of the three Protestant interpretations of the Christian faith. The Greek Orthodox Catholic Church is moving in the direction of ecclesiastical organizations under the control of the State. Roman Catholics recognize a dual allegiance to the King and to the Pope. Kings occupy the seats of the mighty. Territorial sovereignty and national self-determination endow regal power with the ancient Roman *imperium*, the right to command, and thus, with the rise of modern nations, a new Age of Absolutism begins.

XV

The Emancipating Mind

"Give me liberty, to know, to utter, and to argue freely according to conscience, above all other liberties."—JOHN MILTON.

EMANCIPATION is the release of the individual or the group from the bondage or the restriction created by social environment. It is the liberation of the individual from the yoke of the community and of the institutions through which the community expresses and enforces its will, including the traditions, customs, and folkways that form an integral part of its social structure; or it is the liberation of a weaker community from the coercion of a more powerful community.

Social control is necessary to an ordered society and is therefore an essential element in the preservation of any civilization. The institutions through which this social control is exercised function coercively, educationally, and persuasively. The family illustrates these three modes of action, the goal of which is the development of the child. The imperative need of social control tends naturally to an overemphasis upon authority and upon the institutions through which this authority becomes effective. The stability of the social order rests upon the maintenance of the authority of its conserving institutions. "The individual withers but the world is more and more." The exercise of coercive power is accompanied, both in men and in institutions, by the desire to acquire greater power, and this tends to develop into the will-to-power, predominant in those who administer the affairs of the institution.

The history of mankind is the record of the conflict between two interpretations of life; the one, giving to personality the highest place, seeks to direct all the agencies of social control toward the development of the individual; the other, recognizing that this development depends upon the stimulation and the control of the growing personality by its environment, seeks through social

169

pressure, often coercive in character, to compel the individual to become that which it is deemed he ought to be.

Jesus held that every institution existed as a means to an end, the end being the welfare of the individual. Even an institution so hallowed in the life of the nation as the Sabbath existed primarily as a means of furthering the well-being of humanity: "The Sabbath was made for man." He placed "the child in the midst" and condemned every influence, every educative process, every coercing method within the social order that failed to make central the welfare of that child. He championed all human rights that the individual needed to exercise in order to live in the world as a son of the Highest. Institutions he approved only as a means to an end, the end being the development of the individual into the moral likeness of God. He refused to compromise his position, though by doing so he might have gained control of all the coercive institutions that dominate the social order, "the kingdoms of this world," and chose rather to mold the lives of men by instruction, admonition, and persuasion. The creation and the use of coercive means, especially by coercive religious institutions, has been the Great Heresy of Christian history, a betrayal in every respect like that of Judas, in that Christ has again been placed in the hands of sinners; a betrayal which has blackened the pages of history with religious wars, religious persecutions, and with every kind of wickedness, all undertaken and performed under the guise of promoting the true Christian faith. Viewing the facts as an impartial historian, Lord Bryce says, "Half the wars of Europe, half the internal troubles that have vexed the European states, from the Monophysite controversies in the Roman Empire of the fifth century down to the *Kultur Kamp* in the German Empire of the nineteenth, have arisen from theological differences or from the rival claims of Church and State." [60]

The right of private judgment, which involves the principle of religious liberty, was the intellectual justification of the Protestant Revolution; yet the Reformers, as soon as they had formulated their articles of faith, organized their own ecclesiastical institution and secured the protection of their princes, repudiated freedom of conscience and gave their approval to coercion by the State in the interest of religious uniformity. The Inquisition carried on its excessively barbarous coercive measures in all Roman Catholic lands, and the Protestants, with less cruelty and to a lesser extent, persecuted those who would not agree with them in doctrine and practice. The Protestants, though they had exercised the rights which grow out of religious liberty, were unwilling to extend these rights to any who differed with them in the interpretation of the Scriptures.

Too hastily we may condemn the Reformers as inconsistent and hypocritical and selfish. The contemporary Anabaptist movements which sought to promote complete religious freedom were overwhelmed, their leaders were persecuted to death, their basic teachings were so grossly misrepresented that for nearly three centuries the principles which they sought to establish were generally and most vigorously condemned. The Lutheran, the Calvinist, and the Anglican movements in all probability would have met with a similar fate if no coercive measures had been employed by them. This leads to the consideration of the conditions and the circumstances under which it is proper and right for any social institution—the family, the school, the State, the Church—to employ coercive measures and to limit the free exercise of individual rights.

The exercise of authority is coextensive with organized social life. An institution without some kind of authority is inconceivable. Three vital questions arise:

1. Is the authority derived from a source which possesses rightful sovereignty?

2. What institution possesses right of coercion?

3. Under what conditions are coercive measures justly exercised?

The source of the authority, the right to exercise the authority, and the circumstances which require coercive action are the primary subjects for consideration. In the family, the authoritative head is the parent; in the school, the teacher; in the State, the ruler; in the religious body, whoever exercises overseership, and in each the entrustment with power involves inescapable moral obligations on the part of those possessing and exercising this authority.

The source of all rightful authority is an ideal and universal moral order, while the right of any particular executive of an institution depends upon the existence and the maintenance of a correct relationship to this order by him and the institution he represents. The Christian affirms, not only that such a moral order exists but that in the character of God this ideal moral order in all of its perfection is found and that whoever "resisteth the power, resisteth the ordinance of God." The Christian contention is that the exercise of authority is a divinely approved method, that the institution should be so related to God that its acivities will indicate a faithful endeavor to carry out the will of God, and that the proper goal of all institutional effort is the stimulation and the strengthening of the purpose within the individual to live in the world as a loving, obedient child of God To this end Christianity seeks to Christianize all institutions. The Christian valuation of any institution therefore is measured by its devotion to moral and Christian ends.

As society becomes more highly organized, institutions increase in number and variety. In modern life, the territorial sovereignty of the State is the basis of the legal existence of every institution even the family, for whose establishment a marriage license must be procured from the State; and also the Church, whose ownership of property depends upon some form of legal incorporation. The State, in the exercise of its sovereign powers, may establish system of religion to promote national morality, just as it enacts a system of criminal law to reduce wrong-doing. For thousands o years this course has been followed in civilized lands. Nearly all national governments which recognize the Christian religion have asserted the right to enforce religious conformity. The State except in a few instances where a theocracy has been attempted Geneva and the Colony of Massachusetts being illustrations recognizes no higher goal than its own collective, material an moral welfare, and, with this end in view, the majority of the Christian States, until comparatively recent times, have used coercion in some form to suppress dissent.

Territorial sovereignty, self-determination involving self-defense and the maintenance of national honor are asserted by the State as inalienable rights. The promotion of the well-being of all i citizens is recognized as an obligation of the State and right coercion is based on this obligation. As John Stuart Mill says, "The sole end for which mankind are warranted, individually and collectively, in interfering with the liberty of action of any of their members is self-protection." War, if not for aggression, is the nation defending itself against a foreign enemy; punishment of criminals is the nation defending itself against enemies within its own boundaries; taxation is coercion in the interest of procuring the funds necessary in protecting its citizens and promoting their general welfare.

If the State determines that the propagation of treasonable teachings threatens its peace and sovereignty, it possesses the legal right to protect itself against the danger. If the State is convinced that the dissemination of certain religious doctrines has political implications which threaten the security of the State, it has the same legal right to suppress such teachings. On this ground, the Roman Catholic kings and princes support the Inquisition, the Lutheran princes and Anglican kings coerce Calvinists and Independents. The legal right of the State is undeniable; the question of moral right remains to be determined, and this will be settled by the character of the Christian religion itself.

The proper expression of the Christian religion is to be found in either conformity or confession. If submission to certain sacred rites, if obedience to an ecclesiastical authority, if the acceptance of creeds promulgated by this authority and the ordering of one's life in harmony with the instructions of its legal pastors be the conditions of Christian discipleship, then conformity not only makes one a Christian, but no one can be a Christian without this conformity and therefore every phase of legal and social pressure is permissible in order to secure this desirable end. On the other hand, if the voluntary transfer of the control of one's life to God as revealed in Jesus Christ, resulting in the enthronement over the inner life of the will of God as supreme in all matters, and if all outward religious forms have value only as they give expression to the saving experience to which the individual testifies, then coercion in any form militates against the development of the saving Christian experience.

The State and the Church both assume institutional forms but with differing functions and objectives. The one seeks the tem-

poral welfare of its citizens; the other, the eternal blessedness of
mankind. The one is compelled to exercise coercion in the maintenance of its stability and its territorial sovereignty; the other
by using coercive measures destroys voluntariness as the principle
of action in the individual. The vital question is whether one
can become a Christian only by a free, voluntary, and therefore
moral response to the claim of Jesus Christ as the Lord, who is
given control of the individual's life, or may he become truly a
Christian in some other way. In the New Testament this moral
response is the condition of discipleship, and its expression is the
act of one who is exercising religious liberty. Confession, preceded by a personal trust in Jesus Christ and followed by baptism
in his name, is the requirement of Church membership in the
Apostolic Period.

The basic difference in the interpretations of Christianity
throughout all Christian history grows out of the definition of a
Christian. Is he one who has been baptized into the fellowship
of a divine institution, the Church, or is he one who believes in
and obeys Jesus Christ? If the former, coercion is not only permissible but commendable; if the latter, coercion is indefensible
in that it renders increasingly difficult, if not impossible, the moral
response to the appeal of Christ.

The Protestants sought first to reform the Roman Catholic
Church. Failing in this, they set up ecclesiastical establishments,
State Churches, where the ruling powers were favorable. They
continued to endorse the principle of coercion in order to secure
conformity in doctrine and practice. Another movement, different
in character, more radical in its objective, sought to restore the
primitive Christian faith, based upon the principle of voluntariness, whose exercise incontestably depends upon the personal
enjoyment of religious liberty.

These radical groups, most of them known as Anabaptists, form
the religious aspect of the Emancipating Mind, and they possess
for the modern world a significance greater even than the Reforming movements, because they carried the principles they espoused
to their logical conclusions, and sought to create a new social
order by making the individual central in religion rather than the
religious institution.

The Emancipating Mind is the fusion of all groups of thought interested in freeing themselves and others from every form of unjust coercion, namely coercion not necessary to welfare of mankind, fertilized by a passion for individual liberty but restricted often to the securing of that liberty in the field to which the special attention of the particular group is directed. Since the Middle Ages, co-operation among all groups seeking the attainment of every rightful liberty that is attached to any human relationship has steadily increased. The common purpose which fuses these groups together, even when their ideals and programs are in conflict with one another, is a common devotion to freedom and an emancipation from every phase of unjust coercion. From the assertion of papal supremacy by Gregory VII (1073-1095) to the present hour, rightful liberty has been the most important civil issue in all lands where Christian civilization has prevailed.

The Renaissance, with its revival of classical learning, stimulated intellectual freedom, promoted humanism or the appreciation of culture, inspired a contempt for Scholasticism, the great bulwark of papal absolutism; quickened the study of the Scriptures in the original languages, and exposed the impostures of the Roman hierarchy. Through the invention of printing the literary works of liberal-minded scholars were widely distributed and eagerly read. Beginning in Italy, the Renaissance, during the fourteenth, fifteenth, and sixteenth centuries, created an intellectual atmosphere favorable to the progress of freedom of thought. Some of its notable leaders supported the Reformers, others gave at least nominal adherence to the Papacy, and others still, like Erasmus, strongly assailed the leaders of the Reformation. Copernicus, Galileo, and Bruno, all Roman Catholics, rejected the geocentric theory and laid the foundations of a new interpretation of the heavens. Philosophical speculation, historical criticism, and natural science were seeking freedom from ecclesiastical and political coercion.

Under the rise of Nationalism, the kings gain their freedom but the peoples are merely transferred from the absolute rule of the Pope and the Emperor to territorial sovereigns who possess a like absolute authority over them. The emergence of the Middle Class, who through the changed economic conditions are acquiring wealth, and the world expansion which follows the discovery of America, serve to enrich, extend, and strengthen the yearnings of men toward a greater freedom of action. The Reformers, like the kings in the realm of government, seek for themselves liberty but approve coercion by the State in promoting and establishing their interpretations of Christianity.

The Renaissance promoted intellectual freedom and scientific inquiry; nationalism, the freedom of kings; the new economic order, greater freedom of action by the successful; the Reformation, religious freedom from papal supremacy under the protection of the State—liberty for the scholar, the king, the merchant, the Protestant, but for the sincere dissenter no liberty at all based upon the rights of man or the teachings of Jesus regarding human brotherhood and the free exercise of personal faith.

Toward the close of the Middle Ages and during the period of the Reformation, the demand for religious liberty came from groups of Christians who espoused the separation of Church and State, who despaired of reforming the Roman Catholic Church and who sought to reorganize the believers in Christ into bodies patterned upon the ecclesiastical model given in the New Testament. All accepted the Scriptures as a divine revelation and posited as an inalienable right the privilege of the individual to read and to interpret the Bible for himself, and having found, as he believed, the truth, to obey its teaching unhindered by any external authority.

The Roman Catholic gave the central place to the Church as a divine and saving institution; these liberty-loving groups made the individual central, salvation being a personal trust in and obedience to the precepts of Jesus as given in the New Testament. The vast majority composing these bodies were peasants, possessing little learning; but among their leaders were some of the finest scholars and the most courageous spirits of the age. Deserving of mention are: Carlstadt, a member of the University of Wittenberg; Conrad Grebel, trained at Vienna and Paris; Rinck, eminent Greek scholar; Hübmeier, a learned priest, who revolted against the Roman Church and spread his views throughout Switzerland and portions of Austria; Menno Simons, a former priest, the founder of the Mennonites; Hans Denck, the rector of a school

in Nuremberg; Schwenckfeldt, a Silesian nobleman; Johannes
Companos, educated in the University of Cologne; Michael
Servetus, trained in the universities of Sargossa and Toulouse;
Gherlandi and Francesco della Saga in Italy and Socinius in Po-
land. Clearly, the movement did not lack distinguished intellect-
ual leadership.

Since these freedom-seeking Christians uphold the right of
private interpretation of the Scriptures, wide differences develop
among them as to doctrine and practice. However, they agree in
holding that only those who have an experience of religion, being
"conceived by the word of God and born of faith," possess the
right to Church membership; therefore, they baptize either by
pouring or immersion only those who profess to have had this
experience, though they previously may have been baptized in
infancy. For this reason they are called Anabaptists, Rebaptizers.
They call themselves "Brethren," "Believers," "Christians." The
Reformers are aiming to reform the old Church of the Bible;
the Anabaptists, to build a new Church from the Bible. Holding
that the centuries intervening between the Apostles and their own
times are covered by "the apostasy" the Apostles foretold, they
undertake to restore the Church of the New Testament, composed
solely of spiritual persons—a regenerated church membership. In
the interest of religious liberty, they repudiate any connection
between Church and State; in the interest of preserving a regenerated Church membership and the right of a child later to
exercise his personal religious liberty, they reject infant baptism.

The Anabaptists are pacifists who are willing to die rather than
bear arms. Capital punishment they strongly oppose. They deny
the right of any Christian to hold any political office in which
coercion is used. They practice self-denial and tend toward a
Christian communism. Some of them, despairing of social justice,
participate in the revolt called the Peasants' War in 1525, resulting in the slaughter by the princes and nobles of Germany of probably one hundred thousand of the oppressed within ten weeks.
Others, also led by those who claim prophetic powers, repudiate
pacifism, set up a theocracy in Münster which they rename the
New Jerusalem. When the city falls before the attack of the
Roman Catholic Bishop and his allies, a reign of terror ensues,

"all suspected of lack of sympathy with the new regime being remorsely slain." Persecutions by Roman Catholic, Lutheran, Calvinist and Anglican, fierce and unrelenting, follow, and thousands of Anabaptists die for their faith.

"Judged by the reception it met at the hands of those in power, both in Church and State, equally in Roman Catholic and in Protestant countries, the Anabaptist movement was one of the most tragic in the history of Christianity; but judged by the principles which were put into play by the men who bore this reproachful nickname, it must be pronounced one of the most momentous and significant undertakings in man's eventful religious struggle after truth." [61] As Harnack says, these Anabaptists were three hundred years ahead of their time. They emphasized voluntariness in religion, private interpretation of the Scripture, and freedom of conscience; further, they stressed the evil inherent in infant baptism, since it makes for an infringement of the right of the child in exercising later the privilege of a free religious choice. Thus they laid the foundation upon which the social structure of religious liberty has been reared.

The modern governments which in recent times adopted the principle of the separation of Church and State have done so with little realization that the thousands of Anabaptists who gladly gave up their lives as a voluntary sacrifice and who, after their martyrdom, were everywhere scorned and maligned by prejudiced historians, were the ones who made possible for the future generations freedom in the realm of religion, and by their tragic protest against every form of state and ecclesiastical coercion inaugurated the movement toward complete religious liberty.

The Renaissance, restoring the ancient Greek attitude toward nature, man, and the enjoyment of life, inspired the study of science, stimulated nationalism, introduced the movement to which in Germany is given the name of the Enlightenment, and prepared the way for utilitarianism, or the valuation of institutions and corporate activities on the basis of their promoting human comfort and material prosperity, this being the new guiding principle in social action. These movements contributed to the better understanding of the physical world, the growth of democratic institutions, and the creation of an industrial civilization.

The expansion of human knowledge and the centering of interest upon the welfare of man, tended to lessen the influence of organized Christianity and to restrict the coercive powers exercised by the Roman Catholic and the Protestant State Churches. In the Protestant lands especially, the spirit of nonconformity manifested itself. Aided by the growing sentiment in favor of the exercise of human rights, it gradually permeated popular thought, and the result was the establishment of the principle of religious liberty.

In his work, On the Liberty of the Christian Man, Luther gave a correct definition of the Christianized Mind, though in his relations to those with whom he differed he failed to live up to it: "Every man, because of his faith, is a free lord of all things, subject to none; every man, because of his love, is in bondage, a servant of all."

Religious liberty for the individual is a freedom bounded by his knowledge of the truth, restrained in its exercise by love, and directed toward a goal which is a voluntary conformity in word and deed to the will of God. It is to the interest of the State to safeguard such an individual in enjoyment of this liberty; for thereby his moral progress is assured, and the moral integrity of the State is increased as such individuals become more numerous. A State founded upon the principles of justice flourishes as its morally and religiously law-abiding citizenry grows in influence and power.

The field of action by organized religion, Christian or non-Christian, properly is limited to admonition, education, and persuasion; while the range of coercive administration by the State is circumscribed by its power to protect itself against any acts that violate the civil laws which are grounded upon sound moral principles, even though it may be claimed that the violations are inspired by a religious motive.

The American way of life is the product of the aspirations and the untiring endeavors of those who sought freedom from every form of religious coercion in order that they might devote themselves to the emancipated pursuit of mystical Christian piety as they saw it portrayed in the New Testament. Their objective was a form of religious liberty in which by civil law they would be neither enjoined nor molested. As Ernest Sutherland Bates points out, "The ideal of self-government was brought to America by the Pilgrims; the separation of Church and State was derived from the Baptists; the right of free speech was the development of the right of conscience, established by Roger Williams and William Penn; the equality spoken of in the Declaration of Independence was an outgrowth of the equality practiced by the Quakers. Democracy was envisaged in religious terms long before it assumed a political terminology."

The student of history can discern in the present global war a parallel to the religious issues which were present, though not always articulate, in the American Revolution. The religious objective today, as seen if not openly proclaimed by the evangelical bodies of this country, is the realization of a goal in which the sovereignty of God is acknowledged, the freedom of religion is guaranteed, the proclamation of the Gospel of Christ is given free range in all lands, the principles of democracy are enthroned as the ideal basis of earthly governments, and a new world order is to be established by the victorious United Nations, committed to the preservation of an enduring peace and inspired by good-will toward all mankind. The strength and the weakness of the American way of life as it relates to religion will be considered in the study of the Denominational Mind.

XVI

The Denominational Mind

*"The realm of religion is entirely beyond the scope of the State. * * * *
Its only relation to religion is to protect all of its citizens in the sacred rights
of conscience, just as it protects them in their rights of person and property."*
—JOHN GARLAND POLLARD.

RELIGION is reverence in action. Its isolated expression is private
worship; its social expression is public worship. Reverence, a
mingling of humility and appreciation, needs conceptual forms
for the defining of its object of worship, and also needs instruction
in the manner in which a satisfying and helpful relationship may
be attained. This need is met by doctrine. Religion is a constant
influence in the life of the individual, and he approaches the religious ideal only as the reverent spirit permeates all experience, by
controlling conduct and by molding a personal character in harmony with his highest ideals. Religion expresses itself as a worship,
a creed, a way of living.

These outward manifestations of the spirit of reverence, which
form observable religious behavior, take on a social character and
thereby call for a degree of social control over worship, belief, and
practice. The degree to which this control shall be exercised is the
ever-present issue in Christian history. The full control of all
the three expressions of religion—worship, belief and practice—can
be fully assured only upon the assumption that there exists an
institution, divinely endowed with a plenary power, in possession
of all infallible truth and in control of the only means of spiritual
salvation and blessedness, and that this institution, exercising all
temporal and spiritual powers, successfully imposes, by the use
of every form of social pressure upon all true Christians, the
acceptance of belief and the direction of worship and practice.
This is the contention of the Roman Catholic Church, and it
rests upon the theory that an external control is an end which

181

must be secured at any cost. The logic of the position demands a complete standardization of worship, belief and practice for all who are recognized by the Church as faithful Christians. Unquestioning obedience to the Roman Church, exercising a divinely bestowed right to command, is the sole test for an individual member. The reign of absolutism in religion attains the fullest expression in Roman Catholicism, and its ideal is the complete subjection of thought and action to the mind and purpose of the Papacy. This goal, however, has never been completely realized.

Denominationalism is a neutral word, derived from denomination, meaning name, and implies a devotion to the principles and policies of a Christian body which undertakes to give a distinct interpretation of Christianity and which devotes itself to the propagation of this interpretation. The Denominational Mind is the union of all elements which fused together create a devotion to a distinct interpretation of Christianity, grounded upon the enjoyment of a varying degree of religious liberty, fertilized by the passion to give a social expression to the religious convictions of a hierarchy or of groups of Christians who accept a definite interpretation of Christian worship, faith, and practice, developed upon the soil of the modern world.

The Denominational Mind is most active and fruitful in the congenial mental climate which exists only where freedom of thought prevails; and while this Denominational Mind promotes division in name and in the corporate actions of the followers of Christ, it arouses in them the sense of greater personal responsibility and evokes a stronger personal devotion to a definite interpretation of Christianity. This makes possible a more generous support of Christian causes and institutions than has ever been voluntarily given to any other historial religion.

No social agency functions without exercising some form of authority, coercive, admonitory, educational, or persuasive. The avowed object of every Christian denomination is the extension of the benefits of Christianity to others, and from this point of view it is a social agency intent upon the fulfilment of its mission. The desire for success in the Apostolic Age leads organized Christianity to seek and to use all available means in propagating its faith—missionaries who preach and teach; the reading and the circulation of an inspired literature, the Old Testament and the books which now form the New Testament; the organization of groups of believers into local churches with worship, including the observance of the Lord's Supper and almsgiving; and the promotion of a loving fellowship and of a high order of moral living by all professing Christians. This is the pattern as given in the New Testament.

The efficacy of forms is taught in the second century. Baptism is declared to be the means of salvation, and the Lord's Supper is interpreted first as a sacrifice of almsgiving offered by the worshipers, and later as the bloodless sacrifice of Christ. The growing power of the bishop, the desire for organic church union, the alliance between the Empire and the Church, the rise of the Papacy, and the recognition of the Church as a divine institution whose head is the vicar of Christ, give to the Roman Catholic denomination in central and western Europe the opportunity of exercising absolute power over all social institutions. Salvation only within the Church, salvation only through baptism, salvation only by submission to the Papacy are the basic conceptions of Romanism, the imposing of which is enforced by every coercive measure available.

The Protestant denominations, save for a few Waldensians, were extirpated in Italy and in Spain, were overwhelmed in France, Bohemia, Moravia, Poland, and Hungary; but they were successful, largely through alliance with the State, in portions of Germany and Switzerland and in Denmark, Norway, Sweden, Holland, Scotland, and England. Except in Geneva, where for a brief period under Calvin, State and Church were identical, the State Church depended upon the State for the exercise of coercive measures. Each of these Protestant state bodies formed denominations which used directly or indirectly coercive, admonitory, educative, and persuasive measures.

The Christian groups which accepted some other interpretation of Christianity than the one to which the State gave approval and support, sought the establishment of the principle of toleration, with its relief from coercion. By 1650 there were in Europe, including the State Churches and the two Catholic bodies, the Greek and the Roman, twenty-three denominations, each undertaking to define the proper modes of worship, to formulate its doctrines in confessions of faith, to maintain its standards of Christian living and to propagate its interpretation of Christianity.

Devotion to a distinct and comprehensive interpretation of Christianity is the distinguishing characteristic of the Denominational Mind. The denomination is sustained because groups of Christians hold that this interpretation more nearly expresses the spirit, the truth, and the essential character of Christianity than other competing interpretations, and that loyalty to the best one knows demands the continued support of this denomination for the establishment of the true Christian faith.

Racial, political, social, and economic factors lead frequently to subdivisions of those who are in practical agreement as to the accepted interpretation of Christianity. A spiritual unity within these exists and waits only a favorable opportunity for an organic expression. The strength of denominationalism inheres in the free devotion of its members, inspired by loyalty to Christian truth as they understand it. The denomination, as a social agency, offers itself as the necessary and the most effective means of establishing this understanding of Christian truth. However, the historical survey of the rise of the denominations does not reveal always the type of free action that the above principle suggests.

Each distinct interpretation of Christianity rests upon a basis of agreement and disagreement with other interpretations. The spiritual leadership of Jesus Christ is accepted by all professing Christians. The Bible is also recognized as a guide in faith and practice. Christianity, it is affirmed, affords spiritual benefits surpassing any other religion. Differences arise as to the divinity of Christ, the means of salvation, the value and authority of the Bible, the method of admission to church membership, the authority of the denomination or church, the value of the sacraments, the acceptance of creeds, the relation of Church and State, the orders of the Christian ministry, the authority of the clergy, the type of church government, the forms of public worship; and the doctrinal basis of salvation, of growth in grace, and of the future life.

If the history of the origin of these denominations, over two hundred and fifty in the United States alone, is enmeshed in political and other secular elements, the conflicting beliefs and practices of the followers of Christ in modern times presents at first sight a confusion worse confounded.

The furniture of the Christian place of worship suggests the deepest cleavage in these varied interpretations of Christianity. In the one, the worshipers turn their faces toward the altar; in the other, toward the pulpit. The one grounds salvation in the sacraments, and the officiant is a priest; the other grounds salvation in a personal trust in Jesus Christ, and the leader of worship is a preacher of the Gospel. To the former belong the Eastern Churches, the Roman Church, and the Anglo-Catholic group in the Church of England and its ecclesiastical off-shoots; to the later, all evangelical Christian bodies, who require the profession of a personal faith in Jesus Christ as the prerequisite to full membership.

The two groups accept the divinity of Christ and acknowledge him as Saviour, but differ as to the means of salvation. The one affirms that baptism is necessary to salvation; the other, that faith alone is necessary. The one holds to sacramentarianism; the other, to evangelicalism. The one develops a highly elaborated hierarchical organization in which the Episcopacy, the rule of the bishop, in the Roman Church specifically the Bishop of Rome, is central; the other, while ordaining some to the ministry of the Word, recognizes the universal priesthood of all believers. The former groups have sought and secured the support of the State, and, except in Soviet Russia and in Roman Catholic countries which have adopted the separation of Church and State, they still enjoy the support of the State; the latter groups, except the Lutheran State Churches of Germany, Denmark, Sweden and Norway, and the Presbyterian church of Scotland, sustain no such relationship.

In the sacramentarian group may easily be discerned the influence of the Hellenistic Mind, especially in the emphasis placed by the Greek Catholics on orthodoxy; the influence of the Roman and Sacerdotal Minds, especially in the emphasis placed by the Roman Catholics upon the Papacy; and the influence of the Nationalistic Mind, especially in the Church of England, which seeks through the theory of the Apostolic Succession of her bishops to interpret the National Church as being in the unbroken line of descent from the Holy Orthodox Catholic Church, which had in the third century made the sacrament of baptism the basis of salvation.

The evangelical group, rejecting tradition and all centralized church authority founded upon the claims of the Popes, accept the Bible and the Bible only as authoritative and have organized their systems of doctrine, their forms of church government, their modes of worship, upon their understanding of the teachings of the New Testament.

The multiplication of denominations results from religious liberty, one phase of which is the right of private interpretation of the Scriptures, accompanied by the freedom to live in accordance with one's own religious convictions. The number of the denominations today is therefore not so surprising as the fact that they are not more numerous.

Humanism, the cultural movement which accompanied the Protestant Reformation, insists upon the right of the individual to determine for himself by research and by rational reflection what is the truth in every line of thought. This attitude of mind leads to the adoption of the scientific method and the strengthening of the scientific spirit. Humanism, recognizing the intellectual rights of the trained individual mind, contributes much to both political and religious liberty.

Voluntarism, holding in harmony with the New Testament that Christianity is a divine tender of saving grace to be obtained through a personal faith in Jesus Christ, conditions salvation upon a purely voluntary relationship of the believer with God, unobtainable through any other means. Therefore civil or ecclesiastical coercion or social pressure of any kind or character cannot create the saving Christian experience. This contention, which is the basis of the Anabaptist movement and later the Anti-Pedobaptist protest in England and in the American Colonies, finds its logical consummation in complete civil religious freedom and the separation of Church and State.

Modern denominationalism may be said to have its beginning with the Peace of Westphalia when Roman Catholics, Lutherans and Zwinglians, are granted within defined limits the right to exist undisturbed. Religious absolutism slowly gives way to religious toleration, as religious toleration is now giving way to religious liberty.

The denominations differ widely as to the authority which each, as a social agency, exerts over its own members and as to the right they claim to possess in influencing and controlling secular social life. Except in the Society of Friends and a few minor groups, baptism is the method by which the individual is inducted into church membership. Infant baptism enables the two Catholic bodies and the State Churches to embrace within their folds all who are subjects of the civil authority, thus making church membership and citizenship co-extensive. Where the union of Church and State did not or does not now exist, the compulsory baptism of infants, through the co-operation of parents and church officials, creates an actual or potential membership and enables the church to include all members of families connected with it. The extent of the authority exercised by the denomination depends upon the definition it gives to itself as an institution, whether it conceives of itself as divine or as partly divine and partly human.

The elements of division which enter into denominationalism, at first sight, appear to be linguistic, historical, doctrinal, sacramental, social, moral, and administrative, with racial, cultural, economic, and psychological elements also present. However, all these are subsidiary; the basic difference lies in the definition each denomination gives to itself as a religious institution or church, the authority it exercises, the functions it performs, and the specific mission it undertakes to fulfil.

The New Testament presents the Christian Church as a body of believers in Jesus Christ, meeting together for mutual edification. The Church is simply the institution to which the disciples of Christ belong. It exists to maintain public worship, to proclaim Christian belief, and to promote Christ-likeness of character, "Where two or three are gathered together in my name, there am I in the midst of them," is the earliest of all descriptions of a Christian church. An ideal spiritual body, composed of all believers everywhere makes up the Church of Christ, called sometimes the flock, the body of Christ or the bride of Christ. Ignatius

(c. 115), writing to the Christians in Smyrna, says, "Where Christ is, there is the Catholic (Universal) Church." Tertullian (b. 150-160), who says, "Outside of Christ there is no salvation," is followed by Cyprian (c. 200), who says, "Outside of the Church there is no salvation," and who also teaches that there is "no church where there is no bishop." Personal attachment to Jesus Christ is being supplanted by loyalty to an institution, and the termination of the process is reached in the contention of the Roman hierarchy that outside of the Roman Church there is no salvation, that the Roman Church and the Kingdom of God are identical, and that the Roman Church possesses the right to exercise all temporal and spiritual authority. Coercion, the right to persecute, is inherent in the constitution of the Roman Church because it is declared to be a divine institution and as such to possess the divine right of an unconditioned authority and monopoly in the realm of religion and in all human affairs.

The Roman Church possesses, on this assumption, a position superior to the Scriptures; therefore it has from time to time forbidden laymen to read them, condemned translation into the vernacular, incited civil authorities not only to the burning of Bibles, but even to the burning at the stake of those who possess copies of the translations, and in more recent times has defended on the ground of its obscurity, the withholding of the Bible from the people. Persuasion is a means rarely used by the Roman Church. Its educational program begins with special instruction as to the divine origin of the Church and the supremacy of the Papacy. The Roman Catholic Church is a denomination that uses coercion, admonition, education, and sometimes persuasion to promote an interpretation of Christianity in which the institution is represented as possessing absolute authority on earth.

The Greek Catholic Church rejects the Papacy, centers authority in the action of the ecumenical or general councils held before the severing of relations with the Roman Catholic Church in 1054, adjusts its organization to the civil authorities in countries that recognize the Church as the official Church, and emphasizes its traditional liturgy, but has contributed little to education or social betterment. Its weakness has been disclosed in its present plight within the Soviet Republics.

The evangelical denominations agree in accepting the Bible as the authoritative guide in worship, faith, and practice. Each endeavors to prove that its form of government, confession of faith, and Christian life conform more closely to the teachings of the New Testament than those of other religious bodies. Following the Reformation, the denominations that are willing and able to secure the support of the State, use coercive measures to destroy all other interpretations that seek corporate expression. The dissenting denominations suffer many penalties for their nonconformity, and seek the establishment of the principle of religious toleration, while many of their adherents, with the development of Colonial America, find an asylum in the New World.

Given the right of reading and interpreting the Bible, it follows that honest differences as to its teaching will arise; and if the individual posseses the privilege of following the dictates of his conscience, as he does in the United States and in some other countries, he recognizes that as a true Christian he must do all that he can to promulgate the truth as he sees it. Therefore he associates himself with others of a like faith. Loyalty to Christ demands nothing less than this. "Men of light and leading who have reached conclusions of fundamental importance, not otherwise sufficiently recognized, have become the founders of great evangelical denominations," [62] and bodies so formed have become the most indestructible of all voluntary social organisms.

Those in the United States that hold most tenaciously to the evangelical principle limit their membership solely to those who give evidence of being truly regenerated, recognize the spiritual parity of all believing Christians, and form their local bodies upon the principles of a spiritual democracy. These evangelical bodies lay great emphasis upon voluntarism, use persuasion as the method of extending their membership, encourage education, especially the religious training of the young, deny that there is any grace-giving element inherent in the sacraments, and reject the compulsory baptism of infants, on the ground that it is an invasion of the potential religious liberty of the infant, who is necessarily at this time incapable of hearing the Gospel and believing in Jesus Christ. Admonition is based upon New Testament precepts, and coercion is limited to the dismissal of unruly members from the fellowship of the church. Under this description, varying in matters lying outside of the above statement, there are, according to the 1936 Religious Census, more than fifty denominations, of which the Baptist family, nineteen in number, is by far numerically the strongest.

Denominationalism in the United States has been imported and indigenous. During the Colonial Period nineteen religious bodies, including the Church of England, the Congregationalists, the Dutch Reformed, the Lutherans, the Friends, the Roman Catholics, the Baptists, the Presbyterians, the United Brethren, the Moravians, and the Mennonites, established congregations, while nine new native denominations came into existence, totaling twenty-eight. By 1850 the number was increased to fifty-three; by 1900, to one hundred and twenty; by 1916, to two hundred; and by 1926, to two hundred and thirteen. Racial and linguistic differences account for many of these religious divisions. The nature and function of the Lord's Supper divide Lutherans, Calvinists and Zwinglians; the mode, subject, and function of baptism separate the Baptist and Pedo-baptist groups; doctrinal emphasis, often on minor theological points, accounts for many more divisions while the three types of polity, the Congregational, the Presbyterian and the Episcopal, have played an important rôle in dividing many who are practically agreed as to doctrine.

The worth to Christianity of a denomination is measured by its reverential spirit, its intellectual consistency in harmonizing tested knowledge and revealed truth, its efficiency as a social agency directed toward Christian ends, its ability to inspire its membership to live Christlike lives, its power to command the loyalty of its constituency through personal service and sacrificial generosity in carrying forward its program of missionary endeavor and its success in exhibiting in personal and communal life the ascendancy of the governing principles of the Kingdom of God. The denominations whose influence and numbers steadily increase are notably successful in emphasizing some, if not all, of these features.

Denominationalism within the United States exhibits organized Christianity functioning without legal restraints. The multiplicity of the sects is the despair of those who cannot conceive of Chris-

tian unity except in terms of organic church union. They dream
of a united Christendom in terms of an institutionalized ecclesiastical monopoly. Unity amid diversity, in which devotion to Jesus
Christ is grounded in voluntarism, is not the goal of their efforts.

The last two centuries of Christianity reveal within the United
States the consequences that follow the enjoyment of religious
liberty. The Census of Religious Bodies in the United States,
1936, reports the Roman Catholic membership, which includes its
entire population, as 19,914,937, largely foreign-born or descendants of foreign-born who have come to this country since 1880.
There are thirty-seven denominations which trace their ecclesiastical descent from some one of the State Churches in the Old
World. At least thirteen denominations derive their doctrine and
polity from the Reform led by John Calvin, while nineteen others
have adopted the name of Methodist, indicating a connection
with the evangelistical movement of the eighteenth century, led
by John Wesley. To the latter might be added thirty-two other
bodies, particularly those which emphasize holiness in Christian
living, that have come into existence largely through the influence
of leaders who were formerly Methodists. The democratic group,
emphasizing religious freedom and voluntarism, most of them im-
mersionists, embrace fifty bodies, of which the Baptists are by far
the most numerous. In general, the Methodists and the Baptists
stress persuasion or evangelism; the Presbyterians, education and
doctrine; many of the smaller groups, especially the Holiness
bodies, perfection, and admonition; the nationalistic group, the
preservation of their linguistic and cultural inheritance and a devotion to the doctrine and polity of the parent State Church; the
sacramentarian group, ecclesiastical authority and uniformity in
worship.

Denominationalism, grounded upon religious liberty tenders to
every individual the privilege of choosing the religious faith to
which he will give allegiance. The Bible is held as an authoritative
guide to faith and practice, and its study and personal interpretation are encouraged by all Evangelicals. Christian education has
been greatly stimulated. The Gospel has been proclaimed at
home and abroad. Competition has proved to be as beneficial in
religion as in business. The bodies which have shown the greatest

growth and have been strengthened the least by immigration are those that have exercised the least social pressure and have used persuasion as the prime means of propagating their interpretations of Christianity.

Every form of religious coercion diminishes as religious freedom is extended. The trend is in the direction of greater liberty, which points to the continuance of denominationalism. With the growth of Christian loyalty to the convictions which unite the group into a denomination, there is coming an appreciation of the interpretations and the ministries of other groups, resulting in a larger Christian fellowship and an inter-denominational co-operation. As this spirit grows, denominationalism will cease to be sectarian, for the various groups will be spiritually united in love and loyalty to Jesus Christ. A number of these bodies have entered into organic union and others are in the conference stage. The emphasis is being placed upon the elements of agreement found in these Christian divisions, and this emphasis is being intensified by the recognition of the serious danger confronting all religion everywhere throughout the world.

XVII

The Scientific Mind

"A little philosophy inclineth a man's mind to atheism, but depth in philosophy bringeth men's minds about to religion."—FRANCIS BACON.

THE OUTSTANDING FACT in the modern religious situation is the trend toward the de-spiritualization of all life. A lessened emphasis upon the supernatural logically follows the interpretation of religion as a purely natural human experience. The loyalty of vast multitudes of humanity to their inherited religions is in many ways more active than ever before in human history, and this quickened devotion may have been evoked by a sensing of the crisis which all the religions of the world now face. Christianity is bearing the brunt of this world-wide attack. Since it claims to be the only religion worthy of all acceptation, and possesses an acknowledged pre-eminence in lands where western learning is most widely diffused, the denial of all supernatural objectivity has created for Christianity the greatest and most difficult intellectual problem of its long and eventful history. Confessedly, the mental climate in which the modern man lives lies within scientific latitudes, and his intellectual life is stimulated by the ozone of the scientific spirit. More and more, the educated man has his habitat in the observable world of phenomena; claims to hold only that which he is able to prove, and is becoming more indifferent, if not more critical and impatient, toward every religion that affirms a supernatural experience of heavenly grace.

The Scientific Mind is the fusion of all groups of thinkers who posit orderliness in the universe, who seek a clearer understanding of facts, their interrelationships and their rational implications; fertilized by a passion to discover, to know, and to describe accurately the phenomenal aspects of the world in which we live; based upon the theory that the consequences which follow antecedents illustrate universal and invisible law, enabling one rightly to interpret all the changes that occur, from the activities of the atom to the whole cosmic process. The method of investigation is the assumption of a hypothesis followed by experimentation, the observation of results, and a generalization which is applicable to all like situations. The soil out of which the Scientific Mind grows has a stratum of magic, underlaid by another of myth; and therefore the scientific study of the Scientific Mind requires that our investigation shall begin with myth and magic.

There are five periods generally recognized in the development of science: Primitive Myth, Pseudo-Scientific Magic, Pioneer Observation, Mathematical Measurement, and Biological Evolution. Each presents a distinct way of thinking about the world in which we live, based upon an accepted theory which undertakes to account for the changes that are going on in the universe. These divisions are not chronological, but represent varying levels of human culture.

The lower races are still in the Myth Period. They interpret the forces of nature as ruled by rival gods, and whatever science or trustworthy knowledge they possess is inextricably enmeshed in their religious beliefs and practices. The universal trend is toward the identification of individual gods with natural forces. The priests are the possessors of whatever knowledge exists and they use it for the strengthening of the cult. The study of seasonal and stellar changes is very old.

The Babylonian priests use their scientific knowledge in working out an elaborate system of astral divination and in the exorcising of evil spirits by magical rites; the Egyptian priests employ their discovered facts in the interest of attaining, through magical means, salvation after death. Comparatively early, under the influence of Greek philosophy, the conception of a theogony, a world ruled by gods, gives place to a cosmogony, a world ruled by natural principles; impersonal forces or elements supplant the divinities of the Greek myths.

The basis of modern science is laid by Thales, Heracleitus, Anaximenes, Anaximander, Empedocles, Anaxagoras, Democritus, Pythagoras, Plato, and, greatest of all, Aristotle. Each is a philosopher, seeking to explain the universe in terms which posi-

orderliness as universal. During the period between 300 B.C. and
A.D. 500, the Greeks are getting nearer and nearer to scientific
truth. A level of culture, confessedly restricted in area, is attained,
in which magic and superstition are beaten back.

The Dark Ages, with the return of the supremacy of magic, follow; and the thirty generations of Greek speculation, with much
scientific achievement, is succeeded by thirty generations of
Græco-Roman and Medieval speculation, with little or no scientific progress. Rome inherits a bias in favor of superstition and is
tolerant toward all provincial cults. The belief in magic is nowhere opposed throughout this period. "Magic can be found in
the arts, in astronomy, in chemistry, in mathematics and in medicine, down through the very alphabet of knowledge." [63] Astrology
develops into a learned superstition with astrologers, toward the
close of the Middle Ages, serving as honored advisers of royalty
and the rich nobility. Alchemy, or chemistry wedded to magic,
founded upon beliefs in the transmutation of metals, in the universal medicine, in the philosopher's stone, and in the elixir of life,
wins the confidence of Medieval Europe. The earth is the center
of the universe; man is the end of creation; the Roman Catholic
Church possesses the keys which open the doors of heaven to
man; magic, though sometimes condemned by the Church, is universally recognized, and its powers are greatly feared. Within these
limits, credulity seems to possess no bounds, and the science of the
Period of Magic is primarily concerned with "the task of bringing
system into superstition."

The Age of Pioneer Observation, based upon the assumption of
orderliness in nature, begins with Nicholas Copernicus (1473-
1543), whose astronomical theories are not published until shortly
before his death, thirty years after his discovery that "the sun,
sitting on the royal throne, governs the family of the stars." The
fiery Bruno (1548-1600) thinks out the Copernican system to its
end, and declares the stars to be solar systems, each the center of
a new universe. For this, he is condemned by the Church authorities and burned at the stake. Tycho Brahe (1546-1601), the first
great observer in astronomy, over a period of twenty years carries
on his investigations, in the observatory erected through the generosity of the King of Denmark. Johann Kepler (1571-1630),

working over these calculations, discovers the elliptical paths of the planets and their speed limits. Galileo (1564-1642), turning the newly invented telscope heavenward, confirms the laws of Kepler, and by his experiments with falling bodies, dropped from the leaning tower of Pisa, destroys "the old dualism—the belief that there are two realms, the heavens above, perfect and unchangeable, and below the earth, imperfect and changeable. In brief, the universe now becomes one, heaven is brought to earth and earth is put in the heavens. There are no longer superior and inferior, but all bodies have equal rights." [64]

Galileo discovers with his little telescope the phases of Venus and Mercury, the four moons of Jupiter, the spots on the sun, the mountains on the moon, and the rings of Saturn. In his work, *The Two Chief Systems of the World*, he gives, in dialogue form, the arguments for the old and the new theories of the universe, the argument for the latter being much the stronger. He is condemned by the Church and forced to recant his declaration "that the earth moves."

Isaac Newton (1642-1727), the discoverer of the law of universal gravitation, formulates the principle of the unity of the physical universe by proving that all the various bodies within it "obey a common mathematical law."

Francis Bacon (1561-1626) introduces the inductive method, that of reasoning from a part to a whole, from the individual to the universal, from particulars to generals, as the only correct mode of elaborating facts. This philosophical induction infers that whatever has been observed or established as to a part, individual, or species may on the ground of analogy be affirmed or received of the whole to which it belongs.

Science, at the close of the Age of Pioneer Observation, posits an ever-changing universe in which Being is giving place to Becoming, and Becoming in every phase reveals the operation of mathematical law. The interpretation of the physical world is grounded upon unceasing change, exhibiting an orderliness which may be described in mathematical terms. This theory underlies the achievements of science in the age that follows, in which new emphasis is placed upon induction as a method of scientific discovery. To Galileo must be given the credit for creating mechanics as the mathematical theory of motion, thereby giving to the scientist a sound basis for his experimentation. By isolating simple forms of occurrence, the scientist is able to subject them to measurement, on the ground of which he formulates the underlying mathematical law. All natural phenomena, according to the theory, are in essence motions.

Science, limiting its investigation to phenomena, erects as its goal the discovery, within the processes of nature, of mathematical law. The philosophers, who follow the lead of science, interpret Nature as bodies in motion, thus freeing themselves altogether from the control of theology, and they create a materialistic system of philosophy, in which the thesis is propounded that the universe is a machine. The ancient Pythagoreans found the abiding essence of the world to inhere in mathematical relationships; the Age of Pioneer Observation, directing its study primarily toward the heavenly bodies, closes with the foundation laid for "empirical Pythagoreanism," as the reliable and trustworthy method of scientific investigation,

From the viewpoint of the history of thought, three epoch-making facts are to be observed: 1. The field of Science is strictly defined as the study of the motion of bodies; 2. All observation and experimentation is made upon the basis of mathematical law, and measurement is adopted as the scientific method; 3. Science is divorced from theology and the philosophy which bases itself solely upon scientific conclusions creates materialism; for if the universe be a mechanism, nature is de-spiritualized and there is no place left within it for the supernatural. The conflict between Science and Theology begins. The issue is: "Can the universe be explained in its totality by natural causes that illustrate the mathematical principle?"

The Age of Mathematical Measurement extends from the adoption of the mathematical theory in the investigation of nature to the publication of *The Origin of Species* by Charles Darwin in 1859. The progress of science during the period is marked by the introduction of mathematical notions into subjects which formerly were not thought to be mathematical, thereby creating new sciences, such as chemistry, physics, electro-magnetism, and other related subjects. The qualitative conceptions of alchemy give way, following the discoveries of Priestley (1733-1804) and Lavoisier (1743-1794) to the theory of chemical elements entering quantitatively into combination, the mathematical basis of which is discovered by Dalton (1766-1844) in his atomic theory. Experiments made by Gilbert (1540-1603), Du Fay (1698-1739), Galvani (1737-1798) and others, prepare the way for Michael Faraday (1791-1867) and Clerk Maxwell (1831-1879) to unify the study of electricity, magnetism, and light, under the same general mathematical principle. The theory of the conservation of energy, set forth by Helmholtz (1821-1894), furnishes a final systematic generalization, applicable to all the physical sciences and completes the conquest of the mathematical theory in the investigation of the physical world.

France, with her great algebraists of the seventeenth century, leads in the development of pure mathematics. In no other country is the scientific spirit stronger or is scientific knowledge more widely diffused. Germany develops a magnificent system of universities, which emphasize research more than the mere teaching of knowledge, and from 1825 onward their laboratories enrich immeasurably the scientific understanding of the world. England furnishes a great array of scientific names of the first order, each carrying on his investigations within his own chosen field. France leads in the number of scientific works; Germany, in scientific research; England, in fructifying scientific ideas.

The introduction of the mathematical principle into the investigation of nature stimulates the formulation of new systems of philosophy and creates new issues in the field of religion. Descartes (1596-1650) endeavors to harmonize the new science and the old religion. He holds that the world is a machine and that man is also a machine possessed by a soul or mind. He posits, as the single principle of highest and absolute certainty, the existence of consciousness: "I think, therefore I am." He is searching for the elementary truths of consciousness, and of these self-consciousness is the first. All things that are as clear and as distinct as self-consciousness must be equally true. These he calls innate ideas, and among them he places the existence of God.

Spinoza (1632-1677) undertakes to give to philosophy a mathematical form. He identifies God with Nature, from one point of view, "the universal world-essence," from the other, "the sum-total of the individual things in which this essence exists." Spinoza's doctrine of God may be described as a mystical pantheism. Leibnitz (1646-1716), the inventor of the differential calculus, recognizing the trend which makes mathematics the basis of all empirical knowledge, endeavors to unite the religious and the scientific interests of his day by reconciling the teleological or the purposive view with the increasingly popular mechanical interpretation of the world. He posits life as the principle to be used in explaining nature, and he concludes that the universe exhibits the purpose of God.

The Calvinism of the eighteenth century reinforces teleology by emphasizing, in its doctrine of God, divine omnipotence, and in its doctrine of Providence, divine immutable decrees. Science, philosophy, and theology starting from different positions, travel toward a point of agreement, a deterministic interpretation of the universe. The first accepts mathematics as a guide; the second, reason; and the third, the Bible interpreted as the revelation of the sovereignty of God and His eternal decrees.

A spiritual fatigue possesses all Christian bodies, Roman, Anglican, Lutheran, Reformed, and Independent alike. Deism, holding that God exists wholly apart from the physical universe and that God's operation upon it is purely mechanical, formulates a religion which is declared to be natural, in that no belief is held which does not conform to the canons of reason. This movement, rising in England during the last half of the seventeenth century and continuing through the eighteenth, illustrates the impact of the Scientific Mind upon English and later Continental thought. La Mettrie (1709-1751), followed by Holbach (1723-1789), popularizes Materialism, the belief that the universe can be sufficiently explained by the existence and the nature of matter. The thought movement of the eighteenth century, called by the Germans *die Aufklärung* or "The Enlightenment," receives its impetus from the skepticism of Bayle, from the scientific doctrines of Newton and from the theory of knowledge propounded by John Locke. Lessing, Mendelssohn and Herder in Germany, Voltaire, Rousseau, Condillac, D'Alembert and Diderot in France lead in the development of the movement on the continent of Europe.

From Copernicus to Immanuel Kant (1724-1804), the leaders of thought, whose point of view is that of the Scientific Mind, are striving to explain all the changes that are going on within the universe by measurement, or the application of mathematical principles. The hypothesis which they adopt is that the universe and all the bodies within it are mechanical, and therefore may be mathematically described. The world is a machine and is run by mechanical forces. Christian apologists, like Archbishop Paley in his "*Evidence of Christianity and Natural Religion*," argue that a mechanism presupposes a mechanician. Leibnitz declares that mechanism cannot explain the world of microcosms.

Kant, purposing to vindicate the fundamental verities of religion, namely, the beliefs in God, immortality, and freedom, addresses himself to this question: "What does the intellect supply, so as to bring into the casual material gained by experience the logical qualities of universality and certainty?" His treatment of the three main points of his theory of knowledge, "the nature of time and space, the difference of appearance and reality, and the formative or active principle of the human intellect," leads to the conclusion that knowledge is not merely collected, arranged, and abstracted but "it is essentially also created" by the human reason. "The starry heavens above, and the moral law within" fill him with holy awe, the former furnishing verifiable knowledge of reality called natural science, and the latter, with its immediate knowledge of good and evil, making available "another and equally indisputable revelation of truth." He gives the primacy to the knowledge and the affirmations of this moral world within, which he calls the realm of the Practical Reason.

The scientists of the Age of Measurement under a mathematical sign, seek to conquer the universe. Kant, more than any other philosopher, stays their victorious advance. The conflict between mathematics and morals begins. Not until the Scientific Mind has extended the reign of the mathematical principle over the whole domain of mind, will religion, though bitterly assailed, be overcome. So long as man is conscious of a personal moral responsibility, reverence will express itself in action, and the foundation of religion will stand secure. Science has a realm coextensive with law; morality has a realm coextensive with personal freedom; and religion or reverence in action has its factual existence in the experience of the individual who is sure that he is free and therefore responsible to God.

The extension of mathematical theory to organic life marks the beginning of a new epoch in scientific history and ushers in the Age of Biological Evolution. "Just as Newton took the idea of gravitational attraction and transformed it into an impersonal law of a force that varied inversely as the square of the distance and directly as the product of the masses, so Darwin took the poetic metaphor of the struggle for existence and transformed it into an impersonal cause." [65] Newton laid the foundation of the modern physical sciences; Darwin, of the modern biological and mental sciences.

Evolution, in its simplest form, posits orderliness in universal change, and the student who adopts this theory seeks, through the application of some accepted scientific method, to formulate his observations and the results of his experiments into thought as ordered knowledge. The range of his investigation extends from the nebula to the solar system with its encircling planets, from the electron to the profoundest thought of man. The goal of his effort is a generalization which places all observable phenomena under the law of continuity, or cause and effect. Interpreting cause and effect as merely the antecedent and the subsequent in time, he describes the process in terms which presuppose the mathematical principle. This method, when applied to the study of the mind, becomes Behaviorism, the basis of which is the interpretation of personal behavior as a psychical mechanism.

The fundamental ideas of Darwinism are natural selection, variation, and the struggle for existence; the purpose being to explain how the present forms of life come, how species and races have become so widely differentiated, and why other forms of life have altogether disappeared. Darwin and those who follow him unite the organic and the inorganic, mind as well as matter, under the reign of natural law. Evolution soon becomes the ruling idea in all the sciences that deal with human nature.

Science, through its new understanding of the physical world, through its discovery of natural forces and of the methods by which these forces may be harnessed to serve humanity, creates

our modern industrial civilization. All institutions of higher learning throw wide their gates to the incoming of the teachers of
Modern Science, which is grounded upon the theory of evolution.
The phenomena of religion are subjected to the scrutiny of scientific investigators. Western learning and scientific knowledge become synonymous. The Scientific Mind gains the ascendancy
in modern thought, and faith in Science is given a primacy over
all other beliefs in the minds of an increasing number of thoughtful men.

Christianity has been forced by the Scientific Mind to face a
new and disturbing problem, in many ways the most critical in all
its history. "As 'the reign of law' was verified in one region after
another of the universe open to our investigation; as a growing
acquaintance with the immeasurable range of the physical order
in time and space dwarfed more and more all human concerns in
comparison of their material environment, as proofs of the intimate connection of the bodily organism with mental life accumulated, Christianity, with its miracles, its anthropocentric scheme of
things, culminating in the affirmation that God was incarnate as
an individual in our species, its promise of a life after death,
seemed to many to be fighting a losing battle against a 'naturalism'
whose outlook was more in harmony with our new knowledge of
the material world." [66]

Thoughtful men, facing Evolution, fall into one of four groups:

1. Those who accept it as an established doctrine and build
their philosophy of life upon it;

2. Those who hold that in the evolutionary process is seen
God's chosen way for accomplishing his divine purpose in the
universe;

3. Those who recognize the theory as possessing great practical
value as a guide to scientific inquiry, which they limit to the measurable aspects of the phenomenal world;

4. Those who deny the theory *in toto*, on the ground that it
cannot be brought into harmony with divine revelation.

Thus Modern Science has laid the foundation for disbelief in
God, and this disbelief, spreading throughout the civilized world,
has burst forth in the Blitzkrieg against God.

XVIII

Modern Science and the Christian God

"The Christian religion, in its essence, is a doctrine of God and a life in God."

THE ACHIEVEMENTS of modern science have been so rapid and so transforming that it is difficult to visualize the world of even fifty years ago. The machine, as the instrument for the production of economic goods, has largely supplanted the work of human hands. Industrial civilization is running in high gear, with applied science at the steering wheel. The air brake, the block signal, the automatic car coupler have promoted the safety of railway travel. The typewriter, the telephone, the cash register, the adding machine have transformed the conduct of business. Electricity illuminates the streets, while the trolley car, the automobile and the electric light signal contribute to the rapid movement of urban masses. The transparent photograph film and the moving picture machine have created the world's most popular amusement. The phonograph and the radio are bringing into the American home every form of amusement and cultural enjoyment which the ear can enjoy. The mowing machine, the grain harvester, the disk plow and the gas-driven tractor are compelling farm laborers to become skilled mechanics. The battleship, the submarine, the bombing plane, the use of T.N.T. and the increase of artillery-bearing tanks, have multiplied the horrors of war. Communication the world over has attained the speed of light; and the inhabited globe has become a whispering gallery. These inventions have changed the ways of living in all civilized lands.

The intellectual environment of the modern man differs widely from that of his fathers. The immensity of space, the vast stretches of time, the pettiness of this earth contrasted with the total reach of the stellar universe, the study of the autobiography of our planet read by turning the leaves of its geological strata, have so modified modern conceptions that the man of today, in very truth, looks out upon a new heaven and a new earth. The belief in the uniformity of all natural processes is more prevalent and the attitude of suspended judgment in regard to all things that cannot be incontestibly proved, is more widespread than ever before in human history. In such a climate, any suggestion of the supernatural is viewed with suspicion.

The present belief is that consciousness is dependent upon a constantly ever-changing environment, that all sensations that enter into the material of human experience are vibrations to which the senses respond, and, further, that if all motion suddenly ceased, immediately unconsciousness would be the doom of every human mind. The older view was that the mind possessed fixed ideas that corresponded to fixed, unchangeable realities. So our fathers thought and spoke of man as a being; of God, as the Supreme Being; of matter, as unchangeable; of fire, water, heat, air, as elements; of the soul of man, as an entity, and of the powers of man as faculties. The development of the new conception of the universe, in which everything from the electron to the procession of the solar systems, is declared to be in ceaseless motion, represents the greatest reconstruction in human thought since man began to reflect upon his relationship to the world in which he finds himself.

Science maintains that energy is the basis of all things, and that the universe, from its smallest conceivable particle, the baby electron, estimated to be a four hundred thousandth part of a full-grown atom, to the celestial universe, now reckoned to extend at least over a space of 180 quadrillion light-years, is a cosmos in motion. Evolution is the assumption, proclaimed as a scientific doctrine, that all cosmic changes, from the inconceivably infinitesimal to the procession of the stars; from the unicellular structure, the simplest form of life, to the brain of a Socrates, always and everywhere exhibit orderly change and that therefore everything in the universe reveals the presence and the operation of natural law. A belief in God is not necessary to the calculations of the scientists or the conclusions they reach.

When the scientists entered the domain of religion and developed the three disciplines, the psychology of religion, the history of religions, and the comparative study of religion, a new situation emerged. Limiting their investigations to the observable aspects of religion and assuming all religions to be phases of social evolution, these students interpreted this broad field of exploration as a purely human process, which in its noblest forms of behavior contributed to the conservation of socially approved values.

Thus it has come about that the conflict of the Christian faith is no longer with the scientific statements that contradict the Christian traditional position but with the scientific explanation of all religions, including Christianity. Recent writers are sensing this and are calling upon the leaders of every religion throughout the world to co-operate in defending the fundamental claims of religion, namely, the reality of the objects or Object of worship. This is the underlying appeal of the Appraisal Commission of the Laymen's Foreign Mission Enquiry, as given in the book issued by the Commission and entitled Re-thinking Missions. It is not the scientists' new view of the universe but the new interpretation of religion which has transferred the conflict between Science and Religion to a wholly new terrain. It is the postulate that religion is "a human enterprise, an organization of human life, an experience, a social bond and an aspiration," [67] which is forcing religionists everywhere to defend the validity of their beliefs.

The charge is made that scientists who retain some religious faith do so only by compartmentalizing within the individual personality two patterns of thought, whose integration they refuse to attempt. "If the biologist who is an evolutionist in his laboratory, is, while in church, a believer in special creation, the Virgin Birth, miracles and bodily resurrection of the dead, it is only because two aspects of his personality are separated. If brought into contact in the course of discussion or during preparation of a statement of his views, a reorganization would be necessary." [68] It is these two patterns of thought, the scientific and the religious, which today are in conflict

Since scientific subjects largely predominate in the curricula of the American institutions of higher learning and since, in most of these schools, the scientific explanation of religion is the one given in the classroom, it follows that college men and women of today in increasing numbers are able to preserve a semblance of loyalty to their inherited Christian faith only by the retention of these two patterns of thought, one organized about the scientific method and the other, about the religious beliefs taught them in childhood. If the mind insists upon consistency of thought, an inner conformity is sought. The easiest way out is either conformity without conviction or a cultivated indifference to the imperative claims that religion makes. Probably a large majority of college graduates are taking one or the other of these two courses.

These conditions create in the United States, and indeed throughout the civilized world, the most ominous situation evangelical Christianity has ever faced. "Is there a God?" has suddenly become the outstanding question in modern thought. Liberal Christians are ceasing to proclaim the God and Father of our Lord Jesus Christ as the Object of an unrivalled human devotion, on the ground of His eternal existence, power and holiness, and are seeking, through the use of the scientific procedure, to find in the complicated and contradictory phenomena of the world's religions, including the lowest as well as the highest, some common principle, scientifically established, on which to ground an idea of God.

Many take more advanced positions. They affirm that religion will continue even if God, immortality and rewards and punishments play no part in religious thinking. Some are saying that man will be able to live more worthily if he surrenders all hope of a future existence. A growing number of highly educated men express the conviction that a belief in God is not essential to religion. If the word, God, is retained by such writers, the meaning is so thinned down and rarified, his divine powers are so humanized and emasculated and his objective existence so discredited, that the devout Christian cries out, "They have taken away my God!" A popular school, defining religion as man's effort to conserve the highest known social values, interprets the Christian's God as the spirit of the Christian group, inspiring its members to bring in the Kingdom of Heaven. He is real, as the college man's Alma Mater is real; He is real as the child's Santa Claus is real, "but his reality is to be found in the realm of human society rather than in the realm of cosmic processes."

Another group of thinkers, led by H. N. Wieman of the University of Chicago, are defining God in terms of axiological objectivity: "God is that character of events to which man must adjust himself in order to attain the greatest goods and avoid the greatest ills." [69] "God is precisely that object, whatever its nature may be, which will yield maximum security and abundance to all human living, when right adjustment is made. With this definition of the term, it cannot be doubted that God exists." [70] Professor Wieman pleads for the use of the scientific method in the study of the religious experience, apparently rejects in his philosophical statements the authority of any historic revelation and concludes that "the exact nature of God is still problematical and may be for many years to come."

The Christian doctrine of God, as enunciated in the historic creeds, was given rational form in a period when problems were solved by philosophy rather than by scientific experimentation. The intellectual development of the past four centuries has thrust upon Christian thought the necessity of a new apologetic. The Christian revelation of God was made in the life of Jesus of Nazareth, was translated into communicable literary form by the writers of the New Testament and enthroned as the sovereign center of inward control by the followers of Christ, who testified to the regenerating effects produced by its acceptance. Like effects have been produced in all the succeeding generations of the past, and devout living Christians everywhere bear witness and declare with gladness that they too have reproduced the experiences of the early disciples of Jesus, have been released from the enslavement of sin, and possess a vitalized serenity arising out of an enduring fellowship with God.

Christian theologians, giving today an intellectual interpretation to the Christian religion, posit and have always posited in Ultimate Reality or God three apprehensible phases. These are the self-existence, the self-disclosure and the self-impartation of God, which correspond in the New Testament and in Christian theology to the familiar terms of "the Father, the Son and the Holy Spirit." These form the incontestable elements of the Christian revelation of God. No one of them can be left out if the Christian character of the revelation is to be faithfully preserved. The

Christian religion in its essence is "a doctrine of God and a life in God."

The early Christian thinkers lived in an age that was as thoroughly philosophical as the present is scientific. Their discussions and controversial debates led to the formulation of the doctrine of the Trinity, as expressed in the Nicene and the Athanasian Creeds, and this expression was framed in current Greek philosophical terms. The Reformers accepted the historic creeds of the undivided Catholic Church as authoritative and centered their thought upon soteriology, the doctrine of salvation, stressing personal faith in Christ and salvation through divine grace.

Largely because of the scientific interpretation of religion, attention in all circles of serious thought has been directed within recent years toward the idea of God. Leading university professors have debated in a popular periodical, *The Christian Century*, the question, "Is there a God?" The book they have published, comprising their extended discussions, calls forth from John Dewey, the socially-minded but skeptical philosopher, the following comment:

"Anyone who has faced the full intellectual scope and depth of the change in the idea of the universe and of man's history, has no alternative but surrender of the older conception of God or else a broadening out of it to meet the change in the conception of the universe and history to which the God believed in is related. . . . As far as this broadening leads to greater tolerance and humaneness, it is of course to the good. But intellectually, it falls in with the change from *the* God to *a* God; it chimes with the use of the most colorless and indefinite word in the English language and with the thinning down and rarefying of the meaning of the object to which the term refers." [71]

It is not a denial of the inspiration of the Bible, a rejection of the deity of Jesus Christ or an insistence upon man as being the product of an evolutionary process, that forms the chief issue the supporters of the Christian faith today are compelled to meet; it is something even more fundamental: "Can the idea of the triune God, as held by Christians, be brought into logical harmony with the prevailing conceptions that have become personal convictions in minds hospitable to modern thought?" If this harmony is se cured, it must be achieved by showing the reasonableness and the factual or scientific character of the Christian revelation of God.

All that we know, we know within human experience. The only hope that man may reasonably entertain for acquiring any knowledge of God, if there be a God, rests upon the possibility that God is a communicating God, competent to adjust Himself to human conditions and limitations so as to enable man to receive and to understand a divine revelation. The laws that govern human communication furnish the conditions that have to be met, while the range of the human capacity to understand, fixes the limits of man's apprehension of the revelation. As Jesus says, "I have many things to say unto you, but ye cannot bear them now." For man to receive a revelation from God presupposes that God desires to communicate with man, that He meets the conditions of human communication and that the revelation when made is expressed in symbols that the human mind can understand. This is the Christian assumption or postulate regarding divine revelation.

One of the most important human characteristics is that man is a speaking animal. He is able to converse with others. The human personality is a communicating personality. Education is simply organized communication. All teaching, all preaching, all reading, as well as all conversation, illustrate the activity of one mind communicating with one or more other minds. Propaganda is communication in the interest of a program; literature, the thought of the author apperceived by another through the printed page; art, the symbolic presentation of the artist's ideal in visible form, evoking the appreciation of the beholder.

Communication is grounded upon commonness of experience in those who hold converse with one another: a common language, common interests, common knowledge, common points of view and, to a greater or less degree, a common purpose. In the analysis of any communication, we find in the communicator three distinct apprehensible phases which form a threefold relationship within the communicating personality, and to these may be given the names of the subject, the object, and the eject.

The genesis of the human communication lies within, and is the product of, the communicating personality. The source of the communication is the inner or subjective aspect of personality.

The self, as subject, sums up all past experiences, embracing the subconscious as well as the conscious stream, and is the originating source of all that is ever communicated. To this apprehensible phase of the communicating personality is given the name of the subjective selfhood.

The communication, whenever made, is the active, expressive aspect of a communicating personality in which language, or some other available vehicle, is used as the bearer of thought. The personality, viewed from this standpoint, is the objective selfhood, which is always present and active in the processes of communication.

The communicator, before a communication is made, must find in the experience of the one to whom he communicates an area of experience, belonging to and common to them both When strangers casually meet, conversation, if they have a common language, begins and the ascendant purpose in each is the discovery of a commonness of experience. This is done by a process of mutual exploration, which may be described as an ejection, leading to mutual inferences of like experiences, opinions interests and purposes common to them both. The teacher seek first to discover what he has in common with his pupil, and with this body of common knowledge clearly defined, he communi cates added information in such a form as to be understood, an thereby enlarges the content of common knowledge in the min of his pupil. This apprehensible phase of a communicating per sonality should be fully recognized and an appropriate name for i is the ejective selfhood.

Philosophy, and in large measure psychology, has overlooke this most important and essential aspect of personality, which w have chosen to call the ejective selfhood, preferring to limit it interpretation to the subject-object relationship, observable in e: perience. The study of an isolated individuality, which ignore its social contacts and relationships, cannot furnish a true an complete understanding of human experience. Personality mu: be viewed as including the subjective selfhood in which all con munication originates; the objective or expressive selfhood, whic frames and utters the communication; and the ejective selfhoo whose activity precedes and accompanies the communication.

A common language unites men and enables them to become the bearers of a common culture. A common social heritage binds together great bodies of people, creating thereby social organisms of a complex and most durable type. Common religious beliefs, purposes and ideals make for spiritual fellowship, which is the Christian term for commonness.

There are sufficient data in human experience for even the most scientifically minded among us to set up the hypothesis of God and on this basis to search for Him, "if haply we might find him." In approaching this part of our inquiry, we are reminded that the orthodox method is to assume that man is somewhat like God. This is a proper procedure if one follows the deductive method, starting with the statement that man is made "in the image of God."

This procedure is not possible, if we are to approach the inquiry in a scientific way. We must begin with the study of human experience. Knowing the definite restrictions that limit man in the reception of any communication, human or divine, the first question to be answered is, "What are the conditions, man being so cabined, cribbed and confined, which God must meet in order that man may receive and apprehend a divine revelation?" This reverses the anthropomorphic approach, and instead of saying that "man is somewhat like God," we postulate, "the only God that man can know must be in some respects like man and the structure of the mind of God must therefore be somewhat like that of the mind of man." Since there are certain laws that govern man in receiving and in making communications, we infer, on the ground of the universality of the principle of relatedness, that they must also be operative in God if He seeks to communicate with man.

The only God man can know must be known, if known at all, within human experience. If God be personal, He cannot be known by man unless He is a communicating God and seeks to communicate with man; and if He communicates so that man apprehends, He must conform to the limitations and laws that condition man's reception of any and every communication. Not only must God be personal, but He must possess the capacity of a divine adjustment to human limitations. If God be a revealing

God, the structure of the divine mind must be somewhat like the human mind. We can have no conception of what God may be, as He transcends the utmost reach of human experience, but we do know that if He be a communicating personality, we will find in Him a trinity corresponding to the trinity we find in ourselves.

The subjective selfhood of the communicating or revealing God is the ultimate source of the power, the order, the truth, the wisdom, the holiness, the love which are mediated in the several realms of human knowledge and are grasped by human minds as discoveries or revelations. The Christian name for God, viewed thus as Ultimate Reality, is Father. Upon him everything is dependent for its existence, and in this sense, He is the Absolute that the idealistic philosophers affirm.

The divine objective selfhood is the temporal, continuous active manifestation or revelation of God and is the expressive aspect of the divine Communicating Personality. The Logos is the word used in the Gospel of John for the divine expressive selfhood. All that man can know of God is known through the Eternal Logos who once tabernacled among men, bearing the name of Jesus. The earthly ministry of the One whom Christians acknowledged as Lord, was an episode, a flashing divine revelation within the limits of a human life, in the Eternal Self-disclosure of God.

The Christian God, we often say, is Christlike; but the Christian believer asserts also that all the knowledge of God we can ever have, is mediated through Christ. The world was made by him. He is the light that lighteth every man that cometh into the world. The principle of relatedness which enables us to apprehend the unity of all worlds actively exhibits his presence, power and wisdom. He is the expression of all the truth that man has found or ever will be able to find. As the Christian believer reviews divine revelation, he declares that the One, whom we know in history as Jesus of Nazareth, created the light; called unto Abraham; wrestled with Jacob; spake to Moses in the burning bush; led the children of Israel in the Wilderness; dwelt as the shekinah in the Temple; grew vocal in the messages of the prophets; "in the fullness of time" humbled Himself, becoming "in fashion as a man," and sojourned for a brief period in a human body. He lives on, penetrating the whole universe, active in every moment and present everywhere. His cosmic mission continues and will end only when "all rule and all authority and power," hostile to God the Father, shall be abolished, and all things shall be brought into harmonious relatedness, so "that God may be all in all."

The ejective phase is primary in communication because it is the originating condition in the reception of any and every communication. No man may hope for a revelation of God in whose personal experience there is nothing that can be found, as common both to God and to himself. For the majority of evangelical Christians, this common area is first experienced in a condemnation of personal sin that finds its expression in true repentance. The moral consciousness precedes this experience, and in this sense the normal evangelical experience is an outgrowth of the moral life. Wherever God finds in any individual such an area of commonness, however limited it may be, he can make to that one a self-disclosure, a revelation. If the inner life however is so disorganized and deranged, that evil is called good and good evil, an attitude which Jesus declares to be blasphemy against the Holy Spirit, no divine revelation can be made. Such a one cannot be forgiven, because there is no common area of experience between God and him on which to ground such a personal relationship.

The Holy Spirit therefore may be defined as God entering into social relations with man, and co-operating with the individual as he strives to extend within his own life the thought and the rule of God, thus enlarging the human-divine area of commonness. Koinonia is the New Testament word that is translated as "communion." It means the commonness that partners or common owners possess. The frequently recurring phrase in the Epistles, "the communion of the Holy Spirit," describes this area of human experience which the individual Christian possesses in common with God.

The ejective selfhood of God in the New Testament, usually called the Holy Spirit, determines the limits and stimulates the enlargement of this area. The supreme goal of the Christian's endeavor is so to control and to direct his creative acts that they shall express the principles that inhere in the nature of God. The Christian, devoting himself to this high enterprise, does not toil on alone and unaided: "God worketh in you both to will and to do." God ejects Himself into responsive human life, imparting Himself as "a spirit of power and of love and of a sound mind." Millions of Christians testify to this presence of God in their lives.

The revelation of God in Jesus Christ recognizes and affirms the orderliness in physical processes, the achieving of truth through rational processes, and the moral obligation to fulfil the demands of duty. The purpose that dominates his earthly life is not that of teaching science, philosophy or morality. Had he taught science, his field would have been sense data; philosophy, ideas; morality, ethical principles. His mission was to integrate personality: "He came to seek and to save that which was lost." He seeks to integrate the individual personality by inspiring the acceptance of a new inner control through which intelligent self-interest gives way to a triumphant generous-heartedness, a dynamic grounded upon a living fellowship with God. The standard of moral conduct is a generous-hearted disinterestedness: "Whatsoever ye would that men should do unto you, do ye even so unto them."

Jesus reveals God as self-imparting Fatherliness: "God so loved the world that he gave his only begotten Son, that whosoever believeth in him should not perish but have eternal life." The ideal of life is a love, inspired by Christ, that forgives wrong done, that serves sacrificially those in need, that in performance exceeds the demands of duty, that appreciates the good, the true, the beautiful, and that unifies all the activities of the individual life by ordering and doing everything to the glory of God. The responsive personality, striving to achieve this higher life, comes to know God more and more as love integrates, as the highest ideals control and as the Spirit of God guards the thoughts, the aspirations and the purposes in Christ Jesus. The Christian revelation of God is the Best News ever given to man. It affirms the love of God for man and the competency of man to live in communion with God. Every true Christian seeks to share this experienced revelation with others.

The New Testament gives a literary account of the ministry of Jesus, describes the activities of the Apostles and furnishes to receptive minds the ideas that Jesus and his followers proclaimed; but the true revelation of God is experientially known only to him who trusts, loves and serves God and his fellow men, and who gladly expresses in conduct his devotion to the ideals that Jesus embodied. Whosoever does this becomes a Christian man, a witness to the Christian revelation of God and a living witness to its truthfulness.

It is recognized that the interpretation of the Christian doctrine of the Trinity, as outlined above, is different from the one enunciated by the theologians of the fourth century. Their creeds were expressed in the terms of the current Greek philosophy, and much of their verbiage is difficult for us to apprehend, because the whole cultural background of their thinking has undergone more than a radical change; it has practically ceased to exist. With the passage of time, an age dominated by philosophy, has been succeeded by another that is now under the spell of the scientific spirit. It is maintained, however, that the historic creeds and the view here presented are in essence the same and that the latter possesses a practical value because the Christian doctrine of the Trinity is expressed largely in psychological terms. The primary purpose of this presentation is to show that the Christian revelation of God, viewed as a process, does not violate the recognized principles that underlie all communication and that the evangelical confession is therefore neither unreasonable nor incredible.

XIX

The Temptation and the Fall of
Modern Nations

"Then was Jesus led up of the spirit into the wilderness to be tempted of the devil."—MATTHEW.

THE PRINCIPAL EVENTS in the life of Jesus were birth, baptism, temptation, inaugural address at Nazareth, preaching the Gospel of the Kingdom, teaching, healing, training of disciples, death and resurrection.

The significance of his temptations has never been fully or properly evaluated. No individual, no group, no nation, no race can seriously contemplate the issues of life without entering into the three temptations that Jesus overcame, because the desire for security, the desire to be important and the desire for power are, for all who thoughtfully face the future, universal and inescapable.

The first temptation which came to Jesus, following his forty days of fasting, was to use his God-given resources in transforming loaflike stones into bread, and this dealt with his physical security. This testing comes in myriad forms to every individual as well as every social organization. Jesus found in the Hebrew Scriptures the light and leading to make his decision; "Man shall not live by bread alone, but by every word that proceedeth out of the mouth of God." Facing any decision that called for action, Jesus sought first to know the will of God. The recognition of the sovereignty of God, linked to a dominant desire to do the will of God, is the saving element in every temptation. However urgent the immediate need and however desirable and reasonable its satisfaction may seem, the ultimate control of action for every one who seeks the highest good inheres in the revelation of the divine purpose as it relates to the moral and spiritual development of man into the likeness of God.

216

As Jesus contemplated his Messianic mission, the desire for its speedy and successful accomplishment must have had strong appeal. To fling himself from a pinnacle of the temple and to appear unharmed before the crowds gathered in its courts offered a dramatic opportunity to impress his claims upon the people who were waiting and praying for the coming of their Messiah. The consciousness of possessing supernatural powers, the specific promise of divine protection given in one of the Psalms, and the urge to forward as quickly as possible his divine mission on earth, combined to make this a real temptation. Again he found in the book of Deuteronomy the guidance he needed: "Thou shalt not make trial of the Lord thy God." A miracle involving the suspension of the law of gravity had in it no moral appeal and ran athwart the divine purpose to woo man to trust in the forgiving and empowering God. The goal of Jesus was to seek and to save the lost, to bind those he found into a divine fellowship and, through the extension of this fellowship, to achieve a world community—the Kingdom of God.

The third temptation of Jesus dealt with the purpose of God as related to human institutions—the kingdoms of the inhabited earth. The strategy of Satan in the two temptations had failed. The issue is now more closely and clearly drawn. The authority over the kingdoms of the world—including all social organizations that exercise rule—is promised, provided Jesus, recognizing that evil is firmly entrenched in human life, will direct his future endeavors, giving a proper respect to this evident fact. The transformation of all mankind into the children of God is forever blocked, so Satan insisted, not only by the sinfulness inherent in human nature, but also by the evil that permeates the social order. Since the continuance of civilization, whatever its form, is conditioned upon the active functioning of institutions and social agencies, in which good and evil are inextricably intermingled—so runs the argument—the Messianic mission of Jesus cannot succeed unless a compromise is reached, based upon the acknowledgment of evil as coexistent with organized society. To this argument Jesus answers: "It is written, Thou shalt worship the Lord thy God and him only shalt thou serve."

Jesus turned from the winning of organized society to the winning of individual men and women, one by one, trusting them to transform the social institutions and agencies into the pattern of the Kingdom of God, though many centuries might intervene before this objectve should be attained. From this time forward, he likens the processes of the growing Kingdom of God to the sower going forth to sow, the enemy sowing tares, the seed growing secretly, the pervasive power of the leaven thrust into the meal. For his followers, he envisages persecution by the vested interests both civil and religious and for himself, sufferings and death at the hands of sinful men. His last message to his disciples is a summoning to an age-long and world-wide mission: "All authority hath been given unto me in heaven and on earth. Go ye therefore and make disciples of all nations, baptizing them into the name of the Father and of the Son and of the Holy Spirit; teaching them to observe all things whatsoever I commanded you; and lo, I am with you all the days, even unto the consummation of the age." The basic decisions Jesus made in his three temptations reappear in the methods to be used and also in the goal of the efforts of his followers, until the end of the world.

All modern nations have faced, or are facing, the three temptations Jesus resisted: economic security, national prestige and world power. Those nations that have fallen exhibit the tragic consequences of their fateful decisions, which affect not themselves only but the whole world.

The peoples of earth, distressed by living conditions, listened eagerly to those who promised plenty and prosperity through a new social order. These men, calling themselves Leaders, soon became rulers, exercising dictatorial powers. The people were willing, even eager to surrender their political rights for assured abundance of material goods. The parliamentary system which accompanied the establishment of constitutional governments throughout the world, was given up or destroyed in a score of European countries. The moral principles that undergirded international law were ruthlessly violated and all references to God as the judge of these nations was blasphemously derided. This was the price, and those who paid were so anxious to see stones turned into bread that they gave little or no thought to the truth that "man shall not live by bread alone."

All the social evils that plague mankind have their source in a secularization of life that either refuses to obey God, ignores the claims of God or denies the existence of God.

The modern nations that have fallen into the temptation that Jesus resisted, like him, have had a sense of mission. Under this spell, one goal they were seeking was national prestige. The desire to be important, to enjoy prestige, to be recognized as superior, kindles the imagination of national groups and of ambitious and discontented races.

Nations and races, like individuals, have hidden, and often suppressed, a subconsciousness in which are mingled envies, hatreds, bitternesses, prejudices, the memories of cherished wrongs, yearnings for vengeance, cravings for things denied, dreams of conquest and visions of grandeur. In a period of social upheaval and economic dislocation, the man who has the hardihood to make vocal these suppressed desires, who is able to envisage the triumphant realization of everything the populace wants, and who can frame a course of action that promises dominion and glory for the nation or race, makes an irresistible appeal, and the people blindly but enthusiastically follow him. Thus the new rulers climbed into the seats of the mighty and the nations that had turned away from God found themselves the prey of totalitarian governments.

Turkey is a striking illustration of the complete reconstruction of a people, the repudiation of an old religion long supported with fanatical zeal and the erection of a thoroughly secularized State which has thrown the idea of God overboard. Speaking to the Turkish people, their leader, Kemal Ataturk, declared: "I have known all nations. I have studied them on the battlefield, under fire, in the face of death, when the character of a people is laid naked. I swear to you, my people, that the spiritual strength of our nation transcends that of all the world." [72] The appeal was to the long suppressed desires of the Turkish race and the response was given in the establishment of the Republic of Turkey, a completely secularized State, as atheistic in its structure as its leader was atheistic in his personal beliefs.

One by one, nations, in whose subconsciousness dreams of vengeance, conquest and glory have long lain suppressed, fell into the third temptation of Jesus—the will-to-power. Claiming an unrivaled sovereignty over their people, their leaders ruthlessly violated the moral principles that undergird international morality, and, going farther, blasphemously ignored and derided the right of God to the worship and the service of mankind. Religion, if granted continued existence in its organized life, was compelled to submit to a national policy that enthroned the State and reduced the individual to the status of a center of energy to be used by the State. These nations have deified Nationalism, either by rearing national gods or inculcating the belief that the idea of God, whether He be Allah, Jehovah, or the Father of our Lord Jesus Christ, is a menace to public welfare. The immediate origin of the Blitzkrieg against God thus may be traced to modern nations falling into these three temptations that Jesus resisted.

One more question remains to be answered: "Why have these modern nations, each imposing a new and different ideology for the reconstruction of its social structure, reached a common conviction and attitude toward the belief in God?" Japan, Russia, Turkey and Germany have strikingly different conceptions for the organization of society, yet they are in practical agreement as to the unrivaled sovereignty of the State and in their rejection of a belief in God. The desires for economic security, national grandeur, and world power are not an adequate explanation.

An outstanding characteristic of international culture is the high regard given to scientific knowledge. The nations that lead in the Blitzkrieg against God welcome and eagerly utilize the discoveries of science and the inventions that these discoveries have made possible. Indeed scientific knowledge is one of the foundations in each of the differing ideologies the nations have adopted for the reconstruction of the social order. All the leaders in totalitarian lands pay high tribute to science and seek the aid of distinguished scientists in the development of the nation's natural resources. The influence of scientific studies upon religious belief needs to be considered in any serious investigation of the rise of the attack upon God in those countries where the assault has the support of the government.

While the Blitzkrieg against God is unmistakably a direct outgrowth of the new idolatry of Nationalism, its origin may be traced to the secularization and the despiritualization of modern life, which has its deep roots in the soil of humanistic science. The average layman, responsive to present-day cultural influences, regards the authority of science as absolute. "He accordingly allows to science an extra-human, which is to say a superhuman authority. . . . Science becomes a god, somewhere out in space. . . . This elevation of science into a dogma, which is probably the largest tyranny of our time, has destroyed our perception of the place of authority in art, religion and social morality." [73]

The nations which today are using their political power to destroy the belief in God bow down before Science, as in ancient times other nations prostrated themselves before the images of their gods. This deification of Science, accompanied by the denial of God, docs not promote a world community devoted to the human welfare, because Science is unmoral and is equally capable of being used for the furtherance of solely selfish as well as altruistic ends. Thus the nation, exercising an absolute sovereignty over its subjects and recognizing no higher power than itself glorifies Science and at the same time usurps the sovereignty of God by deifying the State.

The scientists who carry on their work of description of physical processes, asserting that they have no need for the hypothesis of God, have laid the foundation for a profound skepticism as to the possibility of any religious knowledge. The reality with which they deal is the ceaseless flow of cosmic change. When religious phenomena are brought to their attention, they reject the view that believers, in their worship and their devotion to the well-being of mankind, are brought into a relationship with a divine Being, and therefore they interpret religious behavior as wholly subjective in its origin, to be treated upon the assumption that there is no overruling Providence in the affairs of men. This is the source of the view that religion is man-made, and since religion demands so much of time, effort and futile sacrifice, it would be better for mankind to recognize that it has no basis in reality and, therefore, to seek some more reasonable basis for the promotion of the betterment of the human race. This doctrine—perhaps dogma is the better word—leads logically to the position now taken by the nations that are warring against God, that is, that belief in God is a hindrance to the progress of mankind. The war for human freedom in which the democracies are united against the Axis Powers is only one phase in the most portentous phenomenon in the whole history of the human race—the Blitzkrieg against God.

Throughout this work, the significance of language in the formation of great human societies has been repeatedly emphasized. The essential basis of community consciousness is communication, in which language is the most important factor, giving form, meaning and continuing expression to the culture, which a social group, bound together by a common speech, is able to produce and to perpetuate. "Language," says John Stuart Mill, "is the depository of the accumulated body of experience to which all former ages have contributed their part and which is the inheritance of all yet to come."

The most striking linguistic fact in modern times has been the spread of English speech. Three and one-half centuries ago, three and one-half million people used English. Latin was then the language of the scholars; French, the court; English, the common people. Within this comparatively brief period, the use of English has increased nearly a hundredfold.

English, as the carrier of fructifying ideas, is the best vehicle in existence for the spread of the principles of civil and religious freedom. No other culture gives so high an evaluation to the sanctity of personality or defends with so much vigor the rights of the common man. The continued extension of the English language creates a culture favorable to free speech, free governments and free churches.

The program of Winston Churchill, endorsed by President Roosevelt, which envisions the world-wide use of basic English, is a plan which has within it the possibilities of extending throughout all lands beneficial and enduring freedom. While there have been and are in the English-speaking world many internationally known savants who deny the existence of God, they have not been able to inaugurate any social or political reorganization grounded upon the denial of deity. No English-speaking group or government has completely fallen into the temptations that Jesus resisted. The Blitzkrieg against God is led by nations that do not use English and therefore do not share in our English cultural inheritance.

The World War between the Axis Powers and the United Nations is reaching its climax. The wealth, the manpower and the material resources of the whole world are being thrown into the struggle. Tens of millions of men and women are in the conflict. Whoever wins, victors and victims alike, will be overwhelmingly impoverished, if not bankrupted. The rehabilitation of devastated lands, the restoration of a world order, and the establishment on a sound basis of a durable and righteous peace call for sacrifices in many ways greater than the war itself.

The nations now at war have one goal in common—the creation of a world community. Germany and Japan envisage a new world order, to be attained through world conquest; the United Nations, through some form of world federation for the permanent perservation of peace. War is a process that heightens and intensifies the feelings of oneness on the part of the peoples who together participate, creating thereby a community consciousness, achieved through the use of military force. The United Nations possess this consciousness of community, brought into being through a common determination to compel the unconditional surrender of the Axis Powers. In the populations involved, in the exercise of all-out prodigious effort, in the expenditure of material wealth and manpower, the United Nations form the greatest and most powerful community in action that the world has ever known.

This Global War, with all its horror and destruction, is in the process of bringing into existence an international community consciousness upon which may be reared the structure of the World Community, which, if wisely designed and directed, will guarantee a just and durable peace. This can be accomplished only as those who gather at the Peace Conference resist the temptations that came to Jesus in the wilderness.

The clue to history is discovered in the age-long workings of the providence of God, frustrating the evil purposes of men and nations and granting to the meek, the gentle, the peace-loving the right to inherit the earth. "He increaseth the nations and he leads them captive. He taketh away understanding from the chiefs of the people of the earth, and causeth them to wander in a wilderness where there is no way. They grope in the dark without light; and he maketh them stagger like a drunken man." The stars in their courses are fighting against the modern nations who, having adopted ideologies that would encompass the toppling of God from His throne, seek economic security, national prestige and military power in order to become world conquerors. They have taken up the sword, and by the sword they shall perish.

The road toward a righteous and durable peace is long, hard, unpaved and skirts many a precipice. If the victors fall into the temptations that confronted Jesus and make a treaty for world peace that leaves out the recognition of the sovereignty of God, another war more terrible, more devastating than the present struggle will begin before the babies of today reach maturity. The tragic world crisis will not be met by the United Nations winning the war, but by the restoration and the extension throughout the world of a vitalizing all-dominating faith in God as Sovereign and Judge of mankind. If the decisions of the high contracting Powers are to bring forth lasting benefit for humanity, God's presence must be felt, and His revealed will must be sought in the coming Peace Conference.

The Blitzkrieg against God is losing something of its fury. The Russian Embassy gave one-half of its Washington issue, January 30, 1943, to the appeal of the patriarchal incumbent of the Holy Russia Orthodox Church, Sergei, Metropolitan of Moscow, and to the New Year's message of the Russian Baptist Church addressed to all Evangelical Christians and Baptists under the yoke of Nazi invaders. Six months later, Sergei, with the tacit consent of the Soviet Union, was installed as the official head of the Russian Orthodox Church. The same day January 30, 1943, Adolf Hitler, in a pronouncement to the German people, declared, "God will be a just judge," a new note in his addresses.

A voice from the Philippines cries, "There are no atheists in the fox holes of the Bataan Peninsula." Rickenbacker and his companions, drifting helplessly over the wide expanse of the Pacific, draw together their rafts for prayer and the reading of the New Testament, and find strength and comfort in the words of Jesus.

Man is incurably religious, and in God's own time the Blitzkrieg against Him will be only a poignant memory. When this horror passes, those who trust in God will pray with a deeper earnestness and with a better understanding: "Our Father who art in heaven, hallowed be thy name. Thy Kingdom come. Thy will be done, as in heaven, so on earth."

XX

The Mind of Contemporary Christianity and the Future of the World

"Thy Kingdom come. Thy will be done in earth, as it is in heaven."
—The Lord's Prayer.

As ONE SURVEYS the successive linguistic cultures of the past nineteen centuries, a striking paradox is clearly in evidence. The Christian faith has been dependent upon these cultures for the conveyance of its message, but their reaction has always tended to a modification, if not a radical distortion of its original Christian form and meaning. Linguistic cultures have been a help and a hindrance to the propagation of the pristine Christine faith.

The Aramaic, the Greek, the Latin, the Teutonic, and the English languages, to name the most significant, have been the necessary vehicles that enabled the missionaries of the Christian faith to share their cherished beliefs with those whose culture was grounded in another language. Thus, on the one hand, the expansion of the Christian enterprise has been accompanied by the enrichment of Christian teaching and, on the other, by the introduction of thought-patterns that have weakened, distorted and sometimes denied the essential truth of the Gospel itself. The expression of the Christian faith has been compelled to conform to the mold of the cultural earthen vessel in which it was being deposited.

This generation is the heir of all the good and the evil that the centuries have wrought since that day when Jesus commissioned his followers to make disciples of all nations. The task which the Master outlined was age-long and world-wide, and took definite form in the preaching of the New Testament period as repentance toward God and faith in the Lord Jesus Christ. Those who went forth as the heralds of this divine revelation commanded men everywhere they went to turn from sin and to give the control of their lives to God as mediated to man in Jesus Christ. Their message was summarized in the words: "Believe on the Lord Jesus Christ and thou shalt be saved." The Good News they proclaimed assured in the present life a redemption from the dominion of sin, and in the life to come an eternal blessedness.

The modifications and the distortions of the simple Christian message, evident to any thoughtful student of these cultures, are

1. New requirements declared as necessary to salvation;
2. The enthronement of an intellectual interpretation as possessing something superior to, and more essential than, simple faith in Christ;
3. The setting up of a centralized ecclesiastical authority, claiming absolute sovereignty in temporal as well as spiritual affairs;
4. The union of Church and State, with an accompanying interaction that deadens a functioning spirituality,
5. The wide-spread growth of a humanistic science that has denied to God a place in the acquirement of a better and a more extended knowledge of ourselves and of the world in which we live.

Aramaic culture, with its meticulous observance of the current applications of the Mosaic law, furnished within the New Testament churches the background and the dynamic of the Judaizing movement, whose exponents stoutly asserted: "Except ye be circumcized after the manner of Moses, ye cannot be saved." Thus a rite was given equal, if not greater, importance than the faith that cleanses the hearts of believing Gentiles. While Judaic Christianity practically disappeared before the close of the second century, the assumption that a rite is an essential act in the Christian religion still prevails in all sacramental bodies which hold baptism to be essential to salvation, and these bodies have within their folds nearly eighty per cent of the world's Christian church membership. Only in the English-speaking areas may be found a majority of Christians who believe that faith in Christ, and that only, is necessary to Christian salvation.

Philosophical speculation permeated the Græco-Roman world as scientific knowledge pervades modern life. The missionaries of the Christian faith, entering the areas of Greek culture, won the adherence of men of standing. There arose in these new converts the desire to reconcile within themselves, and also for the benefit of others possessing like intellectual attainments, reason and revelation, the accepted principles of current Greek philosophy and the historic manifestation of divine grace made through Jesus Christ. The early teachers in this endeavor were called the Apologists. Another group of thinkers, who had accepted the Christian faith but were more concerned for the preservation of their philosophical convictions than for the propagation of the Gospel, were known as the Gnostics. These held that whatever in the historic revelation, including the Old Testament, which did not harmonize with their philosophical presuppositions should be rejected. Controversy followed. The era of creed-making was inaugurated. Christian theology was born and orthodoxy—right thinking in the realm of religious matters—became the test of Christian faith. In the process, ecclesiastical machinery was developed for the overthrow of heresy. As the power of the Church of Rome increased, persecution of all who dissented from her doctrines became widespread. Protestant State Churches coming into existence followed the example of Rome in proscribing dissent. There is no darker picture in all the history of Christianity. The religious persecution of the Jews, Protestants, and Catholics is today greater than ever before in all recorded time. However this is not grounded upon the preservation of an official orthodoxy, but upon the avowed purpose to destroy the belief in the God of Jews and Christians. This is the Blitzkrieg against God.

The lessons to be learned are that the Christian faith cannot be perpetuated through the use of force and that the New Testament way for the propagation of this faith is persuasion—the witnessing by those who know the power of an endless life to the truth of the Gospel of Christ. The intellectual assent to an orthodox creed does not make the Christian man, but a personal experience of divine grace that integrates the whole of the inner life in loyalty to the Lord Jesus Christ.

The Christian movement in the New Testament assumes the form of local groups belonging to a larger spiritual community that embraces all true believers, and this larger community was called the body of Christ. No group can function effectively without some form of government. These early Christians sought the guidance of the Holy Spirit; recognized the Hebrew Scriptures as a divine revelation, pointing to the coming of the Christ; heeded the teaching of the Apostles and prophets, and set up in each local body officials to lead in an administration of church affairs. The overseer or bishop in Gentile churches managed the funds given by the brethren for the needy, and officially represented the church or churches he served in relation to other Christian groups. Influenced greatly by the prevailing Roman conception of the necessity of a centralized authority, the bishops began to assume the powers of ecclesiastical monarchs. The Bishop of Rome claimed pre-eminence and, favored by the fall of the Roman Empire, laid hold upon the right to rule in temporal as well as ecclesiastical affairs. The Roman Church is the heir of the Roman imperial power and the Pope of Rome is appropriately called the Pontifex Maximus. The doctrine of salvation through baptism was followed by another dogma, "no salvation outside the Church." The next step was to declare the Pontifex Maximus to be the Vicar of Christ, reigning over mankind as the world's only rightful ruler. The claim of papal infallibility came in 1870.

According to Roman dogmas, faith alone does not effect salvation, but leads to salvation. The performance of baptism by a legal pastor of the Roman Church, obedience to the Pope as the Spokesman of Christ, and the acknowledgement of the Church as the only legitimate agency for the propagation of the Christian faith are necessary to an assured salvation.

These unscriptural requirements are traceable directly to the influence of Latin culture. The Roman Church claims nearly three-fifths of the world's reported Christian population. With an international organization more highly developed than any other Christian body, possessing the rights of a nation and exchanging her diplomatic representatives with nearly every government on earth; with her claim upon the loyalty of her members that takes precedence over their allegiance as citizens to their own government, the Roman Catholic Church, without exercising physical force directly, is the most powerful totalitarian government on earth. Concern is rightly felt as to the part Communistic Russia will play at the Peace Conference which is to follow the war, but the lovers of religious liberty may properly feel an equal concern as to the proposals that the Pope will seek to incorporate into the final peace treaty. In considering the mind of contemporary Christianity, the uncompromising attitude of the Roman Church in the defense of her dogmas looms as probably the greatest obstacle to the world-wide establishment of religious freedom for every man, everywhere throughout the world.

The union of Church and State following the Reformation was effected through the recognition by the leaders of the Protestant Churches of the need of civil protection and financial aid, and by the rulers of the countries predominantly Protestant of the need of a Christian body that would support the theory of the divine rights of kings and would strengthen in moral and spiritual ways the stability of their existing governments. The State Protestant Church acquired security, prestige and power; the State acquired a dignity and an authority through the State Church's declaration for, and support of, the absolutism of kings as grounded in the will of God, so that whosoever resisted the king resisted God. Under these conditions, there was no place and no protection for dissenters. Utilizing infant baptism for the induction of all the newly born into the fold, the State Church approached in membership the population of the whole country.

Two of the basic principles of the Protestant faith were universal priesthood of all believers, and the right of the individual Christian to read and to interpret the Bible for himself. These doctrines led to dissent, and the persecution of dissenters as heretics and as enemies of the State followed in Protestant lands. Spirituality, or the emancipated pursuit of mystical Christian piety, declined in the laity and in the ministry of the State Church; the services of worship grew more cold and formal, while the Church itself became an increasingly secularized institution through its dependence upon the State.

The dissenters raised the issue in the realm of morals and religion as to the right of the individual to follow the dictates of conscience and to obey the Scriptures as he was able to interpret their meaning. More voices were lifted in the defense of this right, and civil and religious liberty found new champions. In Rhode Island there was set up a government with "full liberty in religious concernments"; the statute of religious freedom, in its original form the work of Thomas Jefferson, severed Church and State in Virginia; the first Amendment to the Federal Constitution, introduced by James Madison, gave to the people of the United States complete religious freedom.

The union of Church and State is a departure from the teachings of Christ, which point to a free Church alongside a free State within a free society. No description of the contemporary Christian Mind can leave out the consideration of the State Church as a force in present-day Christianity.

The mind of contemporary Christianity is in profound confusion, and its primary cause is our present-day humanistic culture. The distortions of the early Christian faith, due largely to successive cultural environments, continue as organic and sometimes appear as controlling features, particularly within those ecclesiastical bodies that stress their historic continuity. Often in times of distress, like the present, there have been revivals of religion. The economic world-wide depression of 1929 did not have this result, and in the midst of our Global War there is little evidence in so-called Christian countries of a turning to God.

There are in the United States 256 different religious bodies officially reported and many more which have not gained the attention of the Census Bureau. Limiting the view to those which are classified as Protestants, two groups are to be noted: Fundamentalists and Modernists. The former stress the Lordship of Jesus Christ, the divine authority of the Bible, the necessity of the new birth and the strict adherence to Christian living; the latter, closer in touch with the current trends of thought, are keenly interested in harmonizing Christian beliefs with the conclusions of competent scientists; are profoundly concerned for human betterment, stressing the Social Gospel, and are active in the promotion of a richer and a more ornate service of worship. Representatives of both groups are found in all of the older evangelical denominations.

Christ made his appeal to the individual, seeking a trustful obedience, and this is stressed by all Fundamentalists. Therefore they emphasize evangelism. They hold that the betterment of society is conditioned upon the number, the influence, and the active devotion of truly regenerated followers of Christ. The Modernists are captivated by the ideals of Jesus, and seek a reconstruction of the institutions and the social agencies which form the environment of the individual. The Fundamentalists need to enlarge their conceptions of Christian service, and the Modernists need to recognize evangelism as primary in the promotion of human betterment.

The New Testament is crowded with incidents of social service, but they are the work of those who have been redeemed by faith in Christ from the power of sin. The truly regenerated believer burns with an enthusiasm for humanity. He recognizes that he renders the highest and most effective social service through the sharing with others his own experience of God's forgiving grace. A solicitude for souls, their moral and spiritual well-being, is the acid test of the Christian in every generation. Where this solicitude has prevailed, history recalls that it has been the dynamic of social betterment.

The world is at war; on every continent battles that will determine the course of future history, perhaps for a thousand years, are being fought. A great number of Christians are profoundly disturbed by the claims of country as opposed to the claims of Christ. In the time of peace, pacifism, both in Great Britain and in the United States, was a popular theme in hundreds, perhaps thousands, of Christian pulpits. It was easy then to preach upon love—the powerless power—as the greatest thing in the world. Many pastors urged their young people to enroll as conscientious objectors. Despite the portents of a World War, public opinion in the English-speaking countries, under the impact of a growing pacifism, demanded the reduction of armaments. Appeasement became the national policy of the principal democracies.

The possibility of the conquest of other lands through the mechanization of war entranced the leaders of the countries that had set up Nationalism as a religion. Thrusting God altogether out of their cruel and selfish plans, Italy, Germany, and Japan inaugurated wars of aggression. World conflict became inevitable. Force, used in time of peace to restrain crime, now had to be exercised in the mastery of the nations, engaging in the commission of crimes against the peace of the world. The necessity for the restoration of order compelled the peace-loving peoples to take up arms.

The evangelical interpretation of the Christian faith has in modern times met with its greatest successes in the English-speaking areas of the world. This fact has a significance which hardly can be exaggerated. No other language equals the English as a carrier of the idea of freedom. Wherever religious liberty prevails, the Gospel has free course. Thus the future of evangelical Christianity and with it the future of the world is conditioned upon the extension of religious liberty. The most essential of the Four Freedoms proposed by President Roosevelt is the freedom of religion. The English-speaking powers, the United States in particular, illustrate the incalculable benefits that flow from religious liberty.

Freedom of religion is more than a possibility in the new world order that will follow the present World War. The opportunity presented to this generation has no parallel in Christian history. A period of convulsion and social change in travail brings forth a more hopeless enslavement or a more fructifying emancipation of the human spirit. Man rises in the scale of value, wherever he is accorded religious liberty. Here is a cause for which the most earnest pleas should be made when the representatives of the victorious nations gather for the Peace Conference. However, these pleas will not be effective unless demand for the freedom of religion is made and is supported by the overwhelming endorsement of the peoples who live under democratic rule. Those who have the keenest and the deepest interest in this matter are the evangelical bodies in the English-speaking lands. The greatest responsibility rests upon them in securing this endorsement.

All who believe that religious liberty is a God-given, ineradicable right, to be recognized and conserved by all human agencies that exercise authority; all who believe that every form of compulsion in religion, whether it be by a religious body or a civil State, is a wrong justly to be condemned; all who believe that religious liberty is the ultimate ground of democratic institutions, and that whenever this liberty is questioned, restricted, or denied by any group, political, religious, or philosophical, every other human right is imperiled; all who thus believe must recognize their convictions as a categorical imperative, summoning them to action—action which cannot be delayed without dire disaster to the future of the world. Humanity is on the march and at this dramatic moment civilization faces the cross-roads of destiny.

More is needed than the legal guarantees of the freedom of religion, even though they are made available for men everywhere throughout the world. Our Christian leadership should first recognize that the Blitzkrieg against God has its roots in the prevailing culture of lands presumably Christian. The secularization of the agencies, education in particular, that have controlled the modes of contemporary thought and action is the soil in which the modern hostility to the belief in God has had its origin. These agencies, the present-day frontiers for Christian missionary endeavor, must be transformed into instruments for the molding of the existing social order into a pattern evermore distinctly Christian. Here is a task to which every follower of Christ, if he be faithful, must dedicate himself. The call is to Christianize society in all of its corporate activities. The kingdoms of this world must be brought into subjection to the Kingdom of our Lord and Christ, always and only by Christian means and processes.

The international spirit of Christianity envisions a world government through which equal justice under law may be administered and the inequalities of life be softened by the strong bearing the burdens of the weak, to the end that the spirit of Christ may dominate the relations of men and gain the ascendancy in the institutions of mankind. In periods of transition and reconstruction, great advances are possible. The establishment of freedom of expression and freedom of religion everywhere throughout the world would give to the proclamation of the Gospel of Jesus Christ an unprecedented opportunity, and as the evangelical interpretation of Christianity is extended throughout the earth, a world community consciousness, centering in God, will be developed which will enable mankind to establish and to maintain peace on earth among men of good will; for this good will is the very essence of an operative brotherhood of man and is the chief Christian obligation in human relations: "Thou shalt love thy neighbor as thyself."

A new apologetic, addressed especially to the intelligentsia, giving in sound and convincing argument "a reason for the hope" we cherish, is most urgently needed. This is a challenge to Christian scientists and philosophers to pay the intellectual tribute to Christianity which our religion deserves. Such an apologetic has an appropriate place in the curriculum of colleges and universities. The time is ripe for a new type of witnesses and teachers of the faith.

The Christian forces of the world need not only themselves to be united in this divine enterprise; they need also the co-operation of Science, Reason and Moral Reform. The following bases are suggested as furnishing the foundation for a better understanding leading to a working together for an enduring world betterment: In the inorganic world there is order; in the organic world, there is life, and in its unfolding there is a movement toward freedom, less in the vegetable kingdom and ever-increasing from the lower forms of animal life to man himself. Order is present, and freedom is evidently the goal of the processes of living things.

The development of the child from infancy to adulthood is marked by four successive adjustments to environment:

1. Physical—This is the field of scientific observation, grounded upon the assumption of orderly change which may be described, and this description is all that science undertakes to do;

2. The Psychical—This is the field in which ideas find symbols for expression in words, and in which those ideas that meet the test of logic are held to be true;

3. The Axiological—This is the field of esthetics, ethics, economics and all other areas in which desires create values. The assumption that rules in this field is that some values are worthy and some are not. All voluntary acts are found here—for striving is linked to desire, and desire is translated into action through judgments of worth;

4. The Religious—Religion is reverence in action, and the content, the character, and the gradation of a religion are determined by the objects or Object of worship.

These adjustments are made in a universe integrated by the principle of relatedness, a principle equally discernible in the electron and the farthest solar system. Man, trying to understand the world in which he finds himself posits order, everywhere exhibited in the changeless amid the ever-changing. He posits the law of continuity in all physical phenomena. He posits the attainability of truth in the realm of thought. He posits oughtness in the realm of his striving. He posits a source for this universal orderliness, he posits an ultimate ground for his apprehension of truth, and he posits in something or some One eternal, this sense of obligation, and in so doing he brings into a working relationship his scientific attitude and his religious faith.

Reverence is inherent in human nature. Man posits, if he thinks consistently, the ultimate source of order, rationality and oughtness in the Object of his worship. But his needs clamor for more than this. His life will soon end. He hungers for the truth as to the meaning of life; his moral weakness and depravity prevent the achievement of his ideals; he is lonely and desires a companionship that transcends anything human. He and all that the universe contains move ceaselessly onward, and his need is urgent.

This religious problem has been solved by tens of millions of men and women who hold that God is the source of order, truth, and righteousness; that He has revealed in Jesus the way to an eternal blessedness, and that the mission of every believer is to proclaim and to establish the Lordship of Jesus Christ, creating thereby a world community—a global fellowship—a lasting peace. The Christian faith in the making of a better world is grounded upon the belief in the God of order, truth, righteousness and love, and there is nothing in this faith that contradicts sound science.

The world crisis calls the followers of Christ to a fresh and a more complete dedication to God, and from this will flow the revival of religion that will reach out to all lands. The cruelties of the present war have restored the conviction of human depravity, and furnish convincing evidence of the reality and the exceeding sinfulness of sin. The austerity of God is being acknowledged and the recognition of this life as a period of probation is receiving a wider acceptance. The old doctrines are coming back into the pulpits of Christian lands, but not in merely conventional forms, depending upon the sanctions of tradition; not as theological formulas, but as vital realities in experience and hope, with the sanction of revelation and the support of history. The Bible is more widely distributed and more generally read. God is waiting to pour out the Holy Spirit upon this generation.

God is in the World War for Human Freedom, revealing in carnage and destruction the disastrous consequences that flow from the efforts of nations to destroy the belief in His existence and sovereign power. God is writing in contemporary history, so clearly that all men may see, that evil, however strongly intrenched in a godless culture and fortified by political power, is self-frustrating, and is doomed to be overwhelmed. God is declaring that the weapons of war, which today are bringing destruction in the air, on the earth, and under the sea, are futile instruments in the promotion of peace and that the divine plan calls for a World Fellowship, composed of men of good will, who under the leadership of Christ will be able to establish peace on earth. God, as mediated in Christ Jesus, is the Saviour of civilization as well as the Saviour of men. The revolt against God will utterly fail. "Except the Lord build the house, they labor in vain who build it; except the Lord keep the city, the watchman waketh but in vain."

References

1. William Newton Clarke, *An Outline of Christian Theology*, p. 1, Charles Scribner's Sons.

2. Harry Elmer Barnes, *The Twilight of Christianity*, pp. 41-42, Richard R. Smith, (120 E. 39th St.).

3. Dark and Essex, *The War Against God*, p. 216, Abingdon Press.

4. *Ibid*.

5. Adolph Harnack, *The Mission and the Expansion of Christianity*, vol. I, p. 84, G. P. Putnam's Sons.

6. Paul Wernle, *Beginnings of Christianity*, vol. I, p. 159, G. P. Putnam's Sons.

7. Morton Scott Enslin, *The Ethics of Paul*, Harper and Brothers.

8. Adolph Harnack, *The Mission and the Expansion of Christianity*, vol. I, p. 206, G. P. Putnam's Sons.

9. George Hodges, *The Early Church*, p. 25, Houghton, Mifflin & Co., Boston.

10. Francis Legge, *Forerunners and Rivals of Christianity*, pp. 8-9, Cambridge Press.

11. Samuel Angus, *The Mystery Religions and Christianity*, p. 14, Charles Scribner's Sons.

12. Francis Legge, *Forerunners and Rivals of Christianity*, p. 21.

13. Epictetus, Discourse III, 13.

14. Cyril Bailey, *The Legacy of Rome*, p. 138, Clarendon Press.

15. E. M. Hulme, *The Middle Ages*, p. 11, Henry Holt & Co.

16. Samuel Dill, Roman Society from Nero to Marcus Aurelius, pp. 267 and 271, Macmillan and Co., London.

17. Francis Legge, *Forerunners and Rivals of Christianity*, p. 1, Cambridge Press.

18. Pyramid of Pepy I.

19. Hisiod, Theogony, p. 123.

20. Adolph Harnack, *What is Christianity?* pp. 194-5, G. P. Putnam's Sons.

21. Adolph Harnack, *History of Dogma*, vol. I, p. 222, Roberts Brothers, Boston.

22. Samuel Angus, *The Mystery Religions and Christianity*, p. 45, Charles Scribner's Sons.

23. *Ibid*.

24. Samuel Angus, *The Religious Quests of the Græco-Roman World*, pp. 77-78, Charles Scribner's Sons.

25. Harold R. Willoughby, *Pagan Regeneration*, p. 280, University of Chicago Press.

26. Adolph Harnack, *The Mission and the Expansion of Christianity*, p. 234, G. P. Putnam's Sons.

27. Samuel Angus, *The Religious Quests of the Græco-Roman World*, pp. 91-92 and 145.

28. Adolph Harnack, *The History of Dogma*, vol. II, p. 305, Roberts Brothers, Boston.

29. *Ibid.*, vol. I, p. 62.

30. *Ibid.*, vol. I, p. 227.

31. *Ibid.*, vol. I, p. 319.

32. Herbert B. Workman, *Christian Thought to the Reformation*, p. 48, Charles Scribner's Sons.

33. Adolph Harnack, *History of Dogma*, vol. II, p. 334, Roberts Brothers, Boston.

34. *Ibid.*, vol. II, p. 105.

35. William J. McGlothlin, *The Course of Christian History*, p. 45, Macmillan and Co.

36. Charles A. Briggs, *Theological Symbolics*, p. 85, Charles Scribner's Sons.

37. George Preston Mains, *Christianity in the Light of Modern Knowledge*, p. 479.

38. John Edwin Sandys, *A Companion to Latin Studies*, p. 299, Macmillan and Co.

39. Virgil, *The Aeneid*, Book VI, II, 847-853.

40. Justin Martyr, *Op. XII*, p. 2.

41. Cecil John Cadoux, *The Early Christian Attitude Toward War*, p. XIII, Headley Brothers, Limited, London.

42. Francis Legge, *Forerunners and Rivals of Christianity*, p. 29, Cambridge Press.

43. Rufus M. Jones, *Studies in Mystical Religion*, p. XX, Macmillan and Co.

44. Henry C. King, *Theology and the Social Consciousness*, p. 77.

45. H. C. Moberly, *Atonement and Personality*, p. 316, Longmans, Green & Co.

46. Adolph Harnack, *What is Christianity?* pp. 191 and 193, G. P. Putnam's Sons.

47. Adolph Harnack, *History of Dogma*, vol. II, p. 142.

48. *Ibid.*, vol. IV, pp. 304-5.

49. Louis Duchesne, *Early History of the Church*, vol. III, p. 45, Longmans, Green & Co.

50. Adolph Harnack, *What is Christianity?* pp. 258-9, G. P. Putman's Sons.

51. H. C. Lea, *The History of Sacerdotal Celibacy*, p. 181, Macmillan and Co.

52. George Preston Mains, *Christianity in the Light of Modern Knowledge*, p. 578.

53. H. C. Lea, *The History of Sacerdotal Celibacy*, p. 17-18, Macmillan and Co.

54. James Westfall Thompson, *Economic and Social History of the Middle Ages*, p. 648, The Century-Appleton Co.

55. Adolph Harnack, *History of Dogma*, vol. III, p. 169, Roberts Brothers, Boston.

56. *Ibid.*, vol. VII, p. 273.

57. *Ibid.*, vol. VII, p. 252.

58. Albert Henry Newman, *Manual of Church History*, vol. II, p. 203, American Baptist Publication Society, Philadelphia.

59. Herbert D. Foster, *Political Theories of Calvinists*, American Historical Review, April, 1916, p. 500.

60. James Boyce, *American Commonwealth*, vol. II, p. 554, Macmillan and Co.

61. Rufus M. Jones, *Studies in Mystical Religion*, p. 369, Macmillan and Co.

62. Albert Henry Newman, *Manual of Church History*, vol. II, p. 420, American Baptist Publication Society, Philadelphia.

63. Isaac Woodbridge Riley, *From Myth to Reason*, p. 155, D. Appleton & Co.

64. *Ibid.*, p. 155.

65. Benjamin Ginzburg, *The Adventure of Science*, p. 310, Simon and Shuster, [1200 6th Ave.].

66. George Preston Mains, *Christianity in the Light of Modern Knowledge*, p. 718.

67. J. H. Randall, Jr. in *Current History*, July, 1929.

68. Clifford Kilpatrick, *Religion in Human Affairs*, p. 472, John Wiley & Sons, [440 4th Ave.].

69. H. N. Wieman, *The Wrestle of Religion with Truth*, p. 14, Macmillan and Co.

70. *Ibid.*, *Religious Experience and its Scientific Method*, Macmillan and Co.

71. *Christian Century*, vol. L, p. 194.

72. Dark and Essex, *The War Against God*, p. 214.

73. Hugh Miller, *Christian Truth in History*, pp. 89-90, Harper and Brothers.

General References

Adolph Harnack, *History of Dogma*, Roberts Brothers.

Kenneth Scott Latourette, *A History of the Expansion of Christianity*, Harper and Brothers.

R. Harold Paget, Editorial Director, *An Outline of Christianity—A Story of Our Civilization*, Dodd, Mead & Co., Distributors.

James Hastings, *Encyclopaedia of Religion and Ethics*, Charles Scribner's Sons.

Index

Altar vs. Pulpit, 185

Alexander the Great, 70, 73, 74, 101, 115

American Education, 20, 33, 54

Anabaptists, 137, 174, 177-178

Anselm, 149

Apologists, 83, 84, 85, 86, 96

Architecture, 150

Aristotle, 73

Astrologers, 109, 194

Ataturk, 35, 219

Atheism, 7, 11, 16-17, 34-38, 218-221

Authority and Restraint, 137, 174, 177-178

Authority of the Bible, 162, 230

Bacon, Francis, 196

Baptism, 66, 81, 88, 125, 137-139, 162, 177, 183, 189

Baptists, 36, 189-191

Barnes, Harry Elmer, 34

Bates, Ernest S., 180

Bellarmine, 126

Blitzkrieg against God, 7, 11, 12, 17, 30-39, 202, 221, 233

Bolshevists, 35-36

Boniface VIII, 158

Book of Common Prayer, 167

Bryce, Lord, 170

Calvin, John, 163-164

Church History, 13-17, 51

Church and State, 15-16, 153, 155, 162, 166-167, 229-230

Church Councils, 100, 167

Church of England, 190

Civilization, 31-34

Clement, 96, 129

Clue to History, 223

Conditions of Revelation, 211-212

Conflicts of Christianity, 13-17

Counter Reformation, 159, 167

Creeds, 95-96, 99-101, 102-103, 147

Cultures,
  defined, 59
  described, 71-80, 84-90, 105-107
  in Christian history, 60-63
  conflicts with, 63-69, 93-101, 114-121, 144-150, 174-180, 204-207, 225-230

Crusades, 149-150

Darwinism, 201-202

Definitions,
  Christian, 13, 174
  Religion, 181

Denominationalism, 182, 183, 190
  Cultural Backgrounds, 180-187, 188-191, 230

Deism, 199

Descartes, 198

Dewey, John, 208

Deniken, 36

Diet,
  Worms, 152
  Speyer, 153

Dispersion, 72

Dissenters, 93, 98, 137, 151, 174-178, 229

Donatists, 140

Duchesne, 140

Early Christian Literature, 85-86

Edicts,
  Milan, 99
  Worms, 152
  Nantes, 165

Eleusinian Mysteries, 115

Elements in Apostolic Thought, 51-52, 55-58, 60-61

Emancipating Mind, 169, 174-176, 179-180, 227, 229-230

English Language, 222, 232

Epochs, 52-55

Eusebius, 100

Evangelicalism, 62, 68, 83, 90, 135, 137, 159, 174, 186, 189-191
Evolution, 201-202, 205, 209
Experience, 22-24

Fundamentalists, 230-231
Four Freedoms, 38, 232
First Amendment, 230

Genius of an Age, 87
Gentiles, 27, 53, 70-80
Gladstone, William E., 6
Germany, 11, 37-38, 151, 162, 177, 198-199, 220
Gnosticism, 92-96
God—
  Conceptions of as held by Jesus, 47
  by Jews, 63-64
  by Early Christians, 90
  by Gnostics, 94
  by Creed-Makers, 99-101
Great Heresy, 170
Greek Language, Literature and Universities, 73-74
Gregory VII, 175

Harnack, Adolph, 56, 82, 89, 92, 94, 97, 138, 154, 178
Hellenism, 81, 84-85, 94-96, 105, 123
Hitler, Adolph, 30, 37
Hughes, Charles E., 16-17
Humanism, 186

Ideology, 30-31, 33-34
Ignatius, 85, 128
Imperium, 109-110
Incarnation, 47
Infant Baptism, 154, 162, 177, 187, 189

Japan, 11, 34-35, 231
Judaism, 13-14, 60, 63
Judaizers, 64-69
Justin Martyr, 85

Kant, Immanuel, 200
Kepler, Johann, 195
King James' Version, 167
Knox, John, 166

Language, 40, 50, 53, 55, 73-74, 105-106, 144, 151, 156, 222-225
Leibnitz, 199
Linguistic Cultures—
  Defined, 59-63
  Described, 71-80, 84-90, 105-107, 144, 146, 189-190
  Conflicts with, 63-69, 93-101, 114-121, 147-150, 174-180, 204-207, 225-230
Locke, John, 165, 199
Logos, 99
Luther, Martin, 15, 137, 152-153, 162, 179
Lutherans, 37, 153, 162-163, 186, 190

Maccabees, 64, 115
Marcion, 92, 94
Marx, Karl, 35
Materialism, 7, 16, 29, 34, 38, 55, 63, 79-80, 193, 199, 202, 204-205, 221
Mein Kampf, 30, 37
Methodists, 191
Mind, 40
  of Christ, 41-49
  Apostolic, 53, 55-59
  Judaizing, 60, 63-69
  Gentile, 70-71, 75, 78-79
  Hellenistic, 81, 84-85
  Theological, 91, 93-98, 101
  Roman, 105-107, 109-110
  Sacerdotal, 112-121
  Ecclesiastical, 123-132
  Mystical, 133-138, 141-143
  Protestant, 151-155
  Nationalistic, 159-167
  Emancipating, 169-171, 174, 176-180
  Denominational, 182, 184-192
  Scientific, 193-202, 204-207, 209, 234-235
Mithraism, 88, 111
Modernists, 230
Mystery Religions, 84, 87-90, 93-94, 101, 147
Mysticism, 13, 22, 24, 26-27, 47, 52, 61-62, 68, 90, 133-138, 141-143,

151, 154, 171, 176-178, 186, 189, 190, 213, 214, 229, 235
Nationalism, 7, 11, 17, 34-39, 159-160, 168, 218-220, 231
National Reich Church, 37-38
Newton, Isaac, 196, 199, 201
Nicene Council, 129, 208
Non-Christian Religions, 28-29
Notable Women Mystics, 142

Origen, 96, 97, 111
Orders, 141

Pacifism, 111, 231
Paganism, 14, 71-72
Papacy, 12, 124, 129-131, 146-151, 156, 158
Paul, 58, 67-69, 126, 129, 137
Pax Romana, 76
Peace Conference, 232
Peace of Westphalia, 161
Persecutions, 66, 107-108, 148, 178
Peter, 26, 46, 65-66, 68, 123-126, 129
Pharisaism, 64, 66
Philosophy, 22-24, 79-80, 93, 99, 134, 200, 234
Pontifex Maximus, 113-114, 228
Presbyterians, 164, 191
Priesthoods, 88, 112-120
Protestantism, 161-167, 171, 174, 183

Reformation, 15, 16, 27, 103, 130-131, 145, 155, 159-160, 176, 181-183, 228-229
Religious Liberty, 16, 17, 24-25, 33-34, 170, 174-180, 182, 189-192, 232-233
Renaissance, 159, 160, 175, 178
Rhode Island, 230
Roman Catholicism, 15, 27, 61-62, 123-131, 144-149, 176, 181-183, 228-229

Roman Empire, 14, 15, 29, 64, 71, 75, 76, 84, 105-111, 116, 122
Roman Law, 76, 109
Rosenberg, Alfred, 38
Russell, Bertrand, 34
Russia, 11, 12, 29, 35-37, 220, 224, 228

Saul of Tarsus, 66
Savonarola, 151
Scientific Mind, 20-24
    defined, 193-194
    Periods of development:
    Myth, 194-195
    Pioneer Observation, 195-197
    Mathematical Measurement, 197-201
    Biological Evolution, 201-204
Scotland, 164
Second Coming of Christ, 62
Society of Jesus, 167
Social Gospel, 230
Spinoza, 198
Synoptics, 47

Theocrasia, 75
Tertullian, 86, 92, 95-96, 103, 111, 128, 139, 187
Theological Mind, 91, 94-101
Tolerance, 116, 183
Torah, 48, 63, 65
Turkey, 11, 35, 219

Virgil, 110
Virgin Birth, 205
Voluntarism, 186

Wesley, John, 137, 190-191
Williams, Roger, 180
William of Orange, 165
World Peace, 224, 232-233, 236
Wyclif, John, 143, 151, 183

Zwingli, Ulrich, 163